International Studies in Entrepreneurship

Volume 47

This series highlights cutting-edge research in entrepreneurship, small business/ SMEs, economic development, and policy. Volumes in the series feature empirical studies, theoretical analyses, practical applications, and policy recommendations in regional and global contexts, and explore a wide variety of topics with regard to entrepreneurship, including demographics, new venture financing, research & development, business creation, labor dynamics, technology management, and education. Springer and Series Editors welcome proposals for research monographs, edited volumes and reference works in all areas of entrepreneurship research.

Kirsten Mikkelsen • Annika Wolf
Editors

Minds, Brains, and Doxa for Inclusive Entrepreneurship

Entrepreneurial Ecosystems for Diverse Entrepreneurs

Springer

Editors
Kirsten Mikkelsen
Jackstädt-Center Flensburg
University of Flensburg
Flensburg, Schleswig-Holstein, Germany

Annika Wolf
University of Applied Sciences Emden Lee
Emden, Germany

ISSN 1572-1922 ISSN 2197-5884 (electronic)
International Studies in Entrepreneurship
ISBN 978-3-031-50163-0 ISBN 978-3-031-50164-7 (eBook)
https://doi.org/10.1007/978-3-031-50164-7

This Springer imprint is published by the registered company Springer Nature Switzerland AG
The registered company address is: Gewerbestrasse 11, 6330 Cham, Switzerland

Paper in this product is recyclable.

Foreword

Can women do tech? As a successful female founder, this is the most common question I have had from journalists and investors even though I have had prestigious clients like the World Health Organization, and with my team I have done really important social work building healthcare after natural disasters, epidemics and wars worldwide.

That was many years ago now, but it is a question women still get asked today, whether they are established in a job or beginners.

Women today still have to justify why they have achieved something. Instead of acknowledging success, a certain amazement always resonates. But gender is only one issue. Reducing achievement to skin colour or origin is unfortunately still a reality for many people. We all need motivated people. With prejudices, because that's all it is, you don't open up society. And society must open up and not just speak, manage and act for a few. Not only for ethical reasons but also to create a transformation. We have to act now. Is it necessary and possible to break this vicious circle? By all means! Is inclusion an important element? Definitely!

In a world characterised by dynamics and change, the concept of inclusion is gaining increasing prominence. But what does inclusion mean, and why is it of paramount importance for our society and economy? This foreword delves into these questions, illuminates the reasons for past deficiencies in achieving inclusion and explains how an inclusive coexistence can positively shape our collective future.

At its core inclusion is the path towards creating a society in which every individual – regardless of personal attributes such as origin, gender, age, abilities and socioeconomic background – has the opportunity to participate equitably in all aspects of life. It involves dismantling barriers that prevent people from realising their full potential and actively engaging in societal affairs. Inclusion isn't just about tolerance; it's about genuine appreciation of the diversity that enriches our world.

But why is inclusion so vital? The answer lies in its comprehensive positive impacts on both society and the economy. An inclusive society not only nurtures social cohesion and mutual understanding but also cultivates an environment in which people with various perspectives collaborate on solutions. This diverse input is critical for innovative ideas and sustainable change. Inclusion strengthens democracy by ensuring that all voices are heard, and it contributes to reducing discrimination and injustice.

However, achieving inclusion has often proven to be challenging. Historically ingrained prejudices, social hierarchies and structural barriers have led to marginalisation of specific groups in society. Whether they are due to cultural biases, limited resources or unequal educational opportunities, the causes of lack of inclusion are manifold and complex. The challenge is to overcome these obstacles and initiate an inclusive transformation.

Only by promoting inclusion in entrepreneurship can the full potential of a transformative impact unfold. When people with different backgrounds, skills and life experiences are given the opportunity to become entrepreneurs, new opportunities for innovation, product development and sustainable economic growth emerge. But how can this happen and what can we do to make it happen?

Public policy can provide the framework conditions. One of the central building blocks for entrepreneurship in Germany is certainly the EXIST funding programme. It finances innovative and sustainable business ideas and is a funding programme of the Federal Ministry of Economics and Climate Protection. Evaluation of the prospective start-up team and start-up idea is explicitly open-topic in EXIST and it addresses all motivated founders. For example, the funding guidelines explicitly refer to the Diversity Charter, which focuses on inclusion and diversity. The newly created EXIST-Women funding line also highlights efforts to promote more diversity in start-ups.

Supporting inclusion in entrepreneurship is not only about access to education and resources, but also about creating a welcoming environment. Universities, incubators, accelerators and investors play crucial roles in supporting founders from diverse backgrounds. At the same time, policies, social awareness and cultural changes are needed to enable inclusive entrepreneurship. Today's pressing problems such as climate change need the ideas of capable founders. They should all be heard and their ideas acted upon.

In the end, yes, of course: women can do tech! All people can do tech! Would I start a business again today? Absolutely! It is a good experience to broaden one's horizons, to get to know other people and to learn responsibility for other people! Is it easier to found a company today? No, it's not! Is it more difficult to start a business today? No! But there is a change in thinking and support. The authors of this book are part of this rethinking and motivators of it. You can feel and see it in a greater diversity of people. You notice that aspiring founders are more aware of the impact of their actions. And you sense that a change in thinking is taking place in science, business and politics, and that inclusion is not only perceived as important but it is actively supported.

This book has been written by experts with years of experience in the field of entrepreneurship. They show that anything is possible if we openly see the diversity of people and support them and show them the way. The authors write openly about the situation, and also about their personal experiences. This is why it is authentic and gives real insights. But the most important message of this book is that we can make a difference right now.

The characteristics of an inclusive entrepreneurial culture may include the following. *Diversity and Inclusion*: An inclusive entrepreneurial culture promotes a broad range of perspectives, experiences and backgrounds. This creates an environment where innovative ideas shaped by diverse life experiences and viewpoints can emerge. *Accessibility*: Inclusion involves minimising or eliminating physical, technological and social barriers to facilitate access by individuals with disabilities and from various life situations. *Equal Opportunity*: An inclusive entrepreneurial culture ensures that everyone has an equal opportunity regardless of factors like gender, origin, sexual orientation and socioeconomic status. *Education and Sensitisation*: Training and awareness raising promote understanding of the importance of inclusion and help reduce biases. *Flexibility*: Inclusive entrepreneurial cultures offer flexible working conditions and schedules to accommodate the diverse needs and commitments of founders. *Mentoring and Support*: Mentoring, coaching and resource offerings help individuals from underrepresented groups develop their entrepreneurial skills and successfully realise their business ideas. *Recognition of Diverse Success Stories*: Inclusion involves acknowledging and celebrating the success stories of individuals from different backgrounds to create role models and inspiration for future entrepreneurs.

True inclusion requires a coordinated effort involving educational institutions, businesses, political institutions and society as a whole. It demands a conscious shift in mindsets and an open willingness to bridge gaps between seemingly disparate individuals. Inclusion necessitates courage, persistence and the recognition that our coexistence becomes richer when we embrace diversity. By encouraging people with different perspectives and abilities to pursue their entrepreneurial dreams, we not only create economic success but also shape a world where everyone has an equal chance to realise their dreams.

Let's start today! This book tells us what we need to do.

Andrea Schuster,
Projektträger Jülich,
Gründungs-, Transfer- und
Innovationsförderung,
Fachbereich Gründungskultur
Berlin, Germany

Contents

Chapter 1
On the Need for More Inclusive Perspectives on Entrepreneurship

Annika Wolf and Kirsten Mikkelsen

No group of entrepreneurs should experience any barrier for starting or developing a business

(Verheul & Thurik, 2001).

The fact that this was stated more than two decades ago data from the Global Entrepreneurship Monitor or national monitors show that not much has substantially changed since then. Women's participation in entrepreneurial activity remains relatively low compared to that of men in most western capitalist countries. Taking intersectionality (i.e., race, age, and sexual orientation) into account, those proportions get sharper. These developments or rather nondevelopments happen despite the fact that entrepreneurial activity has, for a very long time, been translated into economic growth, disruptive innovations, and personal self-fulfillment. And whereas these examples represent different levels of analysis, which are macro-, meso-, and individual levels, it is difficult to treat them separately.

With this book on Brains, Minds, and Doxa, we bring together contributions with a focus on mindsets and competencies of entrepreneurial individuals, the role of entrepreneurship education for these individuals and ideas dealing with the rules and dominant perceptions within the entrepreneurial ecosystem.

We want to contribute to a better understanding of what inclusive entrepreneurship means and how an inclusive entrepreneurial ecosystem can contribute to practically enhance entrepreneurial activity from the bottom-up, with a disruptive power for economic and societal transformation. Some of the contributions specifically focus on the role of stakeholders in shaping an inclusive entrepreneurial ecosystem. It is obvious that not only entrepreneurship research and business-related disciplines hold responsibility in this context but also, for example, architecture and

A. Wolf (✉)
University of Applied Sciences Emden/Leer, Emden, Germany
e-mail: annika.wolf@hs-emden-leer.de

K. Mikkelsen (✉)
Jackstädt-Center Flensburg, University of Flensburg, Flensburg, Germany
e-mail: kirsten.mikkelsen@uni-flensburg.de

K. Mikkelsen, A. Wolf (eds.), *Minds, Brains, and Doxa for Inclusive Entrepreneurship*, International Studies in Entrepreneurship 47,
https://doi.org/10.1007/978-3-031-50164-7_1

communication, as well as social media as they shape the entrepreneurial spatial environment – both physically and digitally. This book covers a variety of issues, philosophical, theoretical, and practical:

1. The conceptual presuppositions of the arguments in favor of the entrepreneurial mindset of stakeholders and entrepreneurship education to build a successful ecosystem.
2. The evidence of entrepreneurship education for developing an entrepreneurial mindset. The relation between the internal and external entrepreneurial ecosystem of institutions in Higher Education for fostering entrepreneurial mindsets.
3. The integration of inclusive and emancipatory aspects in entrepreneurship research and practice.

In today's dynamic landscape, inclusive entrepreneurship has emerged as a pivotal concept, aiming to provide equal opportunities for individuals from all walks of life to embark on a journey of sustainable business creation, regardless of their backgrounds. This endeavor is not only aligned with the overarching goals of achieving smart, sustainable, and inclusive growth but also serves as a powerful response to the ever-evolving environmental, economic, and social challenges of our time. Moreover, inclusive entrepreneurship stands as a potent force for generating employment opportunities and combating the persistent issues of social and financial exclusion.

Central to the agenda of inclusive entrepreneurship are policies and initiatives that extend support to individuals who historically have faced barriers in the labor market and remain underrepresented or disadvantaged in entrepreneurial pursuits. These policies are designed to empower diverse groups, including women, youth, seniors, the unemployed, immigrants, and individuals with disabilities, enabling them to overcome obstacles and tap into their entrepreneurial potential.

A multifaceted approach to inclusive entrepreneurship involves addressing a range of challenges and implementing strategies that enable the realization of this vision. Governments and institutions play a pivotal role in shaping an environment that acknowledges the value of less "conventional" entrepreneurial projects This includes refining regulatory frameworks, facilitating access to financial resources, cultivating entrepreneurial skills through training and mentorship, fostering an inclusive entrepreneurial culture, and strategically aligning actions to ensure that inclusivity remains at the forefront.

The journey toward inclusive entrepreneurship is not devoid of complexities. As economies strive to reinvigorate productivity growth and tackle rising inequality, inclusive entrepreneurship emerges as a pathway to address these intertwined challenges. As authors who have immersed themselves in building entrepreneurial ecosystems and conducting research on entrepreneurship and gender, we understand the intricate nature of creating an environment that truly embraces diversity and the emancipatory power within.

This book embarks on a journey to explore the dimensions of inclusive entrepreneurship, bringing together diverse perspectives from educators, scholars, supporters, investors, and entrepreneurs themselves. Within its pages, we delve into the critical roles of mindsets and competencies, the transformative influence of entrepreneurship education, and the need to challenge prevailing norms within entrepreneurial ecosystems.

In the pages that follow, we shed light on the intricacies of inclusive entrepreneurship that extend beyond gender considerations. Diversity takes on myriad forms – ethnicity, age, social status, physical capabilities, and neuro-diversity, among others. Each chapter endeavors to amplify the voices and experiences of these often-marginalized groups, providing visibility to their unique challenges and potential contributions.

With our focus in this book on Brains, Minds, and Doxa, we endeavor to bridge macro-, meso-, and individual-level analyses, recognizing that these dimensions are intrinsically interconnected. The book not only delves into the mindset and competencies of entrepreneurial individuals but also examines the pivotal role of entrepreneurship education and the underlying perceptions that shape the entrepreneurial ecosystem.

A group of authors Malte Krohn, Dagmar Ylva Hattenberg, Norris F. Krueger, and Cornelius Herstatt open the conceptual discourse on mindsets, both innovation and entrepreneurial mindset. They provide a taxonomy of mindsets that help prevent a proliferation of concepts if one conducts research on innovation or entrepreneurial mindsets. This is of utmost relevance if programs are to be developed to foster those mindsets. They do this by analyzing the three most commonly applied mindset theories from cognitive psychology, educational psychology, and organizational leadership and proceed by reviewing conceptualizations in the entrepreneurship and innovation fields.

As inclusive entrepreneurship requires inclusive ecosystems, an analysis of those is also related to dealing with formal and informal institutions. Lela Grießbach and Kerstin Ettl investigate the effect of these on female entrepreneurs in Georgia. This topic is highly relevant and interesting as it becomes clear that women's inequality in starting a business venture manifests on multiple levels. Georgia is a transitioning economy and not only is entrepreneurial activity in a western capitalistic sense still new, but also its formal and informal institutions are still male-dominated. Applying a qualitative approach, the authors analyze to what extent formal institutions may positively influence women's position in informal institutions and shed light on the emancipatory aspects of entrepreneurship.

The Chap. 3 is a practitioner's view on the image of women entrepreneurs drawn by social media. Rea Eldem, an entrepreneur within the discipline of diversity, elaborates on how the counter picture of the male entrepreneur archetype has led to the construction of a new female archetype of a woman entrepreneur. However, in her view, it is just as exclusive and one-sided as the male entrepreneur. Besides the "new narratives" seem to ignore the role of a person's position in the social sphere and the power the related social structures have. This consequently prevents women entrepreneurs from walking their very own path.

New founded companies today very often benefit from incubators and coworking spaces. These open offices have accelerated entrepreneurial activity as they offer uncomplicated rooms for networking, exchange, and office space for (young) entrepreneurs. For nascent entrepreneurs, this is a chance to overcome some of the liabilities of newness, smallness, and adolescence. However, often coworking spaces follow architectural standards set by design offices and investors. Jona Wolf and Kirsten Mikkelsen discuss this tension against the background of both disciplines – architecture and entrepreneurship – underlying masculine standards. The overall issue is to what extent co-working spaces can actually offer an inclusive environment.

A very personal view is that of the practitioner Ann-Carolin Helmreich. Her chapter grants insights into her own journey and the challenges that she was facing as a member of the startup scene in Berlin. While she was accepting the facts of a male-dominated environment in her early years in different startups, she became an advocate for a more diverse, equal, and inclusive entrepreneurial ecosystem later on. Her story is an impressively honest self-reflection of a person discovering who she is and, thereby, finding purpose – and herself.

Social entrepreneurship has grown to be a main driver for (regional) change and has become an access point for citizens to engage in transformation. With a focus on societal value over profit, those endeavors are most likely to face financial challenges prior to realization. In her chapter, Sandra deBoer presents us with an analysis of two regional initiatives aiming to facilitate social entrepreneurial projects. She evaluates the role of policymakers in creating an entrepreneurial environment that provides access to finance for social entrepreneurs.

The next practitioner, Heidrun Twesten, is an expert in VC funding and shares her insights on how to get in touch with investors – from business angel to venture capitalist. She is also familiar with gender stereotypical and business model-related obstacles for getting fundings for entrepreneurial ventures and highlights the role of a structural transformation to make the startup scene more diverse.

In their Chap. 10 on "inclusivity tax," the authors Alexandra David, Judith Terstriep, and Laila Zahaib investigate migrant entrepreneurship in Germany. Not only do they employ secondary data on migrant entrepreneurs, but they also use verbal data from interviews with migrant entrepreneurs. The plea for a narrative change is to regard migrant entrepreneurs as models and to utilize their experience knowledge, experience, and way of running businesses for establishing a more inclusive entrepreneurial ecosystem.

Inclusivity of entrepreneurial ecosystems is also the topic of the following chapter by Annika Wolf. Through a theoretical and practical lens, she focuses on senior entrepreneurship. With the decline of an active skilled labor force and an aging population with elderly people retiring from the labor market, senior entrepreneurs become an important driver for innovation in achieving sustainable economic growth. Following three examples of senior entrepreneurial ventures, she sets forth specific recommendations to create opportunities for senior entrepreneurs.

Expanding on contributions on the entrepreneurial mindset, Mikkelsen, Berger, and Engelsberger use an exploratory approach with an extended open innovation (OI) measurement tool. As un-unified concepts of mindsets are – both innovation and entrepreneurship – they share the difficult task of measure mindset changes after educational interventions. Hence, a new tool was employed to let students self-assess their changes in dimensions as openness, creativity, positive attitude toward KSS, risk and failure tolerance and entrepreneurial uncertainty, entrepreneurial creation, and collaboration. The chapter aims at providing an argument for other KPI than a number of founding projects.

In his conceptual chapter, Florian Frenz discusses the potential of entrepreneurship education for answering the growing demand of heterogeneity in classrooms, based on the idea that heterogeneity fosters entrepreneurial activity. For this purpose, he examines perspectives on heterogeneity in the educational context, with a particular focus on the various forms of response that teachers can employ to address heterogeneity. Based on that he draws attention to the effectuation logic and design thinking as possible methodological foundation for addressing heterogeneity in the context of entrepreneurship education.

In addition to the entrepreneurial mindset, future entrepreneurs need entrepreneurial competencies. In an investigation among Polish and Chinese students, Sandra Kwit-Misiak and Jinyue Yang investigated how satisfied students are with the quality of teaching and whether this is related to the satisfaction with the development of personal competencies in teaching, which they think are similar to entrepreneurial competencies. They also do so by comparing business and non-business students as well as students who received entrepreneurial education and not.

Große, Liszt-Rohlf, and Baldwin investigate intersectional inequality among university students and the potential influence on their attitudes toward entrepreneurship. They argue that the support for entrepreneurial projects in higher education does not automatically address all students. Rather, intersectional inequality, e.g., social status and ethnicity leading to latent discrimination among those students and eventually resulting in untapped potential. The study seeks to give recommendations for ecosystem builders at universities to create actions that reach out to disadvantaged groups and those who have not considered entrepreneurship as an option.

Ultimately, the aspiration of our book is to contribute to a more profound understanding of versions of inclusive entrepreneurship and its potential to drive economic and societal transformation. By assembling contributions that span the realms of philosophy, theory, and practice, we aim to advance and open the discourse on inclusive entrepreneurship. We encourage stakeholders across various disciplines to collaborate in shaping a holistic, inclusive entrepreneurial ecosystem. Through this collective effort, we strive to pave the way for an entrepreneurship landscape that embraces diversity, fosters innovation, and empowers individuals to chart their own paths to success.

Reference

Verheul, I., & Thurik, R. (2001). Start-up capital: Does gender matter? *Small Business Economics, 16*, 329–345.

Chapter 2
A Taxonomy of Mindsets: Current Conceptualizations and Future Directions for Mindset-Based Research in Innovation and Entrepreneurship

Malte Krohn, Dagmar Ylva Hattenberg, Norris F. Krueger, and Cornelius Herstatt

2.1 Introduction

Why do certain people perceive the dynamic global marketplace as a threat to their organization while others see a world of opportunities (see also Hölzle et al., 2020)? Why are certain individuals attracted to the turbulent and ambiguous environment of startups and scaleups? These and similar questions illustrate that, while research on the topic of behavior in entrepreneurship and innovation has tremendously increased, many answers and explanations are still unknown and searched for.

In a plethora of fields, such as within cognitive psychology (Gollwitzer, 1990), educational psychology (Dweck, 2006), and managing internationalization (Gupta & Govindarajan, 2002), innovation (Kahn, 2018), and entrepreneurship (Krueger, 2007a), scholars zoom in on people's mindset to explore said questions, as to understand why certain people behave differently – more entrepreneurial or innovative than others – while being exposed to the same socioeconomic context. A large amount of research thus already attends to mindsets, proving the concepts'

M. Krohn (✉) · C. Herstatt
Institute for Technology and Innovation Management at Hamburg University of Technology, Hamburg, Germany
e-mail: malte@mindfulstartup.school

D. Y. Hattenberg
Family Business Research Centre, Windesheim University of Applied Sciences, Zwolle, The Netherlands

N. F. Krueger
Center for Doctoral Studies, UOPX, Phoenix, AZ, USA

University of Management & Technology, Lahore, Pakistan

Kyushu University, Fukuoka, Japan

K. Mikkelsen, A. Wolf (eds.), *Minds, Brains, and Doxa for Inclusive Entrepreneurship*, International Studies in Entrepreneurship 47,
https://doi.org/10.1007/978-3-031-50164-7_2

relevance and value. The disadvantage, however, is the consequence of disconnect and proliferation (Podsakoff et al., 2016), as mindsets are widely interpreted. Such proliferation can lead to the development of conflicting measures of a concept and hamper theoretical progress (Podsakoff et al., 2016). Currently, conceptualizations provided in different contexts have indeed resulted in fuzziness of mindset research (French II, 2016), bringing forth difficulties and ambiguities in the academic discourse. Our search for a taxonomy of mindsets aims to clarify the fuzziness as declared by French II (2016). Particularly, we aim to conduct an analysis in domains of entrepreneurship and innovation research and contribute a more systematic means to frame future mindset-based studies in the field – hence, a mindset taxonomy. We believe that entrepreneurship and innovation need to concern inclusive contexts: rather than viewing tangible characteristics, we believe that mindsets should be investigated as instigators of entrepreneurial and innovative behavior. Differentiating people based on their mindset rather than demographic characteristics allows for a more inclusive understanding of the fields of entrepreneurship and innovation. While demographics might still create a bias in the prevalence of an entrepreneurial or innovation mindset between members of certain groups today, many mindset conceptualizations include the notion that mindsets contain trainable aspects. This offers an avenue to realizing a more diverse population of entrepreneurs and innovators in the future.

Our analysis suggests, however, that current research does not fully realize the potential of mindset-based perspective to advance our understanding of a more inclusive view of entrepreneurship and innovation. While French (2016) suggests that scholars should explicate their conceptual mindset background to prevent further proliferation (see also Podsakoff et al., 2016), current scientific practice within entrepreneurship and innovation is still different. An example is the study of Töytäri et al. (2018), who investigate the alignment of mindset and capabilities within a business network for the successful adoption of service-driven innovation. They refer to mindsets as "beliefs, rules, and norms about a proper way of conducting business" (Töytäri et al., 2018, p. 774): they thus frame mindsets as distinctive from capabilities and root their conceptual understanding of organizational mindsets in institutional logics put forward by Thornton et al. (2012). This example illustrates one of the origins for the conceptual fuzziness we – building on the existing literature – observe: Are mindsets in innovation and entrepreneurship best investigated on the individual or collective level? Our analysis suggests that both perspectives seem valid and meaningful. However, future work needs to justify these choices more carefully and contrast them to alternative approaches – our taxonomy is intended to facilitate this conceptual framing in future research.

With regard to the definition of the mindset, one can find similar analogies within entrepreneurship research. For instance, Davis et al. (2016) developed an empirical measurement tool: the entrepreneurial mindset profile. Their definition of the mindset is, however, rather broad:

Definition 1. "The constellation of motives, skills, and thought processes that distinguish entrepreneurs from non-entrepreneurs and that contribute to entrepreneurial success" (Davis et al., 2016, p. 2).

Such broad definitions can on the one hand be helpful as they allow for a broader and inclusive understanding, interpretation, and utilization of a concept. Nevertheless, as French II (2016) addresses, it may also cause confusion and fuzziness, resulting from overlap with other concepts and ambiguity with regard to the facets that belong to which concept. As our analysis suggests a need for more conceptual clarity for mindset-based perspectives, we extend French II's (2016) call for more interdisciplinary mindset research. Heeding our own call, we present a shared mindset taxonomy for the domains of entrepreneurship and innovation to hand researchers a tool for classifications and understandings with regard to the specific mindset investigated across research contexts. The questions raised in the introductory paragraph clearly underscore ambiguous contexts, often represented in entrepreneurship and innovation research (Hattenberg et al., 2021). Moreover, existing research does not point in one clear direction: either innovation or entrepreneurship as a context. For this reason, we wish to include both contexts as our research parameters for developing our taxonomy.

According to Bradley et al. (2007, p. 1761), "taxonomies are formal systems that classify multifaceted, complex phenomena according to a set of common conceptual domains and dimensions" to increase clarity in defining and comparing complex phenomena. We propose that a shared taxonomy of mindsets in entrepreneurship and innovation prevents further conceptual fragmentation and contributes to the quality of mindset-based research in two interconnected fields (Zhao, 2005) by providing a means to clearly explicate conceptual considerations in future studies. Furthermore, robust taxonomies can pave the way for ex-post theory building (Nickerson et al., 2013).

2.2 Innovation and Entrepreneurship as a Research Context

To provide future research with a taxonomy, it is necessary to add contextual parameters to our understanding. Mindset scholars have particularly studied contexts that are important to innovation (Kahn, 2018; Engelsberger et al., 2021; Kuczmarski, 1996; Krohn & Herstatt, 2019; Soni & Krishnan, 2014; Töytäri et al., 2018) and entrepreneurship (Krueger, 2007a; Davis et al., 2016; Hattenberg et al., 2021; Shepherd et al., 2010). Hence, we believe that innovation and entrepreneurship research might benefit from a more consistent theoretical foundation of mindsets. Additionally, while both fields have focused on different forms and degrees of mindsets, both fields still struggle to find clear answers to why some people behave more entrepreneurially/innovatively than others. One reason to explain this difficulty could be that other concepts do not provide the inclusive character that mindsets offer. At the same time, mindset concepts should be contextualized and defined in more specific terms. To lay ground for a mutually beneficial understanding, we clarify how innovation and entrepreneurship can be defined and how they are distinct from each other (Kahn, 2022), yet synergetic (Zhao, 2005). For innovation, we build on Baragheh et al.'s (2009, p. 1334) broad definition:

Definition of Innovation. "[...] the multi-stage process whereby organizations transform ideas into new/improved products, service or processes, in order to advance, compete and differentiate themselves successfully in their marketplace."

Innovation is often discussed in an organizational setting, either describing a process or an outcome (Kahn, 2018). The organizational setting is, however, not binding as many examples in the domain of user innovation show (Herstatt & Von Hippel, 1992). Taking an equally broad view on entrepreneurship, we build on the definition provided by Carlsson et al. (2013, p. 914):

Definition of Entrepreneurship. "Entrepreneurship refers primarily to an economic function that is carried out by individuals, entrepreneurs, acting independently or within organizations, to perceive and create new opportunities and to introduce their ideas into the market, under uncertainty, by making decisions about location, product design, resource use, institutions, and reward systems. The entrepreneurial activity and the entrepreneurial ventures are influenced by the socioeconomic environment and result ultimately in economic growth and human welfare."

While the role of ideas is still central, the focus shifts to individuals carrying out actions and cognitive procedures through opportunity recognition and decision making. The line between innovation and entrepreneurship blurs when we account for behavioral perspectives from the field of innovation management (Goepel et al., 2012) and corporate entrepreneurship (Belousova & Gailly, 2013; Burgelman, 1984). Definitions, however, show that entrepreneurship and innovation are generally distinct fields (Kahn, 2022; Zahra, 2015) and that research focuses on different aspects around the broad domain of creating economic or social value from intentional social interactions that focus on realizing ideas.

The conceptual connection between entrepreneurship and innovation has been discussed in classic economic (Schumpeter, 1934) and management theory (Drucker, 1994) and is still explored in different contexts, such as sustainable innovation and entrepreneurship (Schaltegger & Wagner, 2011). Previous research has suggested that innovation is the source of entrepreneurship, and innovation allows entrepreneurship to thrive by materializing its economic potential (Zhao, 2005). Since understanding mindsets is as imperative to understand innovation (Kahn, 2018) as it is to understand what it means to be entrepreneurial (Krueger, 2007a), a shared conceptual mindset foundation for both fields bears great potential to advance our understanding of innovation and entrepreneurship.

2.3 Research Gap, Objective, and Approach

Previous research has found that mindset conceptualizations vary substantially across and within research domains. However, such an analysis has not been conducted in the domains of innovation and entrepreneurship – domains that have seen a growing interest in mindset-based studies. Additionally, while the fuzziness of mindset research has been explicated, literature has not provided a solution to prevent further proliferation. We suggest that a taxonomy approach provides an effective means to address this research gap: a mindset taxonomy for the fields of entrepreneurship and innovation solving the risk of concept proliferation. Hence, we aim to guide mindset scholars with a systematic taxonomy of mindsets by exploring differences and similarities across conceptualizations in different socio-economic contexts. We do not challenge existing conceptualizations of different approaches to mindset research. Instead, we embrace the complex nature of mindsets, using existing research as our building stones. We clarify the variety of definitions and explain the spectrum of mindset conceptualizations. We have four distinct research objectives:

1. Providing an analysis of established mindset theories
2. Extending the analysis of mindset-based perspectives to the fields of entrepreneurship and innovation
3. Developing a set of common conceptual dimensions
4. Identifying future research avenues to leverage the potential of mindset-based perspectives to advance our understanding of inclusive innovation and entrepreneurship

We review the literature utilizing a nomological approach (Podsakoff et al., 2016) to various conceptualizations of mindsets, as we discuss similarities, distinctions, and boundary conditions. As illustrated in Fig. 2.1, we structure our research approach into four steps based on taxonomy-related methodological considerations (Bradley et al., 2007; Nickerson et al., 2013). Analyzing the three most commonly applied mindset theories from cognitive psychology, educational psychology, and organizational leadership, we proceed by reviewing conceptualizations in the entrepreneurship and innovation fields.

Throughout our iterative process, we continuously derive codes for common conceptual dimensions and develop a code structure (Bradley et al., 2007). We triangulate the codes with earlier mindset research conducted by the first and second authors based on Flick (1992). Lastly, we present our mindset taxonomy and discuss future research avenues on how mindset-based perspectives can contribute to our understanding of inclusive entrepreneurship and innovation.

Fig. 2.1 Research process and paper structure

2.4 Mapping the Mindset Research Field

Concepts are the cornerstone of research. They allow scholars to organize complex phenomena through a common language, facilitating effective communication (Podsakoff et al., 2016). Ideally, concepts allow for distinguishing certain phenomena from other related phenomena. However, what if a phenomenon lacks conceptual clarity? French II (2016) grounded his suggestion regarding the prevailing fuzziness on the finding that scholars from different research streams base their mindset conceptualization on different *root constructs*, i.e., cognitive processes, beliefs, and cognitive filters. We suggest that mindset conceptualizations differ across additional dimensions. Since taxonomies classify complex phenomena (Bradley et al., 2007), it is critical to examine established conceptualizations and provide a foundation for subsequent analysis. Hence, we now analyze published studies from the three main theoretical fields involving research on mindsets, namely, cognitive psychology, (Gollwitzer, 1990), educational psychology (Dweck, 2006), and organizational leadership (Gupta & Govindarajan, 2002).

Cognitive Psychology

Fundamental to this literature is the notion that:

> (…) becoming intensely involved with the solving of a given task activates exactly those cognitive procedures that help task completion. The created mindset (i.e., the sum total of the activated cognitive procedures) should consist of the cognitive orientation that is most conducive to successful task performance (Gollwitzer, 2012, p. 528).

Mindsets are conceptualized as the entirety of cognitive processes that are fundamentally connected to solve specific tasks. Gollwitzer (1990) developed the *mindset theory of action phases* and defined distinct phases in the process of human action, namely, deliberation and implementation. Deliberation concerns the process of choosing between various paths of action, which results in deciding on a goal, as it primes a deliberative mindset (Gollwitzer, 1990). The implementation phase, however, concerns the actual implementation of actions by planning where, when, and how to act (Gollwitzer, 1990). A deliberative mindset's cognitive processes concern assessing the desirability and feasibility of potential goals (Gollwitzer, 1990, 2012). Pioneering research in entrepreneurship focused on the distinction between how relatively novice and relatively expert decision-makers process information differently. Mitchell and Chesteen (1995) proposed a focus on expert scripts but cautioned that cognition-focused research presumes that scripts (and schemas and maps) cannot be captured directly, but it is quite feasible to identify robust cues that signal the presence of expert thinking in that domain. As such, they identified a set of such cues that led to ongoing research that reflects, e.g., an individual's ability and willingness to pursue opportunities (Mitchell et al., 2017). Notably, to understand the outcome of deliberation in the form of, for example, entrepreneurial intentions (Delanoë-Gueguen & Fayolle, 2018), scholars have recently operationalized desirability and feasibility considerations based on the *theory of planned behavior* (Ajzen, 1991). Entrepreneurial intentions provide an empirically investigated connection between the mindset theory of action phases and the theory of planned behavior. Gollwitzer's research is applicable in multiple contexts, such as entrepreneurship (Delanoë-Gueguen & Fayolle, 2018), organizational leadership (Clapp-Smith & Lester, 2014), and frugal innovation (Krohn & Herstatt, 2019).

Educational Psychology

Dweck's (2016) research on the growth mindset and the fixed mindset within educational psychology illustrates how the mindset is open to change and adaptation, allowing us to consider the mind as something that *can be set* instead of a *set mind*. Dweck (2017) applies the growth mindset to performance in education-focused settings. Additionally, Yeager and Dweck (2012) investigated how the growth mindset is functional and essential for academic success, as it provides learning opportunities instead of focusing on setbacks.

Similar to intentions research (Van Gelderen et al., 2008; Ajzen, 1991), Dweck (2016) assumes that beliefs and self-beliefs are integral elements of the mindset. In this regard, French II (2016) highlights that such a belief-based conceptualization of mindsets goes beyond the idea of cognitive processes, which are linked to task completion. Dweck (2016) suggests that beliefs are crucial for a change in the mindset and consequent behavior (see also Krueger, 2009). She argues that adopting a growth mindset leads to innovation and entrepreneurial acts within multiple environments. In fact, Burnette et al. (2020) show that growth mindset interventions have a positive effect on entrepreneurial self-efficacy. Nevertheless, scholars call for more research on growth and fixed mindsets in workplace contexts (Rattan & Ozgumus, 2021), such as innovation and entrepreneurship.

While Dweck (2016) proposes the possibility of mindset changes, she recognizes that adopting a growth mindset is not an easy task. Regardless of the context, changes in beliefs and mindset require facilitations from others in terms of support and policies (Hattenberg et al., 2020; Robinson et al., 2016; Hornsby et al., 2013). Hattenberg et al. (2021) show that the entrepreneurial mindset is adaptable and changeable rather than an attribute that is set in stone.

Utilizing the cognitive and educational streams of mindset research reveals differences across three dimensions. First, in line with French II (2016), scholars conceptualize the mindset based on different *root constructs*, such as *cognitive processes* (Gollwitzer, 1990) or *beliefs* (Dweck, 2016). Second, scholars diverge in how they understand the *nature* of mindsets as either *a set mind* with regard to tasks in certain action phases (Gollwitzer, 1990) or *setting the mind* in response to challenges (Dweck, 2016). Third, Gollwitzer (1990) attributed *behavioral implications* to the deliberative mindset and the implemental mindset across phases of human action. While Dweck (2016) assumes that a growth mindset will have wide-ranging behavioral implications, they are not explicated as clearly as in Gollwitzer's (2012) theory.

Organizational Leadership

In the organizational leadership stream, the global mindset (Clapp-Smith & Lester, 2014; Gupta & Govindarajan, 2002; Rhinesmith, 1992) provides a vast body of research and strongly divergent conceptualizations (French II, 2016). Early contributions conceptualized the mindset as:

Definition 4. "[…] a predisposition to see the world in a particular way that sets boundaries and provides explanations for why things are the way they are, while at the same time establishing guidance for ways in which we should behave" (Rhinesmith, 1992, p. 63).

While this conceptualization follows the pattern of linking certain internal processes to behavioral outcomes, the definition does not resemble the role of beliefs or cognitive processes. We, therefore, identify a third way in which scholars conceptualize mindsets with regard to *root constructs*. French II (2016) terms this third-way *cognitive filters*. Furthermore, subsequent research by Gupta and Govindarajan (2002, p. 117) defined the global mindset as.

Definition 5. "[...] an openness to and awareness of diversity across cultures and markets with a propensity and ability to synthesize across this diversity."

We, therefore, notice major differences among conceptualizations *within* one field of research. This can be explained by our third taxonomy dimension, *contextual embeddedness*: the mindset's environmental relatedness, and specifically the boundaries within which an individual manifests the mindset. The context within which the mindset is manifested can, to an extent, foster or inhibit the mindset and behavioral consequences. Consider, for instance, an organizational environment where resources can be provided or where regulations can inhibit an entrepreneurial mindset (e.g., corporate entrepreneurship, (Belousova et al., 2020)), culture-based boundaries (e.g., Rarick & Han, 2015), or family contextual boundaries (e.g., Ejupi-Ibrahimi et al., 2020). Embedding the mindset conceptualization in its research context is generally desirable (Rattan & Ozgumus, 2021). In that sense, diversity across markets and cultures is inherent in the challenges of successful internationalization (Gupta & Govindarajan, 2002). However, openness, awareness, propensity, and ability broaden the *root construct* dimension of the mindset concept beyond cognitive filters. French II (2016) finds that, overall, the global mindset research stream lacks acknowledgment of previous mindset research from cognitive psychology and educational psychology. Considering the study of Clapp-Smith and Lester (2014, p. 212), we find that global mindset scholars acknowledge this lack of theoretical integration and a *"[...] lack of clarification of what is meant by 'mindsets'."* Consequently, Clapp-Smith and Lester (2014, p. 223) turn to Gollwitzer's (1990) research and redefine the global mindset as:

Definition 6. "[...] a dynamic process by which an effective global leader switches between conflicting and paradoxical cognitive orientations in order to take a fuller view of the environment."

While this conceptualization is more specific with regard to cognitive orientations, it shows how mindset conceptualizations can vary within a research field and how a lack of conceptual clarity can prevail. Furthermore, the global mindset stream diverges from cognitive and educational psychology concerning another aspect. While Gupta and Govindarajan (2002) suggest that mindsets can be cultivated, they discuss this cultivation as a *collective* organizational endeavor. As a collective of individuals with each individual having a particular mindset, organizations are prone to a collective mutual reshaping of mindsets through interactions or new experiences (Gupta & Govindarajan, 2002). We, therefore, propose the *level of analysis* as the fifth dimension of our taxonomy.

In summary, we identify conceptual differences across five dimensions, coded as *root construct*, *nature*, *contextual embeddedness*, *behavioral implications*, and *level of analysis*. Therefore, we expand the work of French II (2016) beyond the notion of differing root constructs. These dimensions cover several underlying assumptions, such as *a set mind* and *setting the mind* for the *nature* dimension. Widening the scope of our analysis, we further refine our mindset taxonomy and confirm the applicability of our dimensions. We focus on the fields of entrepreneurship and innovation, which are in need of further development when it comes to consistent mindset conceptualizations.

Mindsets in Entrepreneurship

Since two decades, mindset-based research has gained attention within the field of entrepreneurship, and this mindset has commonly been termed the entrepreneurial mindset (McGrath & MacMillan, 2000). Shepherd et al. (2010, p. 62) define the entrepreneurial mindset as:

Definition 7. "[…] the ability and willingness of individuals to rapidly sense, act and mobilize in response to a judgmental decision under uncertainty about a possible opportunity for gain."

Shepherd et al. (2010) adapted this definition from earlier research on strategy and strategic implications in the firm (Ireland et al., 2003; McMullen & Shepherd, 2006) and cognitive theories (Krueger, 2007b). Key elements in this mindset definition are ability, willingness, the response to a judgmental decision, uncertainty, and the opportunity for gain, which subsequent research has further investigated and validated. On the one hand, the entrepreneurial mindset is, thus, understood as an adaptive, process-wise developing concept, triggered by certain exogenous stimuli. Therefore, when it comes to the *nature* of the entrepreneurial mindset, it appears to resemble a notion of *setting the mind*. Furthermore, the concept appears goal oriented (i.e., the opportunity for gain) and can, in those terms, be coined as resulting in purposeful behavior. In terms of its *behavioral implications*, the entrepreneurial mindset resembles previous mindset research from cognitive psychology and covers deliberation, goal setting, and implementation-related aspects. On the other hand, further research in the field widens the *root construct* dimension (Kuratko et al., 2020; Noble, 2015; Shepherd et al., 2010).

While Shepherd et al. (2010) created the first tangible definition for the entrepreneurial mindset, research remained fragmented (Naumann, 2017) to the point of being divided over whether it is a concept worth keeping or whether it is proliferated with other concepts causing it to be obsolete in the management literature. Hattenberg et al. (2021) conceptually and empirically validated the uniqueness and value of the entrepreneurial mindset. Kuratko et al. (2020) thoroughly examined the entrepreneurial mindset to unravel it in a comprehensive manner. This resulted in the distinction between emotion (what entrepreneurs feel), behavior (how entrepreneurs engage in opportunities), and cognition (using mental models to indicate how entrepreneurs think). The literature, thus, converges on the idea that the entrepreneurial mindset is a complex and active phenomenon – a rather adaptive one. Specifically, we derive a consensus on specific elements of the mindset: *affect-based*, *skill-based*, and *cognition-based* aspects. Lastly, the field of entrepreneurship begins to investigate the entrepreneurial mindset in different contexts, such as organizational entrepreneurship.

Affect-Based Aspect

Whether the affect-based aspect is named the willingness of an individual to engage in entrepreneurial activities (Shepherd et al., 2010), the entrepreneur's feelings in general (Kuratko et al., 2020; Culkin & Mallick, 2011), the entrepreneur's attitude (Davis et al., 2016), the sensing of an opportunity (Ireland et al., 2003), unspecified motivations (Haynie et al., 2010), emotions (Noble, 2015), or passion (Zur, 2015), one thing appears clear. There is an affective component to the entrepreneurial mindset. The entrepreneurial mindset involves more than what an entrepreneur thinks or what an entrepreneur is capable of. If there is no form of nonrational attachment whatsoever to a possible opportunity, there will be hardly any entrepreneurial action. Essentially, this makes the entrepreneurial mindset unique (Hattenberg et al., 2021). Such findings regarding the importance of affect in innovative and entrepreneurial behavior are reported more often in the literature, indicating its necessity for entrepreneurship or innovation to spark (i.e., Kruft & Kock, 2021).

Skill-Based Aspect

Next to affect, many researchers acknowledge a skill-based component. Described by certain scholars as ability (Shepherd et al., 2010; Mitchell, 2017) and by others as actual skills (Robinson et al., 2016; Noble, 2015), this aspect concerns the trainable element of the entrepreneurial mindset, allowing every individual to essentially strengthen his/her entrepreneurial mindset. This is similar to Dweck's (2017) growth mindset development.

Cognition-Based Aspect

The literature converges on a cognitive component containing aspects, such as mental models (Noble, 2015), effectual reasoning (Patel & Mehta, 2017; Sarasvathy, 2001), and knowledge (Shepherd et al., 2010; Haynie et al., 2010). In the earliest entrepreneurial mindset literature, the main focus was on cognition, as many considered the mindset as purely *set in the mind*. Even in later years, considerable effort went into investigating the mindset's neurocognitive aspect (Kaffka & Krueger, 2018), and it appears evident that cognition is still considered as the main contributor to the entrepreneurial mindset.

Organizational Entrepreneurial Mindset

Researchers recently started to acknowledge the idea that entrepreneurs show themselves in all sorts of shapes. This diversity-driven line of thinking has been applied to the entrepreneurial mindset, which can arise and thrive in specific settings (Belousova et al., 2020). Belousova et al. (2020) investigated the entrepreneurial mindset in an organizational setting and drew two conclusions: there appears to be evidence for an organizational entrepreneurial mindset (Davis et al., 2016), and every employee is capable of developing an entrepreneurial mindset while simultaneously performing his/her daily job (Belousova & Gailly, 2013; Birkinshaw, 1997; Burgelman, 1983). Conclusions such as those drawn by Belousova et al. (2020) implicate that everyone can develop their mindset and, furthermore, that not only the opportunity but also the individual's context matters.

While research on the entrepreneurial mindset is still ongoing, it converges around several key ideas and, overall, the field evolves in its understanding of that particular mindset and a shared definition. Nevertheless, this convergence is yet to be established in the field of innovation management. We, therefore, derive further differences, corresponding codes, and a sixth taxonomy dimension in this research field.

Mindsets in Innovation Management

Several important concepts in the context of innovation received scholarly attention in conjunction with mindset-based perspectives. Innovation has been described as a mindset (Kuczmarski, 1996), and as an integral part of innovation:

> To truly manifest innovation and reap its benefits, one must recognize that innovation is three different things: innovation is an outcome, innovation is a process, and innovation is a mindset (Kahn, 2018, p. 453).

We find, however, that a consistent approach to mindsets in innovation is still lacking, such as a commonly applied definition of an innovation mindset. Empirical studies are scarce or fail to provide a sufficient conceptual integration with previous mindset research. In the context of innovation, we discuss how scholars approach design thinking (Brown, 2008), open innovation (Chesbrough et al., 2006), and frugal innovation (Zeschky et al., 2011) based on mindsets, as we believe these are the most commonly applied conceptualizations and applications of the mindset in the field of innovation.

Design Thinking Mindset

Emerging in the scholarly discourse over a decade ago (Brown, 2008) as a novel and important approach to innovation, design thinking has received considerable attention (Micheli et al., 2019; Starostka et al., 2021). Among other perspectives, such as a process and toolbox, scholars have approached design thinking as a mindset (Brenner et al., 2016) and *"characteristics that describe design thinking correspond to important mindset considerations for innovation […]"* (Kahn, 2018, p. 458). A recent definition of design thinking as a mindset suggests that:

Definition 8. "As a mindset, DT [Design Thinking] refers to the underlying values, cognition and resulting behaviors that, over time, find their way into the beliefs of people and culture of organizations" (Groeger & Schweitzer, 2020, p. 43).

The set of values, i.e., cognitive and behavioral attributes, constituting the design thinking mindset is suggested to be empathy, collaboration, inquisitiveness and openness to learning, acceptance of uncertainty and risk, optimism, playfulness, and tangibility (Schweitzer et al., 2016). We, thus, derive that the mindset in this specific context is characterized by other constructs from the domain of psychology and behavioral sciences, emphasizing the importance of our *root construct* dimension. Furthermore, we notice early descriptive research (Schweitzer et al., 2016) followed by attempts to systemize a cultivation of a design-thinking mindset among students and practitioners (Groeger & Schweitzer, 2020). In the case of design thinking, the mindset is suggested as an inherent part of the concept (see quote above) instead of an antecedent to a successful application of design thinking. Consequently, we propose the *relation to phenomenon* as a sixth dimension. While this relationship of a certain mindset conceptualization (design thinking mindset) to a wider phenomenon of interest (design thinking) differs from the cognitive psychology approach to mindsets, Schweitzer et al. (2016) follow French's (2016) suggestion and discuss the design thinking mindset in relation to Gollwitzer's (1990) mindset theory of action phases. While this represents an attempt to link the context-specific design thinking mindset to existing mindset theory, we suggest a strong divergence of mindset conceptualizations in the field of innovation from previous theory. This divergence also applies to the scholarly discourse around open innovation.

Open Innovation Mindset

Another innovation paradigm receiving considerable attention is open innovation (Chesbrough et al., 2006). Open innovation is commonly discussed as a certain type of innovation process building on facilitating innovation flows across organizational boundaries (Chesbrough & Bogers, 2014, p. 17). Similar to the design thinking approach, scholars address this paradigm with a mindset-based perspective as well (Engelsberger et al., 2021; Salampasis et al., 2015). Going further than the design thinking mindset, open innovation is defined *as a mindset* – rather than aspects of open innovation being represented by a mindset:

Definition 9. "Open innovation is a dynamic organizational mindset that encourages the exploration and exploitation of diverse knowledge inflows and outflows, leading to innovation continuity and incremental organizational change, through the establishment of trustworthy, culturally sensitive and sustainable relationships" (Salampasis et al., 2015, p. 49).

Since the definition states that open innovation *is* a dynamic organizational mindset, it widens the *relation to phenomenon* dimension. We come to a different understanding of what a mindset is, rather resembling the global mindset stream and add beliefs as a *root construct*:

Definition 10. "A mindset (also known as dominant logic, cognitive map, mental model, strategy frame and belief structure) refers to the knowledge structures that top managers use to make strategic decisions" (Salampasis et al., 2015, p. 39).

Such broad implications and characterizations raise the question of boundary conditions for mindset research. However, there also are more narrow conceptualizations. Engelsberger et al. (2021, p. 2) define an open innovation mindset as:

Definition 11. "[…] an individual's values, attitudes, and beliefs that capture an individual's openness towards KSS [Knowledge Sharing and Sourcing] inside and outside the organizational boundaries that are used as knowledge structures to make decisions regarding KSS which is critical to OI [Open Innovation] performance."

This reflects causal relationships between certain root constructs (values, attitudes, and beliefs) and behavior (knowledge-sharing decisions) and links this to organizational outcomes (open innovation performance). Engelsberger et al. (2021) demonstrate the utility of such a specific mindset in the context of open innovation and show that the mindset can be cultivated with dedicated human resource initiatives. Lastly, we turn our attention to the scholarly discourse around frugal innovation and the frugal mindset. The importance of mindset research for frugal innovation was discussed in early publications (Zeschky et al., 2011), but it is still understudied (Krohn & Herstatt, 2019).

Frugal Mindset

Originating from the context of emerging markets (Zeschky et al., 2011), the frugal innovation paradigm found its path into mainstream innovation research (Weyrauch & Herstatt, 2016). Frugal innovations are characterized by a concentration on core functionalities, an optimized performance level, and a significant cost reduction (Weyrauch & Herstatt, 2016). Scholars suggest that organizations need to change their mindset (Zeschky et al., 2011) and develop a frugal mindset (Soni & Krishnan, 2014) to succeed in developing frugal innovations. Indeed, Soni and Krishnan's (2014) typology resembles Kahn's (2018) suggestion that innovation can be thought of as a process, an outcome, and a mindset. They propose that frugal innovation comprises a frugal outcome, a frugal process, and a frugal mindset (Soni & Krishnan, 2014). The frugal mindset is, therefore, part of frugal innovation instead of being an antecedent to frugal innovation, supporting the necessity of a *relation to phenomenon* dimension.

However, while discussing the frugal mindset with regard to concepts, such as effectuation (Sarasvathy, 2001), bricolage (Baker & Nelson, 2005), and improvisation (Moorman & Miner, 1998), Soni and Krishnan (2014) do not provide a definition of the frugal mindset. A systematic literature review reveals that the scholarly discourse mainly focuses on two crucial components of the frugal mindset (Krohn & Herstatt, 2019): First, employees and managers must recognize the opportunities for frugal innovation, and deliberatively commit to initiate and support corresponding initiatives. Second, employees and managers need the right mindset, such as the concepts discussed by Soni and Krishnan (2014), to implement frugal approaches to problem-solving. This perspective mirrors the mindset theory of action phases by Gollwitzer (1990, 2012) and reflects in the proposition to clearly distinguish between the deliberative frugal mindset and the implemental frugal mindset (Krohn & Herstatt, 2019). This distinction facilitates the operationalization of two distinct concepts, measuring potential effects on decision making and, consequently, the effective development of frugal innovations. Krohn and Herstatt (2019, p. 172), therefore, propose that:

Definition 12. "The deliberative frugal mindset is a cognitive orientation, which is characterized by the belief that offering innovations with a substantial cost reduction, a concentration on core functionalities and an optimized performance level provides viable business opportunities and that the individual and organization is capable of taking the necessary actions to successfully develop these frugal solutions."

With regard to the implemental frugal mindset, Krohn and Herstatt (2019, p. 172) state that:

Definition 13. "The implemental frugal mindset is driven by the goal to offer innovations with a substantial cost reduction, a concentration on core functionalities and an optimized performance level. This action focused cognitive orientation is characterized by a tuning towards deepening the understanding of customers' needs and contexts as well as creatively and efficiently using available resources to develop frugal solutions."

The conceptualization of the frugal mindset is clearly linked to the mindset theory of action phases (see Gollwitzer (1990)). However, the conceptualization of the frugal mindset is also strongly *contextually embedded* in the phenomenon of frugal innovations, building on beliefs, which implies that it is possible to change individuals' mindset when it comes to frugal innovations (Krohn & Buse, 2019).

A Taxonomy of Mindsets

In this section, we present our derived code structure following the methodology of Bradly et al. (2007), and we discuss how these codes form our taxonomy dimensions. Furthermore, we discuss how this framework can support scholars in framing their mindset research. Our analysis strategy and results are summarized in Fig. 2.2.

By analyzing differences and similarities across mindset concepts, we derived implicit underlying assumptions about mindsets. The first two authors constantly

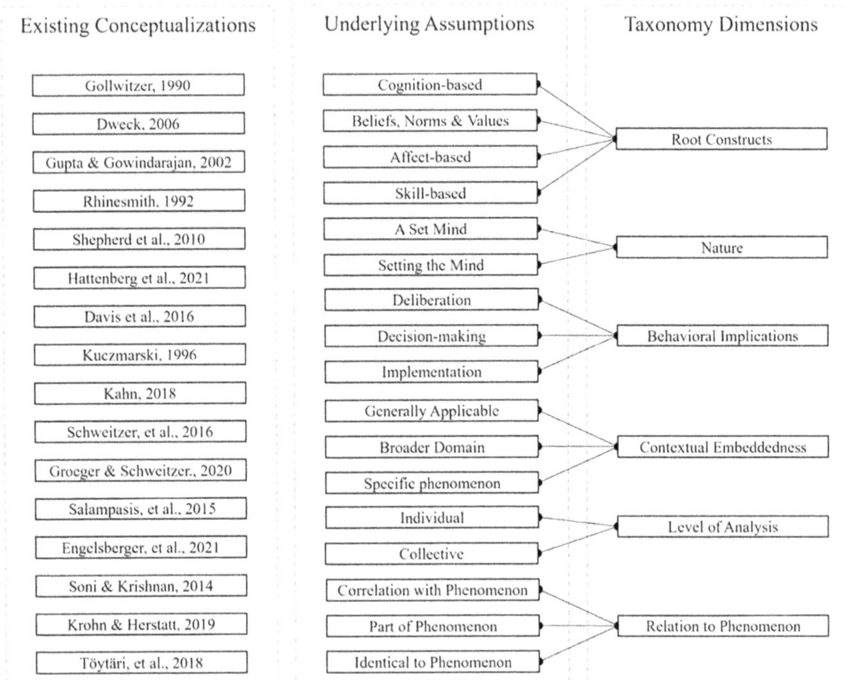

Fig. 2.2 Existing conceptualizations, taxonomy dimensions, and underlying assumptions – graphic based on Gioia et al. (2013)

developed corresponding codes during the review process independently, which we then discussed, compared, and refined. Consequently, we formulated our taxonomy dimensions. In certain cases of our iterative coding procedure, we decided to stay close to the wording of existing concepts (e.g., deliberation and implementation) to avoid contributing to the fuzziness of mindset research (French II, 2016). In other cases, we decided to aggregate assumptions across concepts and facilitate further theory building (e.g., beliefs, norms, and values).

We find that several assumptions influence scholars to frame their research and choose conceptual foundations that fit specific contextually embedded mindsets. An explication of mindset conceptualizations with regard to our dimensions, therefore, appears to be a necessity for research in the field to progress. At the same time, mindset research appears bounded by the dimensions identified in this study. Mindsets are complex phenomena: This is what we can conclude from all earlier research. Apparently, scholars approach this challenge by making use of various *root constructs*, such as cognitive processes (Gollwitzer, 1990), beliefs (Dweck, 2012), emotions (Noble, 2015), abilities (Shepherd et al., 2010), or a combination of constructs (Engelsberger et al., 2021). Most importantly, the scholarly choice of *root constructs* determines how a mindset is operationalized in empirical research.

Additionally, we find that scholars assume mindsets as *static* or *modifiable in nature*. While Gollwitzer (1990) defines the deliberative and implemental mindset with regard to certain behaviors, entrepreneurship and innovation scholars assume that mindsets can be developed (Hattenberg et al., 2020; Krohn & Buse, 2019; Täks et al., 2014). However, we urge scholars to make a deliberative choice about what they try to find out, as we think of our dimensions as continuums. These considerations have implications for study design when it comes to the choice of data collection methods. Furthermore, the assumption that mindset changes are possible speaks for experimental study designs and longitudinal studies.

We identify *behavioral implications* as another dimension. We propose that mindset-based perspectives are applied to create a deeper understanding of important behavioral phenomena, such as innovative behavior in the workplace (Janssen, 2000; Scott & Bruce, 1994), or entrepreneurial behavior (Bird & Schjoedt, 2009). While it is common practice in innovation to explain behavior based on cognitive phenomena, such as intentions (Bartl et al., 2012; Goepel et al., 2012) and entrepreneurship (Kautonen et al., 2013), such narrow perspectives remain limited in explaining more complex behavioral processes. Those narrow perspectives could, thus, be complemented with wider mindset-based perspectives (Delanoë-Gueguen & Fayolle, 2018). This offers the possibility to build on a wider range of interrelated constructs. Arguably, the mindset theory of action phases is widely applicable to *deliberation*, the actual act of *decision making* or *setting a goal,* and *implementation*. However, certain studies in our review assume more specific behavioral implications, such as deliberation-related aspects (Krohn et al., 2020), decision making (Engelsberger et al., 2021), or focusing on maintaining behavioral volition in response to educational challenges (Yeager et al., 2019). Delanoë-Gueguen and Fayolle (2018) show how to combine an exploration of deliberation-related considerations with subsequent action in a longitudinal study. Assumptions about *behavioral implications*, therefore, determine study design with regard to single observations or longitudinal settings. Consequently, mindsets and behavior interact in complex manners and initial qualitative research might elicit a deeper understanding of underlying mechanisms in the corresponding context.

Furthermore, we identify varying degrees of *contextual embeddedness* across mindset conceptualizations. We consider this aspect as a continuum as well, and in this continuum, Gollwitzer's (1990) mindset theory of action phases marks one end of the spectrum, as it is embedded in the wide context of *human behavior*. Progressing on the continuum, we observe *broader domains*, such as entrepreneurship (Shepherd et al., 2010) and more *specific contexts*, such as frugal innovation (Krohn & Herstatt, 2019). In turn, scholars adapt existing mindset conceptualizations to their specific domain or phenomenon. Arguably, research in more specific contexts requires more dedicated pilot work and might have less generalizable implications for other domains.

We also find that scholars make different assumptions about the *level of analysis*. While the cognitive and educational psychology streams focus on the individual, the organizational leadership stream assumes a mutual reshaping of individual and organizational mindsets (Gupta & Govindarajan, 2002). This tendency toward organizational mindsets can be observed in the mostly organizational contexts of innovation (Groeger & Schweitzer, 2020; Salampasis et al., 2015). Beyond the implications for theory and study design, it opens interesting research avenues on the underlying mechanisms of the mutual reshaping of mindsets in organizational settings.

Lastly, by examining existing definitions and conceptualizations, we find that scholars have different assumptions about how the mindset under investigation relates to the wider phenomenon of interest. The *relation to phenomenon* dimension includes *correlations with phenomena* through certain effects, such as open innovation performance (Engelsberger et al., 2021), with mindsets being an integral *part of a phenomenon*, such as innovation (Kahn, 2018), and conceptualizing a wider phenomenon as a mindset (Salampasis et al., 2015).

2.5 Future Research Avenues

Innovation relies on innovative behavior (Goepel et al., 2012; Scott & Bruce, 1994) just like entrepreneurship relies on entrepreneurial behavior (Bird & Schjoedt, 2009), and both disciplines are synergetic in nature (Zhao, 2005). In this chapter, we analyzed and compared mindset research across research fields, and we concluded that mindset-based perspectives are widely applied to understand the entirety of human behavior in the innovation and entrepreneurship context. However, specific mindsets (e.g., the entrepreneurial mindset) appear to relate to their context in complex manners. Our research indicates that the innovation and entrepreneurship research community has not yet established a consistent theory of mindset research, and we believe that our taxonomy provides an important step in developing such a theory. Specifically, our taxonomy is intended to explicate differences and similarities, resulting in six taxonomy dimensions. We strongly suggest that future mindset research aims to link to previous mindset conceptualizations, particularly Gollwitzer's (1990) mindset theory of action phases, and stays within the conceptual boundaries of our taxonomy. Accordingly, the first research avenue is our call for dedicated research on boundary conditions (Whetten, 1989) for the continuums of our mindset dimensions. For example, what is the exact boundary condition to differentiate between a collective organizational mindset (Salampasis et al., 2015) and an organizational culture (Schein, 1985)? Furthermore, we call for more careful *conceptualizations* and a more explicit *contextualization* or socioeconomic embeddedness of future mindset research. The *conceptualization* challenge can be addressed by explicating underlying assumptions regarding our taxonomy dimensions. The *contextualization* challenge is more specific in nature and requires rigorous pilot work.

Compared to the field of entrepreneurship, mindset research within innovation appears to build on a less consistent conceptual basis. Shepherd et al.'s (2010) definition provided an important cornerstone to entrepreneurship, which we now aim to replicate for innovation management. To the best of our knowledge, a commonly applicable definition for a mindset that is conducive to innovation is absent. We, therefore, synthetize mindset-related and innovation-related considerations from Shepherd et al. (2010), Delanoë-Gueguen and Fayolle (2018), Goepel et al. (2012), Gollwitzer (1990), Kahn (2018), Janssen (2000), and Zhao (2005) and propose the following definition:

Definition 14. We define an innovation mindset as the willingness and ability to intentionally create, introduce, apply, and support new ideas as an individual within a work role, group, or organization, and continuously maintain volition to promote idea development along the innovation process to generate innovative outcomes.

While it may be at an early stage to develop a first definition of an innovation mindset, we at the same time believe that such starts need to be made for further developments to take place (see also conceptualization advice from Podsakoff et al., 2016). Additionally, emerging literature has focused on decision-making strategies and anticipatory reasoning in innovation and indicates that such strategies and reasoning are ill-defined as well (Vetorello et al., 2022; Buehring & Liedtka, 2018). Building on this literature and our own findings, we believe that with our first preliminary definition, future research could tangibly investigate how an innovation mindset relates to innovative behavior (Scott & Bruce, 1994) or innovation response behavior (Goepel et al., 2012). Previous intention-based research within innovation management (Bartl et al., 2012; Nedon, 2015) is limited in explaining how organizational members maintain behavioral volition, collaborate, and overcome innovation barriers along the innovation process. Building on Gollwitzer's (1990) mindset theory and applying corresponding study designs from entrepreneurship research, such as Delanoë-Gueguen and Fayolle (2018), bear potential to advance our understanding of innovative behavior and navigating barriers to it.

Furthermore, contextualizing our definition regarding specific innovation contexts, such as frugal innovation and social innovation, could help derive insights with regard to these phenomena. Particularly, it could be interesting to investigate how individuals' minds are set in response to conflicting sets of innovation paradigms. For example, if organizational members' minds are set on a premium-driven innovation logic, does that impede affordability-driven approaches, such as frugal innovation (Krohn et al., 2020)? Mindset-based perspectives, therefore, offer interesting avenues to investigate individual-level path dependency (Sydow et al., 2009). Consequently, it appears interesting to understand how mindset-based change initiatives could help set the mind on a new innovation logic. Similar approaches have produced promising results with intention-based change initiatives (Jimmieson et al., 2008).

Next to this, the field of entrepreneurship offers interesting research avenues concerning mindset research. Where a considerable amount of research has spent time on conceptualizing mindsets (e.g., Hattenberg et al., 2021; Kuratko et al., 2020; Naumann, 2017; Shepherd et al., 2010), research calls for deepening our understanding when it comes to the implication and operationalization of mindsets in multiple contexts (e.g., Belousova et al., 2020; Davis et al., 2016). Our taxonomy provides a first road map for the approach to contextualize the entrepreneurial mindset, and the next step would be to dive into the implications of different contexts. For example, an interesting research question would be, which entrepreneurship-specific contexts foster the development of an entrepreneurial mindset independent of certain demographics. This would contribute to our understanding of the inclusive nature of entrepreneurship.

The entrepreneurship field is currently also open to further debates about the entrepreneurial mindset's behavioral and multilevel implications, as it is difficult to distinguish between mindset and behavior. In any event, the mindset's effects are derived from behavioral implications. Our taxonomy aids future research in strengthening an argument for such a distinction and allows for deriving multilevel implications at the individual, team, and organizational level. Since entrepreneurship does not take place in a vacuum (Hisrich & Kearney, 2011) and contextual embeddedness is recognized (Belousova et al., 2021, 2020), a future research avenue is to explore the entrepreneurial mindset's impact on multiple levels of research.

Lastly, interdisciplinary mindset research to advance our understanding of innovative and entrepreneurial behavior with regard to mindsets offers exciting perspectives. Since innovation and entrepreneurship in themselves are distinct (Kahn, 2022), yet synergetic phenomena (Zhao, 2005), what, then, is the nature of the relationship between the innovation mindset and the entrepreneurial mindset? Are they distinct, synergetic, or even antithetical? Can individuals be driven by both kinds of mindsets at the same time? Does an entrepreneurial mindset foster or impede innovative behavior and vice versa? By proposing a definition for the innovation mindset, resembling the conceptual background of the entrepreneurial mindset, we open avenues to investigate these questions and develop a more consistent theory of mindsets for the innovation and entrepreneurship fields.

2.6 Conclusion

In order to understand innovation (Kahn, 2018) and what it means to be entrepreneurial (Krueger, 2007a), it is imperative to take mindset-based perspectives. We propose that mindset-based perspectives explain behavioral phenomena in relation to root constructs embedded in a phenomenon-specific context – such as inclusive entrepreneurship. Scholars take mindset-based perspectives, because mindsets are considered an important enabler or barrier to innovative and entrepreneurial behavior. Thus, mindset-based perspectives are important for innovation and entrepreneurship as such, and an important tool to understand and realize their synergy. Yet, we find that scholars apply different conceptual approaches. Our taxonomy links six dimensions to several underlying conceptual assumptions regarding mindsets and provides a frame within which scholars can explore innovative and entrepreneurial behavior based on mindsets. We call for more careful *conceptualizations* and *contextualization* of future mindset research to facilitate theory building and prevent a continuing fuzziness of mindset research in the domain of innovation and entrepreneurship.

References

Ajzen, I. (1991). The theory of planned behavior. *Organizational Behavior and Human Decision Processes, 50*(2), 179–211.

Baker, T., & Nelson, R. E. (2005). Creating something from nothing: Resource construction through entrepreneurial bricolage. *Administrative Science Quarterly, 50*(3), 329–366.

Baregheh, A., Rowley, J., & Sambrook, S. (2009). Towards a multidisciplinary definition of innovation. *Management Decision, 47*(8), 1323–1339.

Bartl, M., Füller, J., Mühlbacher, H., & Ernst, H. (2012). A manager's perspective on virtual customer integration for new product development. *Journal of Product Innovation Management, 29*(6), 1031–1046.

Belousova, O., & Gailly, B. (2013). Corporate entrepreneurship in a dispersed setting: Actors, behaviors, and process. *International Entrepreneurship and Management Journal, 9*(3), 361–377.

Belousova, O., Hattenberg, D. Y., & Gailly, B. (2020). Corporate entrepreneurship: From structures to mindset. In *Organizational mindset of entrepreneurship* (pp. 211–233). Springer.

Belousova, O., Groen, A., & Krueger, N. (2021). Corporate entrepreneurship: New insights. In *World encyclopedia of entrepreneurship* (pp. 49–56). Edward Elgar Publishing.

Bird, B., & Schjoedt, L. (2009). Entrepreneurial behavior: Its nature, scope, recent research, and agenda for future research. In *Understanding the entrepreneurial mind* (pp. 327–358). Springer.

Birkinshaw, J. (1997). Entrepreneurship in multinational corporations: The characteristics of subsidiary initiatives. *Strategic Management Journal, 18*(3), 207–229.

Bradley, E. H., Curry, L. A., & Devers, K. J. (2007). Qualitative data analysis for health services research: Developing taxonomy, themes, and theory. *Health Services Research, 42*(4), 1758–1772.

Brenner, W., Uebernickel, F., & Abrell, T. (2016). Design thinking as mindset, process, and toolbox. In *Design thinking for innovation* (pp. 3–21). Springer.

Brown, T. (2008). Design thinking. *Harvard Business Review, 86*(6), 84–92.

Buehring, J. H., & Liedtka, J. (2018). Embracing systematic futures thinking at the intersection of strategic planning, foresight and design. *Journal of Innovation Management, 6*(3), 134–152.

Burgelman, R. A. (1983). A process model of internal corporate venturing in the diversified major firm. *Administrative Science Quarterly, 28*(2), 223–244.

Burgelman, R. A. (1984). Managing the internal corporate venturing process. *Sloan Management Review, 25*(2), 33–48.

Burnette, J. L., et al. (2020). A growth mindset intervention: Enhancing students' entrepreneurial self-efficacy and career development. *Entrepreneurship Theory and Practice, 44*(5), 878–908.

Carlsson, B., et al. (2013). The evolving domain of entrepreneurship research. *Small Business Economics, 41*(4), 913–930.

Chcsbrough, H., & Bogers, M. (2014). Explicating open innovation: Clarifying an emerging paradigm for understanding innovation. In *New frontiers in open innovation* (pp. 3–28). Oxford University Press.

Chesbrough, H., Vanhaverbeke, W., & West, J. (2006). *Open innovation: Researching a new paradigm*. Oxford University Press on Demand.

Clapp-Smith, R., & Lester, G. V. (2014). Defining the "mindset" in global mindset: Modeling the dualities of global leadership. In *Advances in global leadership* (pp. 205–228). Emerald Group Publishing Limited.

Culkin, N., & Mallick, S. (2011). Producing work-ready graduates: The role of the entrepreneurial university. *International Journal of Market Research, 53*(3), 347–368.

Davis, M. H., Hall, J. A., & Mayer, P. S. (2016). Developing a new measure of entrepreneurial mindset: Reliability, validity, and implications for practitioners. *Consulting Psychology Journal: Practice and Research, 68*(1), 1–21.

Delanoë-Gueguen, S., & Fayolle, A. (2018). Crossing the entrepreneurial rubicon: A longitudinal investigation. *Journal of Small Business Management, 57*(3), 1044–1065.

Drucker, P. (1994). *Innovation and entrepreneurship: Practice and principles*. Heinemann.
Dweck, C. S. (2006). *Mindset: The new psychology of success*. Random House Digital, Inc.
Dweck, C. S. (2012). *Mindset: Changing the way you think to fulfil your potential*. Little, Brown Book Group.
Dweck, C. S. (2016). What having a "growth mindset" actually means. *Harvard Business Review, 13*, 213–226.
Dweck, C. S. (2017). From needs to goals and representations: Foundations for a unified theory of motivation, personality, and development. *Psychological Review, 124*(6), 689–719.
Ejupi-Ibrahimi, A., Ramadani, V., & Ejupi, D. (2020). Family businesses in North Macedonia: Evidence on the second generation motivation and entrepreneurial mind-set. *Journal of Family Business Management*, In press.
Engelsberger, A., Halvorsen, B., Cavanagh, J., & Bartram, T. (2021). Human resources management and open innovation: The role of open innovation mindset. *Asia Pacific Journal of Human Resources*, In press.
Flick, U. (1992). Triangulation revisited: Strategy of validation or alternative? *Journal for the Theory of Social Behaviour, 22*(2), 175–197.
French, R. P., II. (2016). The fuzziness of mindsets: Divergent conceptualizations and characterizations of mindset theory and praxis. *International Journal of Organizational Analysis, 24*(4), 673–691.
Gioia, D. A., Corley, K. G., & Hamilton, A. L. (2013). Seeking qualitative rigor in inductive research: Notes on the Gioia methodology. *Organizational Research Methods, 16*(1), 15–31.
Goepel, M., Hölzle, K., & zu Knyphausen-Aufseß, D. (2012). Individuals' innovation response behaviour: A framework of antecedents and opportunities for future research. *Creativity and Innovation Management, 21*(4), 412–426.
Gollwitzer, P. M. (1990). Action phases and mind-sets. In *Handbook of motivation and cognition: Foundations of social behavior* (Vol. 2, pp. 53–92). The Guilford Press.
Gollwitzer, P. M. (2012). Mindset theory of action phases. In *Handbook of theories of social psychology* (pp. 526–545). SAGE.
Groeger, L., & Schweitzer, J. (2020). Developing a design thinking mindset: Encouraging designerly ways in postgraduate business education. In *Design thinking in higher education* (pp. 41–72). Springer.
Gupta, A. K., & Govindarajan, V. (2002). Cultivating a global mindset. *The Academy of Management Executive, 16*(1), 116–126.
Hattenberg, D. Y., Belousova, O., & Groen, A. J. (2020). Organizational conditions stimulating the entrepreneurial mindset. In *Sustainable entrepreneurship and entrepreneurial ecosystems* (pp. 158–176). Edward Elgar Publishing.
Hattenberg, D., Belousova, O., & Groen, A. (2021). Defining the entrepreneurial mindset and discussing its distinctiveness in entrepreneurship research. *International Journal of Entrepreneurship and Small Business, 44*(1), 30–52.
Haynie, J. M., Shepherd, D., Mosakowski, E., & Earley, P. C. (2010). A situated metacognitive model of the entrepreneurial mindset. *Journal of Business Venturing, 25*(2), 217–229.
Herstatt, C., & Von Hippel, E. (1992). From experience: Developing new product concepts via the lead user method: A case study in a "low-tech" field. *Journal of Product Innovation Management, 9*(3), 213–221.
Hisrich, R., & Kearney, C. (2011). *Corporate entrepreneurship: How to create a thriving entrepreneurial spirit throughout your company*. McGraw Hill Professional.
Hölzle, K., Boer, H., & Björk, J. (2020). Driving transformational change—Antecedents and influences of creativity and innovation. *Creativity and Innovation Management, 4*(29), 549–550.
Hornsby, J. S., Kuratko, D. F., Holt, D. T., & Wales, W. J. (2013). Assessing a measurement of organizational preparedness for corporate entrepreneurship. *Journal of Product Innovation Management, 30*(5), 937–995.
Ireland, R. D., Hitt, M. A., & Sirmon, D. G. (2003). A model of strategic entrepreneurship: The construct and its dimensions. *Journal of Management, 29*(6), 963–989.

Janssen, O. (2000). Job demands, perceptions of effort-reward fairness and innovative work behaviour. *Journal of Occupational and Organizational Psychology, 73*(3), 287–302.
Jimmieson, N. L., Peach, M., & White, K. M. (2008). Utilizing the theory of planned behavior to inform change management: An investigation of employee intentions to support organizational change. *The Journal of Applied Behavioral Science, 44*(2), 237–262.
Kaffka, G., & Krueger, N. (2018). The entrepreneurial 'mindset': Entrepreneurial intentions from the entrepreneurial event to neuroentrepreneurship. In *Foundational research in entrepreneurship studies* (pp. 203–224). Palgrave Macmillan.
Kahn, K. B. (2018). Understanding innovation. *Business Horizons, 61*(3), 453–460.
Kahn, K. B. (2022). Innovation is not entrepreneurship, nor vice versa. *Journal of Product Innovation Management, 39*(4), 467–473.
Kautonen, T., Van Gelderen, M., & Tornikoski, E. T. (2013). Predicting entrepreneurial behaviour: A test of the theory of planned behaviour. *Applied Economics, 45*(6), 697–707.
Krohn, M., & Buse, S. (2019). Developing and implementing frugal innovation mindsets in organisations. In *Frugal innovation: A global research companion* (pp. 228–238). Routledge.
Krohn, M., & Herstatt, C. (2019). Vision for frugal innovation: The power of mindsets for transformation. In *Frugal innovation: A global research companion* (pp. 164–176). Routledge.
Krohn, M., Petersen, F., Hochmuth, D., & Herstatt, C. (2020). The deliberative frugal mindset–a model of managerial opportunity recognition for frugal innovation. *Working Paper; Technologie- und Innovationsmanagement,* Hamburg University of Technology.
Krueger, N. (2007a). What lies beneath? The experiential essence of entrepreneurial thinking. *Entrepreneurship Theory and Practice, 31*(1), 123–138.
Krueger, N. (2007b). The cognitive infrastructure of opportunity emergence. In *Entrepreneurship* (pp. 185–206). Springer.
Krueger, N. F. (2009). The microfoundations of entrepreneurial learning and education. In *The handbook of university-wide entrepreneurship* (pp. 35–59). Edward Elgar Publishing.
Kruft, T., & Kock, A. (2021). Unlocking novel opportunities: How online ideation platforms implicitly guide employees toward better ideas by spurring their desire to innovate. *Creativity and Innovation Management, 30*(4), 816–835.
Kuczmarski, T. D. (1996). Fostering an innovation mindset. *Journal of Consumer Marketing, 13*(6), 7–13.
Kuratko, D. F., Fisher, G., & Audretsch, D. B. (2020). Unraveling the entrepreneurial mindset. *Small Business Economics, 57*, 1–11.
McGrath, R. G., & MacMillan, I. C. (2000). *The entrepreneurial mindset: Strategies for continuously creating opportunity in an age of uncertainty*. Harvard Business Press.
McMullen, J. S., & Shepherd, D. A. (2006). Entrepreneurial action and the role of uncertainty in the theory of the entrepreneur. *Academy of Management Review, 31*(1), 132–152.
Micheli, P., et al. (2019). Doing design thinking: Conceptual review, synthesis, and research agenda. *Journal of Product Innovation Management, 36*(2), 124–148.
Mitchell, G. R. (2017). Instill the entrepreneurial mindset. *Research-Technology Management, 50*(6), 11–13.
Mitchell, R. K., & Chesteen, S. A. (1995). Enhancing entrepreneurial expertise: Experiential pedagogy and the new venture expert script. *Simulation & Gaming, 26*(3), 288–306.
Mitchell, R. K., Mitchell, B. T., & Mitchell, J. R. (2017). Entrepreneurial scripts and entrepreneurial expertise: The information processing perspective. In *Revisiting the entrepreneurial mind* (pp. 131–173). Springer.
Moorman, C., & Miner, A. S. (1998). Organizational improvisation and organizational memory. *Academy of Management Review, 4*(23), 698–723.
Naumann, C. (2017). Entrepreneurial mindset: A synthetic literature review. *Entrepreneurial Business and Economics Review, 5*(3), 149–172.
Nedon, V. (2015). *Open innovation in R&D departments: An analysis of employees' intention to exchange knowledge in OI-projects*. Springer Gabler.

Nickerson, R. C., Varshney, U., & Muntermann, J. (2013). A method for taxonomy development and its application in information systems. *European Journal of Information Systems, 22*(3), 336–359.
Noble, C. (2015). Mindsets, mind sets and mind sense. *Prometheus, 33*(4), 411–420.
Patel, S., & Mehta, K. (2017). Systems, design, and entrepreneurial thinking: Comparative frameworks. *Systemic Practice and Action Research, 30*(5), 515–533.
Podsakoff, P. M., MacKenzie, S. B., & Podsakoff, N. P. (2016). Recommendations for creating better concept definitions in the organizational, behavioral, and social sciences. *Organizational Research Methods, 19*(2), 159–203.
Rarick, C., & Han, T. (2015). The role of culture in shaping an entrepreneurial mindset. *International Journal of Entrepreneurship, 19*(2), 119–125.
Rattan, A., & Ozgumus, E. (2021). Embedding mindsets in context: Theoretical considerations and opportunities for studying fixed-growth lay theories in the workplace. *Research in Organizational Behavior*, In press.
Rhinesmith, S. (1992). Global mindset for global manager. *Training & Development, 46*(10), 63–68.
Robinson, S., et al. (2016). New horizons in entrepreneurship: From teacher-led to student-centered learning. *Education + Training, 58*(7/8), 1–32.
Salampasis, D. G., Mention, A. L., & Torkkeli, M. (2015). Trust embeddedness within an open innovation mindset. *International Journal of Business and Globalisation, 14*(1), 32–57.
Sarasvathy, S. D. (2001). Causation and effectuation: Toward a theoretical shift from economic inevitability to entrepreneurial contingency. *Academy of Management Review, 26*(2), 243–263.
Schaltegger, S., & Wagner, M. (2011). Sustainable entrepreneurship and sustainability innovation: Categories and interactions. *Business Strategy and the Environment, 20*(4), 222–237.
Schein, E. (1985). *Organizational culture and leadership*. Jossey-Bass.
Schumpeter, J. (1934). *The theory of economic development, (reproduced, New York (1961))*. Harvard University Press.
Schweitzer, J., Groeger, L., & Sobel, L. (2016). The design thinking mindset: An assessment of what we know and what we see in practice. *Journal of Design, Business & Society, 2*(1), 71–94.
Scott, S., & Bruce, R. (1994). Determinants of innovative behavior: A path model of individual innovation in the workplace. *Academy of Management Journal, 37*(3), 580–607.
Shepherd, D., Patzelt, H., & Haynie, J. (2010). Entrepreneurial spirals: Deviation-amplifying loops of an entrepreneurial mindset and organizational culture. *Entrepreneurship Theory and Practice, 34*(1), 59–82.
Soni, P., & Krishnan, T. (2014). Frugal innovation: Aligning theory, practice, and public policy. *Journal of Indian Business Research, 6*(1), 29–47.
Starostka, J., Evald, M. R., Clarke, A. H., & Hansen, P. R. (2021). Taxonomy of design thinking facilitation. *Creativity and Innovation Management, 30*(4), 836–844.
Sydow, J., Schreyögg, G., & Koch, J. (2009). Organizational path dependence: Opening the black box. *Academy of Management Review, 34*(4), 689–709.
Täks, M., Tynjälä, P., Toding, M., Kukemelk, H., & Venesaar, U. (2014). Engineering students' experiences in studying entrepreneurship. *Journal of Engineering Education, 103*(4), 573–598.
Thornton, P., Ocasio, W., & Lounsbury, M. (2012). *The institutional logics perspective: A new approach to culture, structure, and process*. Oxford University Press.
Töytäri, P., Turunen, T., Klein, M., Eloranta, V., Biehl, S., & Rajala, R. (2018). Aligning the mindset and capabilities within a business network for successful adoption of smart services. *Journal of Product Innovation Management, 35*(5), 763–779.
Van Gelderen, M., Brand, M., Van Praag, M., Bodewes, W., Poutsma, E., & Van Gils, A. (2008). Explaining entrepreneurial intentions by means of the theory of planned behaviour. *Career Development International, 13*(6), 538–559.
Vettorello, M., Eisenbart, B., & Ranscombe, C. (2022). The innovation system roadmap: A novel approach to instil futures-oriented reasoning in strategic decision making. *Creativity and Innovation Management, 31*(1), 5–18.

Weyrauch, T., & Herstatt, C. (2016). What is frugal innovation? Three defining criteria. *Journal of Frugal Innovation, 2*(1), 1–17.
Whetten, D. A. (1989). What constitutes a theoretical contribution? *Academy of Management Review, 14*(4), 490–495.
Yeager, D. S., & Dweck, C. S. (2012). Mindsets that promote resilience: When students believe that personal characteristics can be developed. *Educational Psychologist, 47*(4), 302–314.
Yeager, D. S., Hanselman, P., Walton, G. M., Murray, J. S., Crosnoe, R., Muller, C., et al. (2019). A national experiment reveals where a growth mindset improves achievement. *Nature, 573*(7774), 364–369.
Zahra, S. A. (2015). Corporate entrepreneurship as knowledge creation and conversion: The role of entrepreneurial hubs. *Small Business Economics, 44*(4), 727–735.
Zeschky, M., Widenmayer, B., & Gassmann, O. (2011). Frugal innovation in emerging markets. *Research-Technology Management, 4*(54), 38–45.
Zhao, F. (2005). Exploring the synergy between entrepreneurship and innovation. *International Journal of Entrepreneurial Behavior & Research, 11*(1), 25–41.
Żur, A. (2015). Social problems as sources of opportunity–antecedents of social entrepreneurship opportunities. *Entrepreneurial Business and Economics Review, 3*(4), 73–87.

Chapter 3
The Effects of Formal and Informal Institutions on Women's Entrepreneurship in Georgia

Lela Griessbach and Kerstin Ettl

3.1 Introduction

The impact of formal and informal institutions on women's entrepreneurship has received increased attention among policy makers and scholars globally (Alsos et al., 2017; Estrin & Mickiewicz, 2011; Welter & Smallbone, 2008; Wu & Li, 2019). Institutions affect the nature, pace of development, and extent of women's entrepreneurship, as well as the way entrepreneurs behave (Brush et al., 2018; Smallbone & Welter, 2010). Formal institutions, such as laws and public policies aimed at supporting women and increasing their participation in economic life, may stimulate women's business and entrepreneurial activity (Aidis et al., 2007). Informal institutions, such as cultural norms, may determine the (economic) role and function of women in society, though sometimes to their disadvantage (Welter et al., 2003; Iakovleva et al., 2013).

According to institutional theory, the stronger formal institutions are, the weaker informal institutions and practices become (North, 1991). Consequently, in countries with strong formal institutions, people are more likely to trust state structures, comply with the law, and follow rules and regulations (Mickiewicz et al., 2019). By contrast, in turbulent institutional environments where external conditions change rapidly and major institutional deficiencies may evolve, the population frequently rely on family and friendship ties and informal practices, which are culturally ingrained and accepted in that society, though they may be ethically questionable (Aliyev, 2015). Several scholars have examined institutional factors and their importance for entrepreneurship development in post-Soviet countries (Chepurenko,

L. Griessbach (✉)
University of Siegen, Department III, Business Administration, Siegen, Germany

K. Ettl
Westfälische Hochschule, Bocholt, Germany

K. Mikkelsen, A. Wolf (eds.), *Minds, Brains, and Doxa for Inclusive Entrepreneurship*, International Studies in Entrepreneurship 47,
https://doi.org/10.1007/978-3-031-50164-7_3

2015; Mickiewicz et al., 2019; Welter & Smallbone, 2011). Few studies have focused on women entrepreneurs, revealing that both formal and informal institutions might be constraining for women entrepreneurs in fragile and turbulent environments (Ahlstrom & Bruton, 2010; Smallbone & Welter, 2010). Researchers have repeatedly outlined the importance of institutional changes that enhance the development of new entrepreneurial opportunities, especially for or through women (Estrin et al., 2007; Rugina, 2019; Sätre, 2016; Welter & Smallbone, 2008).

Nevertheless, knowledge about the interrelation between formal and informal institutions in post-Soviet countries remains limited, along with the effects of institutional changes on women's entrepreneurship after the transition process (Griessbach & Ettl, 2020). Furthermore, scholars working on gender and management research in Central and Eastern European (CEE) countries have critically outlined that "there is so few 'CEE' in CEE-related research on women in management" (Rybnikova et al., 2020a, p. 13) and called for more engagement in considering local country- and history-based nuances and peculiarities in conceptual and theoretical perspectives in this regard.

We aim to respond to this call with this chapter, drawing attention to the under-researched context of both formal and informal institutions and their impact on women entrepreneurs and women's entrepreneurship in post-Soviet Georgia, where a large number of democratic institutional reforms have been implemented after the thrilling, but peaceful political change brought about by the so-called "Rose Revolution" in November 2003. The top priority of these reforms was to combat deep-rooted informal, unethical, and illegal practices such as bribery and nepotism, which had been prevalent in all spheres of life, and to move the informal economy into formal structures (Engvall, 2012; Rudaz, 2015). Several studies have documented the successful construction of a suitable free market business environment, involving more people in formal employment, promoting entrepreneurship, and attracting foreign investment (Government of Georgia, 2014; OECD, 2016). At the same time, knowledge of the impact of democratic reforms and informal practices on women's entrepreneurship remains limited. In this context, we follow the assumption that high rates of governance indicators and top rankings – for example, in ease of doing business (Asian Development Bank, 2018; World Bank Group, 2018) – reported on transition countries like Georgia are more likely to focus on the elimination of administrative barriers for local business (Rekhviashvili, 2016; Rudaz, 2012). Such indicators are often used to improve a country's image and to attract foreign investments, whereas "the overall basic institutional framework is still fragile, and the social (informal) barriers are still in place" (Rudaz, 2012, p. 4).

Some research on women's entrepreneurship in patriarchal societies underlines the emancipatory aspect of entrepreneurship showing that despite of advanced institutions in mature markets certain cultural patterns could lead to unequal opportunities and a power imbalance on labor market (Mikkelsen, 2018). In such circumstances, women tend to engage in entrepreneurship in order to overcome these inequalities, gain economic independence, and become free from male dominance (Mikkelsen, 2018). The GEM Report 2014 shows that for women in Georgia, the motivation to engage in entrepreneurial activities is either necessity driven (53.3%) or opportunity driven (46.7%) (Lezhava et al., 2014). According to the report, an average early stage women entrepreneur in Georgia is 45 years old, ethnically Georgian with secondary education, operating either in the capital city or in rural areas. Successful entrepreneurs enjoy a high status in the Georgian society; however, only 26.7% of the female population thinks that they are capable of performing entrepreneurial activities and more than 40% perceives fear of failure in entrepreneurial activities. In addition, the lack of opportunities in the Georgian business environment seems to be an issue for a large number of women (Lezhava et al., 2014).

In Georgia, most women work mainly in low-paid sectors (Asian Development Bank, 2018; World Bank Group, 2018). Even though the number of women in management show impressive results compared to other countries (Grant Thornton International, 2015), there is a significant gender wage gap between men and women, with women earning 64% of what men earned on average in 2017 (Asian Development Bank, 2018; World Bank Group, 2018). In contrast, the Women's Economic Opportunity (WEO) index shows very high scores for women's legal and social status in the country (Economist Intelligence Unit, 2010). However, according to the Global Gender Gap Index 2022, Georgia ranks 55th of 146 countries with a value of 0.731 (with "zero" corresponding to imparity and "one" to gender parity) (World Economic Forum, 2022).

From this perspective, Georgia can be considered a best case of an institutional transformation, having changed from the most corrupt post-Soviet failed state to one known as a "frontier-market" (Rudaz, 2012, p. 4). In 2010, the Georgia Law on Gender Equality was passed that prohibits gender-related discrimination and puts in place provisions for guaranteeing gender equality aimed at ensuring women's safety, providing equality on the job market, and supporting women's involvement in politics (Asian Development Bank, 2018; World Bank Group, 2018). Furthermore, significant steps have been taken in order to increase women's participation in decision-making processes. However, the share of women in politics is still very low and the share of people who favor men in managerial positions is still high. In addition, son preference in the society is still quite strong, which leads to a sex imbalance and thus "missing girls" (UN Women, 2020).

Such contradictory findings from the literature imply the controversial nature of the institutional framework in Georgia, despite tremendous institutional efforts. In this light, we aim to look more closely at not only constraints and prospects of the development of women's entrepreneurship in general but also at the institutional factors that affect the individual paths of women entrepreneurs. This chapter thus advances our knowledge about formal and informal institutions and women's entrepreneurship by answering the following question: *How have formal and informal institutions affected women entrepreneurs and women's entrepreneurship since the Rose Revolution in Georgia, and what does this mean for future development?*

Drawing on results from an (online) focus group discussion with women entrepreneurs from Georgia, we provide initial insights on critical constraints and the supporting factors local women entrepreneurs face. Moreover, we elaborate upon the effects of both formal and informal institutions on women's entrepreneurship development. From several factors representing formal and informal institutions throughout the relevant literature (Rugina, 2019; Smallbone & Welter, 2010), we concentrate on the formal institutions "governmental initiatives," "financial institutions," and "business-relevant education" and the informal institutions "perception of women's role in society," "the use of informal networks of connections and acquaintances," and "gift-giving practices." We thus contribute to expanding the small database on women and management in Eastern post-Soviet countries, which have recently established considerable institutional reforms in order to build democratic institutions and a neoliberal market economy (Aliyev, 2017).

We begin this chapter with a review of the literature on institutional change and women's entrepreneurship development in general, followed by insights about women's entrepreneurship in post-Soviet countries. After summarizing our data design, data generating and interpretation process in the methodology section, our empirical results are presented. After discussing main findings and their implications, we will end with some concluding remarks.

3.2 Theoretical Background

Institutional Change and Women's Entrepreneurship Development

The process of becoming an entrepreneur and the level of a new firms' growth and development is greatly conditioned by their given institutional context (Welter & Smallbone, 2011). Increasing number of scholars have applied an institutional approach to examining entrepreneurship and small businesses in transition economies (Estrin et al., 2007; Manolova et al., 2007; Mickiewicz et al., 2019; Puffer et al., 2010). Accordingly, literature demonstrates how factors such as legal environment, economic incentives, culture, and traditions influence the development of entrepreneurship and the economic advancement of a country. These factors are made up of both formal and informal institutions (North, 1991), which can enable as well as constrain entrepreneurial behavior and activity (Welter & Smallbone, 2011). Formal institutions establish ground rules, such as constitutional, legal, and organizational frameworks for individual actions, facilitating certainty in transactions, as well as encouraging entrepreneurs' utility-maximization considerations (Pathak et al., 2013). Informal institutions refer to codes of conduct, values, and norms (North, 1991), including the uncodified attitudes that are embedded in the society which shape entrepreneurs' decisions (Mikkelsen, 2018; Welter & Smallbone, 2011).

While many studies have concentrated on examining the influences of institutions on general entrepreneurship (which includes both male and female entrepreneurship), assuming that institutions have similar effects on women's and men's behavior, an increasing body of research outlines how gender plays a role, and that there are certain differences in institutional impact on men and women entrepreneurs (Wu & Li, 2019). Existing research has revealed that formal institutions, such as governmental regulations for women, discourage women's willingness to pursue entrepreneurial activity, and thus widen the gender gap in entrepreneurship activity (Estrin & Mickiewicz, 2011). This includes maternity leave policies, restrictions on women's freedom of movement, family policies, and property rights (Welter & Smallbone, 2008). Informal institutions can affect the cultural acceptance of entrepreneurial activities as a career choice, thus shaping women's standing in society and economic function (Brush et al., 2018; Wu & Li, 2019). Moreover, as informal institutions are deeply embedded within a society and its culture, they determine gender roles and prescribe typically "male" or "female" behavior (Ahl, 2006). This supports gender stereotypes in societies that assign certain gender roles for how men and women should act and what their responsibilities in life are (Rugina, 2019). For example, childcare and household chores are mostly associated with women, thus confining them to domestic activities (Wu & Li, 2019). At the same time, certain supportive norms and positive public attitudes toward women's entrepreneurship would encourage women to engage in an entrepreneurial activity (Iakovleva et al., 2017).

With regard to entrepreneurial education, women also experience gender inequality in terms of entrepreneurial competences (Brush et al., 2018; Wu & Li, 2019). This is linked with the fact that even though women are highly educated, working as scientists, medical doctors, and lawyers, or having positions of great responsibility in their jobs, their positions are mostly limited to middle-level management (Rugina, 2019). With regard to entrepreneurship, education can increase women's access to knowledge and the development of their entrepreneurial mindset (Larsen, 2022). The latter will support them in starting a business, no matter whether the knowledge concerns how to run a business or consists of expertise in the business area (Pathak et al., 2013). In transition countries, entrepreneurship is increasingly being recognized as the backbone of economic and social development that has been facilitated by political or economic reforms (Sauka & Chepurenko, 2017). However, as existing research shows, using unified concepts without the consideration of gender specificities in terms of entrepreneurship may not have the intended effects, as the systemic and social constraints for women would continue to exist and still hamper the development of women's entrepreneurship (Griessbach & Ettl, 2020).

Institutional changes – as broadly experienced in post-Soviet countries – can positively influence the development of entrepreneurship in general by removing or lowering barriers to market entry (Aidis et al., 2007). A gender-sensitive perspective incorporates endeavors, which focus on removing or lowering the barriers that constrain women and their entrepreneurial activity (Welter & Smallbone, 2011). Furthermore, institutional change may also result in institutional loopholes that can be identified and addressed by women's ventures (Aidis et al., 2007; Iakovleva et al., 2017). In this context, scholars outline the importance of changes in both formal and informal institutions. Even if formal institutions, such as laws and regulations may enable women to enter entrepreneurship, social norms may still discourage them from engaging in entrepreneurial activities (Pathak et al., 2013). Since informal institutions are deeply embedded in society, they tend to change more slowly than formal institutions (Aliyev, 2015). Conflicting formal and informal institutions build a contradictory framework. This affects entrepreneurial behavior, as entrepreneurs draw on previously "learned" behaviors, which in some cases challenge the formal rules (Mickiewicz et al., 2019; Pathak et al., 2013).

Peculiarities of Women's Entrepreneurship in a Post-Soviet Context

Scholars emphasize the importance of the Soviet gender order in shaping women's standing and role in entrepreneurship (Ashwin & Yakubovich, 2005; Salmenniemi et al., 2011; Sätre, 2016). The Soviet gender order was established through the needs of the state and based on communist ideology and needs to be considered from two perspectives. On the one hand, women were portrayed as being equal to men and able to succeed in any area. In fact, many women were highly educated, working as scientists, medical doctors, and lawyers, or having positions of great responsibility in their jobs, though mostly in middle-level management positions (Rugina, 2019). In the 1980s, the Soviet Union achieved the world's highest female workforce participation rates, with 90% of working-age women employed or in training (Welter & Smallbone, 2010). On the other hand, a so-called "real equality" between women and men, i.e., equal chances and opportunities for personal and career development, was never implemented in the Soviet era (Welter & Smallbone, 2010). Scholars emphasize that the state needed a cheap labor supply for rapid production and manufacturing, so the state empowered women with the aim of utilizing them as a cheap labor source (Shahnazaryan et al., 2016). In fact, only a few women were able to achieve considerable positions among party elites or top management positions in the Soviet economy. Consequently, women were absent from most decision-making institutions (Welter & Smallbone, 2010). Further to the role of women being full-time, paid workers, Soviet feminine identity was highly determined by motherhood. Motherhood was glorified, and household chores were presented as the natural sphere for women (Sätre, 2016). This worker–mother role was translated into the dual responsibility of women not only being successful mothers but also well-educated workers, excelling at their post, never complaining, and contributing to the prosperity of the Soviet Union (Rugina, 2019; Shahnazaryan et al., 2016).

With regard to the role of women in post-Soviet societies and their effects on women's entrepreneurship, it is valuable to consider (returning) women emigrants, who became "transnational mothers"[1] and breadwinners, playing an important role

[1] As a result of migration, women who left their (young) children in their homeland became "transnational mothers", for whom remittances became a means of expressing physical and emotional care for their children (Zurabishvili and Zurabishvili, 2010).

in changing institutions (Zurabishvili & Zurabishvili, 2010). As one response to the economic and political uncertainties of the post-Soviet period, increased unemployment and a decreasing quality of life, women from post-Soviet countries began migrating in greater numbers, through mostly in a nonlegal way, and large numbers of migrants went mostly to EU countries with growing home and elderly care markets (Chachava, 2020). For decades, European labor markets have been increasingly affected by the participation of local women in formal paid employment that has reduced the supply of informal caregivers within families, requiring these families to find alternative, affordable care (Vanore & Siegel, 2015). Migrant women from post-Soviet countries recognized such opportunities for employment in female-focused sectors abroad, with the aim of saving or sending money home in order to advance the economic situation of the family and, in some cases, to start a business after returning (Zurabishvili & Zurabishvili, 2010). One might argue that (returning) emigrant women have a positive impact on the economic advancement of the homeland, as they send a considerable number of remittances and strengthen women's economic role in a society by changing societal norms in accepting women as the breadwinners of the family (Zurabishvili & Zurabishvili, 2010). However, studies show that emigration experiences of women do neither automatically contribute to their own socioeconomic empowerment nor to socioeconomic empowerment of other women in their country (Chachava, 2020). For example, Chachava (2020) found that female immigrants from Georgia learned a lot from observing the experiences of local women in the host country. However, they could neither manage to overcome gender stereotypes and step over the established gender roles during their stay in migration nor after returning to their home country. Accordingly, the behavior of returning immigrant women is still driven by the prevailing gender role "woman as caring wife and mother." To make things worse, immigrant women have adapted to the roles of family breadwinners but men who remained in their homeland in most cases did not take over the domestic work that was done by women before. This led to shortages of care in the families of immigrant women. Although women earned more during the emigration than men in the home country did, men remained the decision makers in families (Chachava, 2020).

Research on women's entrepreneurship in post-Soviet countries has indicated that women are well educated in many post-Soviet societies and that the average education level of men may be even lower than that of women (Rugina, 2019; Rybnikova et al., 2020b). An increasing body of scholars outlines the importance of the educational level of opportunity recognition in starting and growing a business (Ettl & Welter, 2010). Especially in societies, which adhere to male stereotypes and favor male employment, women might restrict themselves through a lack of self-confidence or unsupported fears of failure (Mikkelsen, 2018). Therefore, (formal) entrepreneurship education can support women in acquiring business-relevant knowledge and reducing the limiting effects of low self-confidence, thus increasing the chances of starting a business (Pathak et al., 2013). However, studies focusing on (women's) entrepreneurship in post-Soviet countries have revealed that entrepreneurship and opportunity recognition are less likely to be associated with higher education institutions (Kuriakose, 2013). Regarding women entrepreneurs in turbulent institutional environments, scholars argue that well-educated women might also experience specific barriers where neither business knowledge nor former work experience can help (Manolova et al., 2007). Rugina (2019) found that although the educational level of women in the post-Soviet Baltic countries (which now are the part of EU) is higher than that of men, and the local business environment is considered favorable for entrepreneurs in general, women are more likely to operate here in noncapital-intensive sectors with fewer opportunities for earning a high and sustainable income. This implies that in the context of functioning formal institutions, a high education level of women entrepreneurs does not necessarily lead to growth-oriented ventures. Such diverse and often contradictory research findings suggest that the educational influence on women's entrepreneurial activity in post-Soviet countries requires further examination.

It can be argued that as entrepreneurship was prohibited during the Soviet regime, people could not develop the sense of economic activity that is a characteristic of free market societies. However, existing research underlines the relevance of the attitude women have to daily confrontations of shortcomings caused by the Soviet planned economy (Ledeneva, 1998) and its impact on shaping (post-) Soviet women's entrepreneurial behavior, which women also used after the transition process (Sätre, 2016). As the Soviet state system only partially ensured the inclusion of social services in its planning, social issues remained mostly unconsidered and had to be addressed within informal spheres. Because of the low priority given to the production of consumer goods and the underdevelopment of retail trade, Soviet households were forced to find different ways of overcoming this issue. According to given family structures and the woman's role in the household, it was added to women's responsibility to ensure social security, thus forcing women to engage in informal networks (Sätre, 2016). While women in the Soviet era did not usually hold high management positions, they experienced a lack of "high-level" Soviet network contacts (Welter et al., 2003). Consequently, it can be assumed that, through new "domestic manager" roles, women could successfully manage to overcome shortcomings by maintaining not only contacts with family and friends but also with acquaintances and other informal connections (Ashwin & Yakubovich, 2005), helping them to become somehow entrepreneurial (Rehn & Taalas, 2004; Welter & Smallbone, 2008).

In fact, informal networks of acquaintances and connections were very important within all spheres of life in Soviet society (Aliyev, 2015; Ledeneva, 1998). Informal social networks have been used in many countries after the collapse of the Soviet Union to start a privatization process as the central basis for developing one's own company (Markova, 2016; Puffer et al., 2013). It is notable that social networks are also recognized as an accelerator of entrepreneurial activity in advanced Eastern and Western countries, enabling entrepreneurs to gain access to resources, provide competitive advantage, and facilitate opportunity recognition (Ettl & Welter, 2010; Mierzejewska & Dziurski, 2021). By contrast, in the post-Soviet entrepreneurial environment, networks seem to be inevitable and mostly embedded within an informal context: informal networks are used to overcome institutional voids, such as slow and complicated bureaucracy, rapidly changing, contradictory and weakly enforced legislation, an underdeveloped banking system, unfair competition by obtaining grants, and patron–client relations with donors (Aliyev, 2017; Puffer et al., 2010; Salmenniemi et al., 2011). It is argued that such turbulent environments and entrepreneurship conditions may discourage or exclude women from taking on entrepreneurial activities or thinking about new opportunities for growing their businesses, as women face many (cultural) inequalities restricting their access to required resources. Iakovleva et al. (2013) emphasize that women mostly focus in their businesses on societal issues and desire to solve unmet needs. In comparison, male entrepreneurs tend to focus on traditional business outcomes such as growth or profits (Iakovleva et al., 2013).

However, as previous research has shown, women entrepreneurs in turbulent environments and institutional settings are more likely to use informal contacts and practices, not because they want to engage in unethical behavior, but as a survival and growth strategy (Sätre, 2016). Women reported paying bribes in order to speed up the registration and licensing process. This came in the form of presents, such as flowers or candy for a woman and brandy for a man. Even though women were not always openly told by male officials how much they should pay, they decided to offer presents just to "oil the wheels" of the process (Welter et al., 2003).

3.3 Data and Methods

To obtain insights about formal and informal institutions and explore their effects on women's entrepreneurship in Georgia, we conducted a focus group discussion with Georgian women entrepreneurs from the capital, Tbilisi. A focus group discussion as a qualitative research method enables direct interaction with individuals from the field and obtains their perspectives and opinions on the research phenomenon (Morgan, 1996). As empirical studies on women's entrepreneurship in Georgia and its interlinkage with (in-)formal institutions are scarce, we estimated qualitative data obtained from a focus group discussion a good fit (Blagoev & Costas, 2021). In focus groups, up to ten members participated in a moderator-led conversation (Powell & Single, 1996). For our focus group discussion, we chose a sample of five women entrepreneurs, because smaller sample sizes are more appropriate for gathering in-depth information (Morgan, 1996). In a small group, researchers can get involved more deeply and with more nuance, and are able to act more situation-dependently (Blagoev & Costas, 2021). Furthermore, smaller groups are "more appropriate with emotionally charged topics," generating "high levels of participant involvement" (Morgan, 1996, p. 146). In addition to group size, the level of moderator involvement in a group discussion is of importance, measurable through the number and type of questions, because the moderator can influence the direction of the topics and the group dynamic (Morgan, 1996). In order to give all participants same opportunity to express their opinions (and to encourage those who might otherwise say little), we used only five broad questions as an interview guideline. As our aim was to gather an initial overview of the status quo rather than concentrate on specific topics, we allowed the participants sufficient time to discuss further impulses or ideas.

Due to pandemic travel constraints, we conducted the focus group discussion in September 2021 as a video conference call, using the computer-based software Zoom. Video calling for research purposes has proven useful not only for talking to the respondents but also for seeing and interacting with them in real time, especially where the research population is geographically dispersed (Deakin & Wakefield, 2014). Another advantage of online interviewing is time and space flexibility for participants (Salmons, 2012). An increasing body of research reveals that synchronous online interviewing is often a good alternative to face-to-face interviews (Deakin & Wakefield, 2014).

The language of the focus group was Georgian, the mother tongue of all the participants, including the moderator (one of the researchers and authors of this chapter). The interview guidelines and the participant recruitment were also done in Georgian, thus avoiding any linguistic misunderstandings. The focus group discussion lasted about 90 min and was audio-taped, with the agreement of the participants. The audiotaped material was then transcribed into Georgian without translation, so as not to affect the initial meaning. Based on insights from the literature and their relevance to our research aim, codes and categories were defined and identified, and corresponding passages from the text were allocated to them (Powell & Single, 1996). We translated the results into English, along with the quotations used to support the strength of our findings. To ensure the accuracy of translation, the quotes were translated back from English into Georgian and once again from Georgian into English, in order to ensure consistency. Both authors went through the translated results and discussed the outcomes of the focus group discussion together.

Researchers outline the significance of the researcher's role as an observer in knowledge gaining and in interpreting the data (Morgan, 1996). Therefore, researchers need to be aware of this role and reflect on how their interpretation forms the knowledge that they produce about the objects researched (Blagoev & Costas, 2021). In this regard, we agree that being a moderator (here, one of the researchers) who speaks the language of the participants might be considered problematic, given that the researcher is an "insider," thus affecting the social desirability bias of the participants (Nederhof, 1985). We managed to overcome this by asking indirect questions (Fisher, 1993). The opportunity to be a native speaker indeed helped the moderator to understand the meaning of the statements made by participants, not only on the surface but also by uncovering the deeper context, and then interpreting and generating data with accuracy.

Through the focus group discussion, we aimed to capture women's perspectives on significant factors of formal and informal institutions. This was done in order to identify how these factors constrain or support women and their business development in the country. We anonymized the participants by naming them Participants P1 to P5. Table 3.1 overviews the focus group participants.

Table 3.1 Focus group participants

Name, Age	Activity at the time of the focus group discussion	Engaged in the current activity since:
P1, 37	Fashion designer and textile artist	2014
P2, 24	Online fashion shop-owner and producer of traditional sweets	2018
P3, 60	Jewellery designer	2017
P4, 33	Sales professional	2017
P5, 31	Accountant for the self-employed and small businesses	2019

3.4 Results

Benefiting from Governmental Initiatives

All the participants in the focus group described the overall environment in Georgia as entrepreneur-friendly, although governmental endeavors are most likely oriented toward supporting large businesses rather than small ones. Two participants explained that the government receives more financial benefits from larger businesses, as they pay more taxes. One participant added that as soon as she expanded and transferred her entrepreneurial activity from self-employment into a small business, she faced more regulations, higher tax payments, and obligations. This gave her the feeling of "*working just for the government*" (P1:62). This example indicates how formal institutions influence women-led small businesses in a challenging way.

All the participants had already heard about supporting programs for women entrepreneurs, which are increasingly being offered by governmental agencies, non-governmental organizations, and financial institutions. However, none of them had ever participated in such projects or programs themselves. Almost all of the women entrepreneurs interviewed stated that they had less trust in such programs, because in the past they had experienced themselves or heard from someone that those programs in fact were mostly for established businesses. One woman entrepreneur thought that governmental agencies favored specific branches or highly innovative, high-budget start-ups, and did not pay sufficient attention to women's businesses, which are mostly small. All the participants mentioned the importance of knowing "insiders" within governmental organizations, who can push the promotion of specific businesses or products and thus enable women entrepreneurs to become accepted onto such programs. Two women entrepreneurs added that knowing such an "insider" is also necessary for applying as a participant of markets and festivals run by private organizations. One woman entrepreneur, who creates handmade products (which are typically sold at Christmas markets), noted that although her innovative products are of high quality and sold for acceptable prices, she was not considered as a seller for a local Christmas market because she did not know an insider to support her in getting a place.

For governmental organizations, the participants mentioned that these types of organizations spend considerable money on corporate events and gifts and are therefore desired customers for any entrepreneur. In this regard, the women entrepreneurs stated that so-called "sales intermediaries" are increasingly important. According to the participants, sales intermediaries have good connections to governmental organizations, thus promising (women) entrepreneurs a guaranteed deal in exchange for a percentage of the selling price. This implies that the use of favors and bribes as it has been observed in many post-Soviet countries (Puffer et al., 2013) is still prevalent, despite of recent improvements in formal institutions. All questioned women entrepreneurs noticed that they see this trend rather as a negative development:

> In general, for the development of the economy it is not good, especially for us as we are small players, and those big ones have much greater networks (P2:379–382).

Getting Support of Financial Institutions

All the women entrepreneurs reported that they were not able to grow their businesses without additional financial support. Although several banks offer financial support programs for women entrepreneurs, the women entrepreneurs claim that these banks ask for collateral (as an additional security for loans) which women entrepreneurs cannot provide. According to prevalent traditions, after the marriage women normally do not inherit any capital or property from their family. In their "new" family, it is more likely that the husband or other male family members own the family capital, at least on official documents. Consequently, women in most cases officially do not own any financial capital. Additionally, the participants mentioned that interests on loans at banks are very high, and therefore women entrepreneurs avoid taking the risk of borrowing money from a bank:

> I do not have that much income… If I could, I would not take a risk…From today's perspective I cannot risk it…maybe next year everything will be better (P3:38–39).

Two participants stated that they managed to save money from their former employment for a business purpose. Furthermore, women entrepreneurs reported that they are forced to adjust their price strategies constantly due to the permanent changing and dropping of the national currency:

> Also ... people in Georgia are not able to pay high prices... They [people] do not want these high percentages of high interest rates, otherwise your product is no longer interesting, that is, you should manage your sales so that it is accessible to everyone (P4:43–44).

The participants mentioned that the overall economic instability forces them to deal with customers' low purchasing power, high costs of living, and high purchasing prices in their manufacturing and price building. This limits their profits and forces them to avoid taking any additional risks in order to further develop their business:

> I want to sell more, but for this I need to rent a space, but it is so expensive to rent this space in the city centre...that all my motivation disappears (P3:19–21).

The same is true for rental properties, such as opening a shop or cafe, which are mostly offered in US dollars (that sometimes may be three times higher than the local currency), while women entrepreneurs sell their products in the local currency. The participants complained that this stops them from taking further risks and limits them to selling their products solely online. Additionally, all the interview participants agreed that they lack trust in programs offered by financial institutions in order to support women entrepreneurs, as rules and conditions in these programs do not seem transparent and are mostly oriented toward established companies.

Obtaining Business-Relevant Education

All the participants reported that being well educated is extremely important for women entrepreneurs. Women entrepreneurs who learned and worked in the Soviet time stated that their educational background and working experience helped them in many ways: Combining their "old" and their "new" knowledge positively affected their creativity and success as entrepreneurs. All the participants agreed that specific entrepreneurship education and business knowledge helped them to enhance their customer relationships, to promote their product development, and to increase their turnover. In terms of acquiring business-relevant knowledge, the participants mentioned that there are a considerable number of courses available in this regard. However, they estimate that most of these courses are very expensive and of poor quality. One woman entrepreneur stated that business seminars in higher education institutions are not practice oriented, and in fact do not reflect the reality of the Georgian market:

> That is so, you should have someone who you know, who already has experience with those courses…in order to know how you can achieve your goals. Anyway, you can enrol for training or courses in any field you want, but how good the quality is, that is the question (P5:215–217).

The women entrepreneurs stated that they hire professionals for specific tasks, such as accounting and bookkeeping. They estimated that women in general take (tax) payments more seriously than men:

> They [men] say: My friend doesn't do it, so neither do I. He does not pay anything, so why should I? (P5:227–228).

This statement implies that women seem to follow institutional rules and attempt to meet regulations more likely, whereas men seem to be guided by macho-like behavioral examples neglecting regulatory requirements.

Perception of Women's Role in Society

All the participants underlined the importance of women in developing the Georgian economy, and that they feel less gender-discriminated than before. Additionally, all women entrepreneurs agreed on the strong character of Georgian women, "*who are militant and do not give up easily*" (P2: 289–290), or

> …because a woman can definitely do whatever she wants, and therefore achieve her goal. And she will run her business well, and probably much better than a man (P5:304–305).

Two women entrepreneurs mentioned that in cases in which gender alone might not be a reason for discrimination, the combination of gender and youth can cause problems. Following their experiences, young women entrepreneurs may be considered unexperienced and unserious:

> They all think that I am a little girl, because I am young, they think that they can lie to me, they think I am not able to do business, that I do not know how things work, that I can purchase things, that I am not able to deal with things seriously, they think I am not a real buyer, that I would not be able to carry heavy things (P2:126–128).

They added that it is mostly men who are skeptical of a woman's ability to do business successfully. Therefore, the participants emphasized how important it is that women support and empower each other:

> From what I have observed, it seems that women support women, so women play an important role in empowering women in Georgia (P4:138–139).

Another issue the women discussed here is the societal view of (young) women entrepreneurs and their "choice" between family and business. One interviewee said that in Georgian society it is assumed that young women who have decided to engage in entrepreneurial activities thus reject a family and children. She added that people believe that women are not able to take responsibility for both a family and a business, and that they therefore need to decide on one. Accordingly, women are categorized as family-like or business-like:

> So, if you are doing business, it automatically means that you are no longer interested in family and children, that is, you have taken a different path to any other woman (P2:168–169).

The participants mentioned that women are considered less serious business partners and are often neglected from important business decisions – especially in male-dominated branches. Male colleagues view female colleagues with skepticism, believing that women are not able to fulfill typical male roles equally, as one participant, who had worked for a car-importing company, reported. Women with a family and children face double discrimination at the workplace:

> The first thing they ask is if you have a family, whether you can go on working if your child falls sick, and in that case who you could leave your child with (P5:308–309).

This kind of "family associated discrimination" or stereotyping is not an issue for women entrepreneurs, and participants thought that, in some aspects, women in Georgia experience gender discrimination as employees but not as entrepreneurs.

Not all participants agreed that *all* women experience gender discrimination:

> To tell you the truth, I think about it but cannot recall any barriers I have ever faced because I am a woman (P1:148–149).

Participant 1 (P1) assumed that if women demonstrated their strong characters to others, nobody would dare to discriminate against them. Other participants refuted this opinion, arguing that women often start a business in branches typical for women and do not face discrimination for this reason. However, as soon as they start working in male-dominated branches or in typical male professions, women are more likely to experience discriminative behavior from their male counterparts. The participants stated that women are often perceived as a weak person because of their sex. However, none of the participants wants to give in an image of being "a representative of weaker sex" to achieve her business goals:

> I do not like this role at all, I am very annoyed by this role....On the contrary, I prefer to be considered a strong woman (P2:299–302).

When asking the participants what they think about other women entrepreneurs who started their entrepreneurial activities in the transition period immediately after the collapse of the Soviet Union, they reported that today's entrepreneurship in Georgia is based on entirely different values and principles to those from before. Contemporary women have much more opportunities to start and grow their businesses than two decades ago.

Importance of Informal Networks and Gift-Giving Practices in Doing Business

All the women entrepreneurs interviewed agreed that nepotism is deeply rooted in Georgian society and that women entrepreneurs also tend to use their informal networks of connections and acquaintances as a business strategy, especially because sometimes the only way to manage business operations is by using one's own connections and contacts:

> That is how business is... if you encounter resistance and only this one way is left, and there you can see a possibility, why would you not use it? (P1:336–337).

The participants also agreed that nepotism might discourage women from doing business in their preferred area:

> If you do not have connections in that area, maybe you decide not to start your business in that area but in that which you have connections and acquaintances, because you definitely need someone to support you. (P1:338–341).

This argument points out that the nature of businesses is rather influenced by the entrepreneurs' access to networks than by their ability and skills. Regarding nepotism, the participants stated that without "insiders," who can help and push products forward, "*it would take longer to have a little success, because nepotism is so deep-rooted in Georgia*" (D2:363–364). They emphasized the importance of knowing "insiders," especially at the beginning of entrepreneurial activities, regardless of the level of professionalism: "*It does not matter how good you are…*" (P4:342). At the same time, the participants outlined that nepotism is a constraining factor for the economic development of the country, especially hampering the development of small businesses. This is particularly critical for women entrepreneurs since most women tend to start their small businesses together with their male family member(s). The male co-founders more likely gain recognition and legitimacy as a leader than their female co-founders because men are perceived to be better leaders, especially in patriarchal societies. This can result in structural subordination of women to their male co-founder, which can lead to inequality and hinder the success of the business. However, the participants argued that using informal networks of connections and acquaintances is a kind of opportunity recognition for them personally, which is necessary for successful business operations:

> One should be oriented towards the growth of her own business, no matter in which way… let's say the goal justifies the means (P1:389–390; 396).

The participants believed that gift-giving also facilitates doing business. However, it seems that there are two different reasons for doing so: the first is "*when you get assistance, and you would like to express your gratitude to the person*" (P4:407–408). The second is "*when someone forces you to give them something in exchange for an [informal] service or some assistance*" (P5:411–412). All the participants associated optional gift-giving with an expression of gratitude, and they believed it was something normal in a business context.

> For advancing your business, why not give gifts, if someone helps you with it and takes you and your business further? (P3:418–419).

The participants thought of the practice of gift-giving as an integral part of Georgia's traditions, but also deeply ingrained within the corporate world. Potential business partners use public holidays to send valuable gifts to marketing or sales managers, expecting that this firm will buy their products next year.

3.5 Discussion

In this chapter, we have shed light onto how formal institutions ("governmental initiatives," "financial institutions," and "business-relevant education") and informal institutions ("women's role in society," "the use of informal networks of connections and acquaintances," and "gift-giving practices") affect the overall development of women's entrepreneurship in Georgia. Additionally, we have aimed

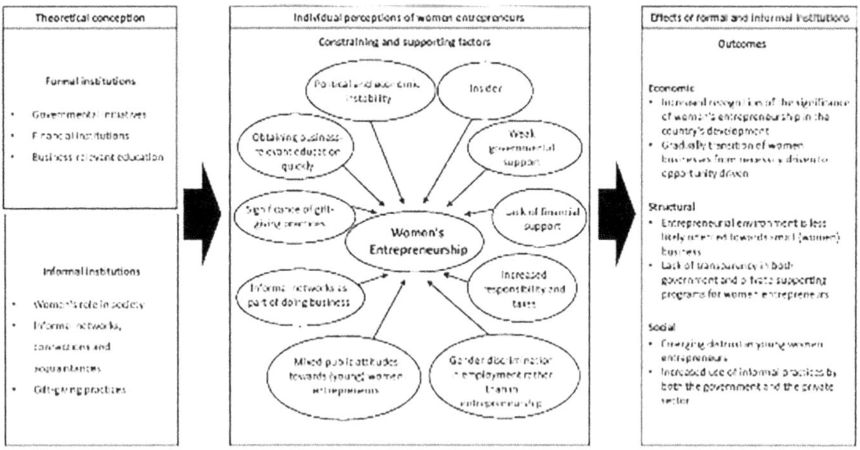

Fig. 3.1 Summarized outcomes, based on theoretical anchors and derived empirical results

to provide insights into the effects of formal and informal institutions on individual entrepreneurial journeys. Figure 3.1 connects our theoretical perspective with the individual view of the women entrepreneurs interviewed and derived outcomes regarding formal and informal institutions in Georgia, on economic, structural, and social levels.

Institutional endeavors taken since the Rose Revolution have managed to improve the overall entrepreneurship environment in Georgia, and more opportunities for women entrepreneurs have emerged. However, the low trust in government programs has forced women to shift their entrepreneurial activity into informal sphere and might have discouraged nascent women entrepreneurs. Although women entrepreneurs are aware of certain governmental support programs for women, the process of conducting programs and communication regarding the programs in general lacks transparency throughout the entire process. Similar results were found in other post-Soviet countries like Russia and the Ukraine (Iakovleva et al., 2013), showing that a lack of transparency, which was typical in the Soviet era, is still prevalent in post-Soviet societies. Furthermore, it seems that governmental support programs do not appeal to women entrepreneurs with different backgrounds, thus leaving out many potential candidates. Local (state) media could be facilitative in informing other women, as well as communicating and promoting successfully completed projects that would encourage more women to make use of these programs.

Financial issues remain a large problem for starting and growing businesses in Georgia today as it is characteristic for many transition countries (Iakovleva et al., 2013, 2017). The unstable national currency and payments in foreign currencies on the local market make women entrepreneurs uncertain about their everyday sales operations and turnover, resulting in a distrust of financial institutions. Issues with high interest and a lack of collateral have existed for decades; however, it seems that neither the government nor the financial institutions have implemented good solutions with financial benefits to women entrepreneurs for their business activities. Furthermore, in terms of cooperation, the focus of financial institutions is directed at larger companies that are financially strong, bring about more publicity with certain programs, and collaborate with established banks. In such an environment, it is more likely that small businesses will stop developing and have to exit the market. Increasing support for women entrepreneurs and small businesses would enable women to enhance their performance and grow their businesses, thus contributing to economic development overall.

Despite simplifications of the labor code made since the Rose Revolution, high rates of unemployment influence the income opportunities and purchasing power of the population. As women's businesses are more likely in low-income branches, and women mostly do not have access to resources and thus ability to produce innovative products, most women entrepreneurs are not able to make short-term big investments by getting fewer profits at the same time. This forces women entrepreneurs, as small business owners, to stay within a low-budget segment of the market. Expanding a business is associated with more obligations and paying more taxes. This strengthens women's belief that it is better to make less profit and pay lower taxes than to make more profit but pay higher taxes. In this regard, we have seen that women have adjusted their sales and operations strategies, limiting their turnover and profit. At the same time, other studies from transition countries show that many women entrepreneurs define their success by monetary values provided through their businesses (Iakovleva et al., 2013). Future studies could take this aspect more closely into consideration and examine the motivations of women entrepreneurs in Georgia in more detail.

Tremendous reforms within the (higher) education system have affected the development of women's entrepreneurship to some extent. In regard to entrepreneurship, the lack of statistical data on the relation between subjects studied, graduates, and their subsequent employment does not allow to make assumptions about how higher education in Georgia contributes to more entrepreneurial activity or performance (Chakhaia, 2013). At the same time, the local education market is overloaded with business-specific training programs, enabling women entrepreneurs to fill the relevant knowledge gaps easily, though the quality of training seems to be crucial. In this regard, we assume that this trend would also encourage women without business-relevant knowledge to start a business after completing such a program. In comparison, in other transition countries like Uzbekistan where (entrepreneurship) education has due to traditional gender roles little priority for women, women entrepreneurs' access to education opportunities is still limited (Welter & Smallbone, 2008). This implies that being closer to the European countries and building democratic institutions helped Georgia to advance its institutions, despite sharing common Soviet past and patriarchal norms with many Asian post-Soviet countries. In addition, based on the findings of Smallbone et al. (2010), which state that institutional change may open up new entrepreneurial opportunities, we argue that offering business-relevant training is an emerging field that individuals recognize as an entrepreneurial opportunity.

It is believed that the success of an entrepreneurial activity for women more likely depends on their personal traits and character. This points to changing attitudes of women in Georgia, who had considered themselves victims of the system, or fighting as heroes (ACT and UNDP Georgia, 2013). This might be linked to an increased number of education opportunities and women's desire and ability to obtain not only general knowledge but also business-relevant education. Castagnetti and Rosti (2011) propose that a high level of education may not always positively affect entrepreneurial activity, because higher education enables individuals to explore better options in paid employment, making engaging in entrepreneurship less attractive. However, in post-Soviet countries with turbulent labor market settings, where employment opportunities and well-paid jobs are scarce, entrepreneurship is often pursued as an opportunity for a stable income and is thus considered a desirable career choice (Kuriakose, 2013). In fact, the results of this study have shown that women entrepreneurs in Georgia are very excited about their entrepreneurial "profession," which they started because of passion and in spite of having obtained a university degree in another discipline. Therefore, it can be assumed that women entrepreneurship in Georgia is gradually transferring from being necessity driven to opportunity driven (Rudaz, 2012). From an institutional perspective, this can be considered as an emancipatory aspect that outlines that entrepreneurship might be shifted from informal to formal sphere when engaging women in entrepreneurship.

We found some evidence that attitudes toward women's standing in society have changed in some respects. Women emigrants, for example, have largely contributed to the empowerment of other women in Georgia and the acceptance of women as family breadwinners, though not entirely changing women's traditional societal roles. On the contrary, according to previous studies, men were usually considered the breadwinners by most families, supporting the idea that men need a better education in order to find a well-paid job (ACT and UNDP Georgia, 2013).

The woman's primary role in Georgia is still linked with motherhood and household chores. Motherhood is glorified, as it is in practice in other post-Soviet societies (Sätre, 2016), and in relation to their families, women face discrimination at work. This seems to be less likely in the context of doing business. Gender discrimination in the labor market may encourage women to choose entrepreneurship over employment, while less gender discrimination in entrepreneurship might result in an increasing number of women in male-dominated branches and professions. In Georgia, this transformation has become especially visible in the wine sector. More and more women have been entering the wine-producing business, while the winemaking tradition was previously believed to be a male-only profession in Georgian culture (Akhlouri, 2010).

Despite some positive links, we have found that a combination of gender and youth is not always associated with successful entrepreneurship, with the argument that young women are weak and unexperienced. This is in line with earlier findings, where women were perceived as successful entrepreneurs only in connection with their husbands, brothers, fathers, or other male counterparts (Jashi, 2005). Furthermore, a new tendency seems to be emerging which clusters young women into business-like and family like women, more likely excluding the successful co-existence of both. However, this indicates that the previous role of a woman being an "all-rounder" has been changed slightly, and women entrepreneurs are now more visible as businesswomen, though not always free from gender stereotypes.

Findings regarding informal networks and gift-giving practices outline the fact that, despite strengthening formal institutions, informal practices are still prevalent in Georgia. Having no connections or acquaintances in a desired branch may force women to start business in another area, likely with more connections. Here, we obtained controversial statements. First, it is believed that the entrepreneurial environment in Georgia is not constraining for women. Second, it seems that using informal networks of connections and acquaintances in doing business is indispensable. Like in many other post-Soviet societies (Markova, 2016), in Georgia, it is believed that an ability to use informal networks as a business strategy is one of the most important traits for entrepreneurs operating successfully.

Noticeably, women entrepreneurs can less likely rely on professional business networks as a formal (or informal) business-supporting organization that might be explained by scarcity or the absence of such organizations (Mierzejewska & Dziurski, 2021). Instead, we have found that the role of an "informal insider" with (potential) business clients, who can push forward and thus enable entrepreneurs to get access, seems to have become prominent. Even though tremendous reforms were conducted in order to combat corruption and eliminate bribery after the Rose Revolution (Rudaz, 2015), this indicates that the "business game" in Georgia is still not played fairly, leaving out the (women) entrepreneurs who do not have important informal connections.

A further constraint to the growth of women businesses is an emerging role of a "business intermediary." Based on good connections with state and private organizations, a "business intermediary" provides entrepreneurs with an informal service for mostly very expensive provisions, enabling entrepreneurs to get the desired order. This tendency also applies to deep-rooted gift-giving practices, which are used mostly by larger companies in order to attract and acquire new business clients informally. In some respects, gift-giving practices seem to be justified when there is no other way to get access to resources, goods, or business connections. This is characteristic of societies with turbulent institutional settings (Welter et al., 2003; Welter & Smallbone, 2008). However, for women entrepreneurs in Georgia, gift-giving in a business context more likely means voluntarily expressing their gratitude when satisfied with services or goods from business clients or partners. This corresponds to the findings of other authors, who outline the importance of the local context in doing business (Smallbone & Welter, 2010) and argue that local norms and peculiarities determine how entrepreneurs think, behave, and make decisions (Markova, 2016; Puffer et al., 2013). This means that there are certain aspects that point to peculiarities, especially in terms of how women entrepreneurs use socially embedded informal practices rather as strategies for advancing their businesses and not intentionally engaging in informal or unethical practices.

3.6 Conclusion

Based on the interrelation of institutions and women's entrepreneurship, this chapter has demonstrated that changing formal institutions does not directly lead to changing informal institutions. Tremendous reforms in Georgia, which were conducted mostly at an administrative level, did not manage to eliminate (unethical) informal practices at all. More particularly, the lack of transparency in governmental operations points to an increased informality within the state bodies that increases public distrust of government support programs. It is therefore important that public programs are communicated with more transparency in order to gain trust within the population. In addition, including gender specific and other diversity aspects like age and ethnicity in entrepreneurship programs can encourage more women nationwide to engage in entrepreneurial activities.

As the present study shows increased opportunities on the market and more accessible resources enabled through recent market reforms support women to recognize opportunities and start a business. However, access to financial capital still remains a big issue.

Furthermore, this chapter has revealed that entrepreneurship enables women in Georgia to overcome gender discrimination issues, which is more prevalent in employment relationships on the local labor market than in entrepreneurial activities. In addition, it seems that women have access to various possibilities to obtain business-relevant education, increase their self-confidence, and enhance their cognitive capabilities. As the study shows women's empowerment is also supported by role models like emigrant women, who significantly contribute not only to their family's economic advancement but also to the country's economic development.

Finally, this chapter demonstrates that women entrepreneurs in Georgia are over proportionally represented in small businesses and low-budget market segments. Therefore, it is important that policymakers focus on small business development using a gender lens since many regulations seem to force women to shift their businesses into informal spheres; or forgo their firms' growth. On the other hand, we show that through entrepreneurial activity women's role in the society has changed to an important economic agent. However, women's success in business is more likely determined by the image of a successful mother. Future research should examine, for example, how state endeavors could contribute to women's economic empowerment without associating them with a mothers' role, thus making single or childless women (entrepreneurs) more acceptable in the society.

We acknowledge that the scope of our research design and the sample size does not allow for a generalization of the outcomes and assumptions made through this study. We used the online group interview method, which might reduce the interaction of participants when compared to face-to-face interviews, thus limiting their discussion ability. Furthermore, as the focus group discussion was conducted and transcribed in Georgian, there is the limitation that, although carefully translated into English, some of the phrases might have lost their initial meanings slightly. In this regard, we emphasize that further studies working on this topic should take the above limitations into consideration and either advance the research design or expand it by using additional methods or samples. As this is one of only a few studies providing first empirical data on the interrelation between institutions and women entrepreneurship in Georgia, we encourage researchers to deepen this knowledge with further theoretical, conceptual, and practical insights. Further research in the Georgian context would enable comparative studies with other CEE countries or mature-market countries, from which policymakers, (female) managers, and (women) entrepreneurs could benefit.

References

ACT and UNDP Georgia. (2013). *Public attitudes towards gender equality in politics and business* [*Sazogadoebrivi damokidebulebebi genderul tanasworobaze politikasa da biznesSi*].

Ahl, H. (2006). Why research on women entrepreneurs needs new directions. *Entrepreneurship Theory and Practice, 30*(5), 595–621.

Ahlstrom, D., & Bruton, G. D. (2010). Rapid institutional shifts and the co-evolution of entrepreneurial firms in transition economies. *Entrepreneurship Theory and Practice, 34*(3), 531–554.

Aidis, R., Welter, F., Smallbone, D., & Isakova, N. (2007). Female entrepreneurship in transition economies: The case of Lithuania and Ukraine. *Feminist Economics, 13*(2), 157–183.

Akhlouri, N. (2010). *Woman and Georgian winemaking* [*Qali da qarTuli meRvineoba*]. Blog Marani.

Aliyev, H. (2015). Post-Soviet informality: Towards theory-building. *International Journal of Sociology and Social Policy, 35*(3/4), 182–198.

Aliyev, H. (2017). *When informal institutions change. Institutional reforms and informal practices in the former Soviet Union*. University of Michigan Press.

Alsos, G. A., Haugum, M., & Ljunggren, E. (2017). Gender equality in regional entrepreneurial ecosystems: The implementation of policy initiatives. In T. S. Manolova, C. G. Brush, L. F. Edelman, A. M. Robb, & F. Welter (Eds.), *Entrepreneurial ecosystems and growth of women's entrepreneurship. A comparative analysis* (pp. 221–243). Edward Elgar.

Ashwin, S., & Yakubovich, V. (2005). Cherchez la Femme: Women as supporting actors in the Russian labour market. *European Sociological Review, 21*(2), 149–164.

Asian Development Bank. (2018). *Georgia country gender assessment*.

Blagoev, B., & Costas, J. (2021). Interpretive inquiry: Constructivist foundations and epistemological consequences. In M. Reihlen & D. Schoenborn (Eds.), *The Springer handbook of the philosophy of management; section: Epistemology of management*. Springer International Publishing.

Brush, C., Edelman, L. F., Manolova, T., & Welter, F. (2018). A gendered look at entrepreneurship ecosystems. *Small Business Economics, 23*(9–10), 768–782.

Castagnetti, C., & Rosti, L. (2011). Who skims the cream of the Italian graduate crop? Wage employment versus self-employment. *Small Business Economics, 36*(2), 223–234.

Chachava, M. (2020). *Paid and unpaid work by migrant women returned to Georgia* [*SaqarTveloSi dabrunebuli emigranti qalebis anazRaurebadi da aunazRaurebeli Sroma*].

Chakhaia, L. (2013). *Strategic development of higher education and science in Georgia*. II - Funding research and higher education financial governance.

Chepurenko, A. (2015). Entrepreneurial activity under 'transition'. In *Context, process and gender in entrepreneurship: Frontiers in European entrepreneurship research* (pp. 6–22). https://doi.org/10.4337/9781785361661

Deakin, H., & Wakefield, K. (2014). Skype interviewing: Reflections of two PhD researchers. *Qualitative Research, 14*(5), 603–616.

Economist Intelligence Unit. (2010). *Women's economic opportunity index: A new pilot index and global ranking from the Economist Intelligence Unit.*

Engvall, J. (2012). *Against the grain: How Georgia fought corruption and what it means.* Central Asia-Caucasus Institute & Silk Road Studies Program, Silk Road Paper.

Estrin, S., & Mickiewicz, T. (2011). Institutions and female entrepreneurship. *Small Business Economics, 37*(4), 397–415.

Estrin, S., Aidis, R., & Mickiewicz, T. (2007). Institutions and entrepreneurship development in Russia: A comparative perspective. *Journal of Business Venturing, 23*(6), 656–672.

Ettl, K., & Welter, F. (2010). How female entrepreneurs learn and acquire (business-relevant) knowledge. *International Journal of Entrepreneurship and Small Business, 10*(1), 65.

Fisher, R. J. (1993). Social desirability bias and the validity of indirect questioning. *Journal of Consumer Research, 20*(2), 303–315.

Government of Georgia. (2014). *Social-economic development strategy of Georgia "GEORGIA 2020".*

Grant Thornton International. (2015). *Women in business: The path to leadership.* https://www.grantthornton.global/en/insights/articles/women-in-business-2015/. Accessed 2020.

Griessbach, L., & Ettl, K. (2020). The entrepreneurial ecosystem and its impact on female managers in transition economies: The case of Georgia. In I. Rybnikova, A. Soulsby, & S. Blazejewski (Eds.), *Women in management in Central and Eastern European countries* (pp. 150–171). Nomos.

Iakovleva, T., Solesvik, M., & Trifilova, A. (2013). Financial availability and government support for women entrepreneurs in transitional economies: Cases of Russia and Ukraine. *Journal of Small Business and Enterprise Development, 20*(2), 314–340.

Iakovleva, T., Solesvik, M., & Trifilova, A. (2017). Motivation of women business owners: Case of Russia, Ukraine and Norway. *Academy of Management Proceedings, 1*, 16600.

Jashi, C. (2005). *Gender economic issues: Tha case of Georgia.* Sida.

Kuriakose, S. (2013). Fostering entrepreneurship in Georgia. In *Directions in development; Private sector development.*

Larsen, I. B. (2022). Fostering an entrepreneurial mindset: A typology for aligning instructional strategies with three dominant entrepreneurial mindset conceptualizations. *Industry and Higher Education, 36*(3), 236–251.

Ledeneva, A. V. (1998). *Russia's economy of favours. Blat exchange: Between gift and commodity.* Cambridge University Press.

Lezhava, B., Brekashvili, P., & Melua, I. (2014). *Global entrepreneurship monitor: Special topic - Women entrepreneurship in Georgia.* Center for Women's Leadership at Babson College.

Manolova, T. S., Gyoshev, B. S., & Manev, I. M. (2007). The role of interpersonal trust for entrepreneurial exchange in a transition economy. *International Journal of Emerging Markets, 2*(2), 107–122.

Markova, N. (2016). *Business ethical norms in Russia: Integrative social contracts theory perspective.* St. Gallen.

Mickiewicz, T., Rebmann, A., & Sauka, A. (2019). To pay or not to pay? Business owners' tax morale: Testing a neo-institutional framework in a transition environment. *Journal of Business Ethics, 157*(1), 75–93.

Mierzejewska, W., & Dziurski, P. (2021). How firms cooperate in business groups? Evidence from Poland. *Central European Management Journal, 29*(2), 63–88.

Mikkelsen, K. (2018). Towards emancipatory aspects of Women's entrepreneurship: An alternative model of women's entrepreneurial self-efficacy in patriarchal societies. In S. Birkner, K. Ettl, F. Welter, & I. Ebbers (Eds.), *Women's entrepreneurship in Europe* (FGF studies in small business and entrepreneurship) (pp. 83–103). Springer International Publishing.

Morgan, D. L. (1996). Focus groups. *Annual Review of Sociology, 22*, 129–152.

Nederhof, A. J. (1985). Methods of coping with social desirability bias: A review. *European Journal of Social Psychology, 15*(3), 263–280.

North, D. C. (1991). Institutions. *Journal of Economic Perspectives, 5*(1), 97–112.

OECD. (2016). *Responsible business conduct in Georgia*. OECD.
Pathak, S., Goltz, S., & Buche, M. W. (2013). Influences of gendered institutions on women's entry into entrepreneurship. *International Journal of Entrepreneurial Behavior & Research, 19*(5), 478–502.
Powell, R. A., & Single, H. M. (1996). Focus groups. *International Journal for Quality in Health Care, 8*(5), 499–504.
Puffer, S. M., McCarthy, D. J., & Boisot, M. (2010). Entrepreneurship in Russia and China: The impact of formal institutional voids. *Entrepreneurship Theory and Practice, 34*(3), 441–467.
Puffer, S. M., McCarthy, D. J., Jaeger, A. M., & Dunlap, D. (2013). The use of favors by emerging market managers: Facilitator or inhibitor of international expansion? *Asia Pacific Journal of Management, 30*(2), 327–349.
Rehn, A., & Taalas, S. (2004). 'Znakomstva I Svyazi' (Acquaintances and connections) – Blat, the Soviet Union, and mundane entrepreneurship. *Entrepreneurship & Regional Development, 16*(3), 235–250.
Rekhviashvili, L. (2016). Counterbalancing marketization informally: Georgia's new-institutionalist reform and its discontents. *Journal of Contemporary Central and Eastern Europe, 24*(3), 255–272.
Rudaz, P. (2012). Entrepreneurship in Georgia. *Caucasus Analytical Digest, 45*, 2–8.
Rudaz, P. (2015). Institutional trust and the informal sector of Georgia. *Caucasus Analytical Digest, 75*, 10–14.
Rugina, S. (2019). Female entrepreneurship in the Baltics: Formal and informal context. *International Journal of Gender and Entrepreneurship, 11*(1), 58–74.
Rybnikova, I., Soulsby, A., & Blazejewski, S. (2020a). Women in management in Central and Eastern European (CEE) countries: "All quiet on the eastern front"? In I. Rybnikova, A. Soulsby, & S. Blazejewski (Eds.), *Women in management in Central and Eastern European countries* (pp. 7–14). Nomos.
Rybnikova, I., Soulsby, A., & Blazejewski, S. (Eds.). (2020b). *Women in management in Central and Eastern European countries*. Nomos.
Salmenniemi, S., Karhunen, P., & Kosonen, R. (2011). Between business and byt: Experiences of women entrepreneurs in contemporary Russia. *Europe-Asia Studies, 63*(1), 77–98.
Salmons, J. (2012). Designing and conducting research with online interviews. In J. Salmons (Ed.), *Cases in online interview research* (pp. 1–30). SAGE Publications.
Sätre, A.-M. (2016). Women's entrepreneurship in Russia: Impacts from the Soviet system. *Journal of Enterprising Communities: People and Places in the Global Economy, 10*(1), 53–69.
Sauka, A., & Chepurenko, A. (Eds.). (2017). *Entrepreneurship in transition economies*. Springer International Publishing.
Shahnazaryan, N., Movlud, G., & Badasyan, E. (2016). From the Cinderella of Soviet modernization to the post-Soviet return to "national traditions": Women's rights in Armenia, Azerbaijan, and Georgia. In *PONARS conference Helsinki*.
Smallbone, D., & Welter, F. (2010). *Entrepreneurship, institutions and institutional change in transition economies*. Conference Paper.
Smallbone, D., Welter, F., Voytovich, A., & Egorov, I. (2010). Government and entrepreneurship in transition economies: The case of small firms in business services in Ukraine. *The Service Industries Journal, 30*(5), 655–670.
UN Women. (2020). *Analysis of the gender pay gap and gender inequality in the labour market in Georgia*. Tbilisi.
Vanore, M., & Siegel, M. (2015). The evolution of gendered migration trajectories from Moldova & Georgia. *Comparative Migration Studies, 3*, 1.
Welter, F., & Smallbone, D. (2008). Women's entrepreneurship from an institutional perspective: The case of Uzbekistan. *International Entrepreneurship and Management Journal, 4*(4), 505–520.
Welter, F., & Smallbone, D. (2010). The embeddedness of women's entrepreneurship in a transition context. In *Women entrepreneurs and the global environment for growth: A research perspective*.

Welter, F., & Smallbone, D. (2011). Institutional perspectives on entrepreneurial behavior in challenging environments. *Journal of Small Business Management, 49*(1), 107–125.

Welter, F., Smallbone, D., Isakova, N., Aculai, E., & Schakirova, N. (2003). Female entrepreneurship in the Ukraine, Moldova and Uzbekistan: Characteristics, barriers and enabling factors and policy issues. In *Women entrepreneurs in the ECE region: Access to financing and ICT*. United Nations.

World Bank Group. (2018). *Doing business 2018. Reforming to create jobs*. World Bank Group.

World Economic Forum. (2022). *Global gender gap report 2022: Insight report*. https://www.weforum.org/reports/global-gender-gap-report-2022/. Accessed October 2022.

Wu, J., & Li, Y. (2019). An exploratory cross-country analysis of female entrepreneurial activity: The roles of gendered institutions. *DE GRUYTER Entrepreneurship Research Journal, 10*, 1–20.

Zurabishvili, T., & Zurabishvili, T. (2010). The feminization of labor migration from Georgia: The case of Tianeti. *Laboratorium: Russian Review of Social Research, 2*(1), 73–83.

Chapter 4
"Deconstruct the Entrepreneur!" No Inclusion Without Diverse Narratives of Entrepreneurship

Rea Eldem

You need to be more visible. You need to be louder. You need to be more assertive. You need to be more confident. You should not be interrupted. You must not sell yourself short. You must not speak too softly. You must not let yourself be overshadowed. You must not be vulnerable. You must be friendly, but not too friendly.

We're good at telling women what to do. Well-intentioned advice, ideas, and suggestions on the auspicious promise of gender equity. They're everywhere, on social media, in advertising, in books, in the workplace, in private, in politics. Buzzwords like women empowerment, women power, and female leadership, and many more catchy phrases link entrepreneurial activities and mindset to the feminine and make it seem that becoming an entrepreneur may just be a handle away from any woman's reach.

Against the backdrop of all these imperatives, one could get the feeling that women are just incapable of advancing as entrepreneurs. Why else would female-led entrepreneurial activity remain low in comparison to that of men? After all, all the tools of the trade are more accessible than ever, specifically catered to women: YouTube videos, Instagram stories, and one LinkedIn post after another. Every minute, a new women's initiative seems to pop up to outline new ways to succeed – as a *female*[1] entrepreneur, a *female* leader, a *female* founder. Women who are not on the fast track by now must surely be beyond help, so it seems.

[1] *Female* in *female* entrepreneur is written in italics throughout this contribution to highlight the gendered and problematic implications of this term.

R. Eldem (✉)
IN-VISIBLE GmbH, Berlin, Germany
e-mail: rea@in-visible.berlin

K. Mikkelsen, A. Wolf (eds.), *Minds, Brains, and Doxa for Inclusive Entrepreneurship*, International Studies in Entrepreneurship 47,
https://doi.org/10.1007/978-3-031-50164-7_4

The goal of this contribution is to sketch out the shortcomings of this approach, which I will call *individualized female empowerment.* I will share observations from practice about how gender equity is addressed in this approach with a focus on social media to demonstrate why it is not helping to foster female entrepreneurship. I will do so by describing the spaces in which entrepreneurship typically happens and shed light on some of the common misconceptions that this ecosystem operates on. I will show how the female entrepreneur is situated within this system and which narratives are opposed on her to make her fit. Lastly, I will provide some ways out.

My perspective on this topic is shaped by my academic and professional background as well as my social position that I would like to disclose transparently. All observations presented are anchored in my role as founder and CEO of IN-VISIBLE, an agency for more gender equality in the working world, for which I have led and accompanied countless qualitative interviews and hosted even more workshops with employees and CEOs in various industries. I have been working with start ups among my clients for five years and have thus had plenty of insights into startup culture.

Moreover, I was the co-captain of the Factory Berlin's Womxn's Circle between 2019 and 2022 and thus had the chance to gain insights into female perspectives around some of Berlin's most interesting innovation and entrepreneurship activities. The framework used for this contribution is, an academic one, however it is enriched by my experiences as a consultant. My perspective is shaped by my own identity as a *white*, female, queer, and able-bodied entrepreneur.

Most of my encounters with stakeholders who have an interest in innovation and entrepreneurship (e.g., through start-ups as clients, during events at meet-ups catered to VCs or advancing entrepreneurs) through my job occurred in rather male-dominated spaces. This is not surprising as even progressive and forward-thinking innovation hubs like Factory Berlin show a gender imbalance in their members. This affects these spaces, and it is safe to say that most other environments in which innovation and entrepreneurship happen, particularly the ones that are tech-focused are shaped by a masculine culture in which women make the minority, if not exception.

Whether this imbalance is caused by the masculine culture in these spaces or whether it is the imbalance that provokes the masculine working culture is an unresolved question that I will not tap into. On a micro-level, this vicious cycle observed in Berlin can give a vivid account of the macro-level issues we are facing regarding female entrepreneurship: an ecosystem designed for and by men with specific codes, practices, and criteria that put the entrepreneur as the subject of interest at the center.

It is this environment in which the *female* entrepreneur is socially positioned. Framed as the feminine counterpart to the (seemingly gender-less) entrepreneur who has traditionally been marked as male, *white*, deeply networked with a robust web of connections and an exceptional comfort level in navigating high-stakes situations, she emerges as the new subject of interest. In order to succeed in the game, the only way for her is to play according to the predominant rules, even though the gendered rules put her at a disadvantage, structurally. Situated with less of a network, less capital, less human resources she can put into the project, less of the "adequate" mindset that is sought after by VCs as well as a business idea that is most likely less relatable and thus proven support worthy by the predominantly male VCs, she starts her journey. Eventually, she comes across some of the obvious gendered hurdles that have been hinted at by numerous research projects (e.g., Balachandra, 2019; Brooks et al., 2014; Kanze et al., 2017).

In search of help, she turns to the Internet and finds a community of like-minded aspiring female entrepreneurs who mutually support each other by sharing affirmations and advice on how to best self-optimize. As of January 2024, on Instagram alone, the hashtag #femaleempowerment had 3.179.506 posts. The steadily growing number of posts share a common pink and red color scheme as well as the clear and uplifting message that she can do it. Accounts of successful businesswomen (and those run by anonymous shady transmitters) are meant to encourage through images, slogans, or memes that build up on positive beliefs about the capability of women and their opportunities in the working world.

The logic used is as follows: existing prevailing negative images of and about women are countered by alternative, usually opposing, messages. These are meant to build women up, to empower them. The word empower contains the word power and empowerment measures are intended to give women power, emotionally. For this purpose, insecurities and stereotypical ideas of and about women are consciously used – in order to counteract them. Thus, the Instagram posts shown below build on precisely these "weak points" in order to turn them into the opposite. An example of a prevailing stereotype is the notion that women are inherently frail or lacking in strength. Therefore, a post suggests that "a strong woman never gives up" (see post below). To provide an alternative to the stereotype that women are insecure when others don't like them, a post would suggest to "smile at people who don't like me"(see post below).

#femaleempowerment Post by @womenempowermentcorner 2020

#femaleempowerment Post by @creativewomencommunity 2020

There's a lot to say about the narratives that are being produced in this rhetoric, many of which are particularly relevant for *female* entrepreneurship. According to social media, the recipe for becoming a successful *female* entrepreneur is to be strong and to rise above societal expectations with a smile on your face. The goal of this approach is to empower women by holding up to them an image of femininity that alludes to outdated beliefs and breaks with them to show: There is another way. And, most importantly, the empowered woman can walk this other way.

This other way offers a seemingly holistic perspective at the successful woman's life and incorporates not only her career but also all other spheres. On Instagram, therefore, under the hashtag #femaleempowerment, alongside messages about the right mindset for the successful businesswoman, an abundance of photos of women's bodies flaunting their diet successes and sharing tips on how to self-optimize beauty, relationships, health, and whatnot, dominate the platform. Although an alternative rhetoric about success and femininity exist, the algorithm incentivizes content in which perfectly groomed bodies that are aligned with heteronormative ideals propagate self work as a means to success. Success, in this logic, is rather question of mindset – that can and should be applied to any sphere of life, from one's looks to actively taking over agency of one's career. As one #femaleempowerment post that is currently trending puts it: "if you want to see change, you need to get out of your comfort zone and face challenges head on" (Boss Babe Brilliant, 2022).

In neoliberal environments, it should not come as a surprise that uplifting women to become entrepreneurs means equipping them with an adequate mindset that allows them to cease more opportunities to become an economical subject that strives for enterprising the self. According to Elias, Gill, and Scharff, global consumer capitalism is one of the main driving forces of some gendered behavior like the one I am describing and the "link between femininity, self- transformation and the body is key to understanding the interplay between gender and subjectivity in the neoliberal era" (2017, 24). This logic is opposed to female subjects who want to advance as entrepreneurs, particularly on social media. This steady emphasis on the individual completely blurs the fact that the resources to succeed at conducting one's life as an enterprise are not equally distributed among individuals and disadvantaged groups have lesser access to opportunities of all kinds.

Angela McRobbie (2009) has shown that young women are increasingly positioned as ideal neoliberal subjects, continually encouraged to make maximum use of opportunities in their personal and professional lives. As body and appearance is increasingly the number one measure of a woman's success (McRobbie, 2013), women absorb this neoliberal mindset in relation to their own physical appearance, transforming themselves to visibly declare management of the body and sexuality (Elias et al., 2017, 24). It is exactly those traits that are very visible on social media posts about *female* entrepreneurship, showcasing linear kinds of femininity aligned with heteronormative beauty standards and lifestyles.

In this framework, women are granted a privileged existence if they make no further demands and submit to the gendered conditions that the system operates on. These conditions regulate inclusions and exclusions and are subject to a market ideal that requires women to obtain a high degree of self-optimization and constant pursuit of personal responsibility: Women are encouraged to make use of the opportunities of the labor market, practice their reproductivity in a self-determined manner and continuously educate themselves to earn enough money to allow for an active participation in the culture of consumption (McRobbie, 2009, 54). The female entrepreneur makes the ideal candidate in this logic, and by shedding the spotlight on young, highly educated, and specifically successful working women, modern societies make visible a kind of womanhood that fits well into new and emerging social and economic arrangements (McRobbie, 2009, 54).

Paraphrasing Deleuze, McRobbie argues that such visibilities are not "forms of objects, nor even forms that would show up under light, but rather forms of luminosity, which are created by the light itself and allow a thing or object to exist only as a flash, sparkle or shimmer" (ibid.). Accordingly, young women's collective power is first and foremost an illusion, created by the spotlight that grants them a shimmering presence – if they reassure specific visual and verbal ideas of femininity. The spotlight presents specific lifestyles and specific women, socially recognizing specific kinds of womanhood that are favorable for neoliberal logics. It never sheds light on those lifestyles and women who do not engage in "a range of practices which are understood to be both progressive but also consummately and reassuringly feminine" (McRobbie, 2009, 54). Thus, the spotlight obscures a part of reality and makes it hard for women to function as female subjects without complying to norms of appearance and self-presentation that are provided by the commercial domain as those technologies of self are the essence of the spectacular feminine (ibid., 54). Social media and pop culture are reproducing those images repeatedly, thereby making certain forms of femininity omnipresent – and marking others as flawed. Online content on *female* entrepreneurship exacerbates this process by perpetuating the myth around the successful *female* entrepreneur who seemingly easily handles the double burden of mother and career woman or any other additional societal expectations that are placed on her shoulders. Online, the "luminosity" of the spotlight is taken to an extreme – successful founder stories are shared, obscuring parts of reality by eclipsing and failing to recognize the system's mechanisms of exclusion.

In a context in which neoliberal discourses emphasize the importance for women to take their happiness into their own hands, the *female* entrepreneur becomes the idealized figure who can have it all. Becoming an entrepreneur is framed as a mindset accessible to young, advancing women who are aiming at being gainfully employed and proving their worth to capitalist society while living up to female expectations, including raising children as newly coined terms such as mompreneur suggest. However, social recognition is only given if she conforms to the expectations that are the base of the social contract that grants her recognition in the first place. She not only needs to come up with a clever business idea, but she also needs to conform to a kind of femininity that is presentable, to the world and on social media. This is a vicious cycle in which women are exposed to the same narratives over and over, and simultaneously become producers and reproducers of these exact narratives.

The described online discourse has very little to do with empowerment as it was initially coined by and is still frequently used in the intersectional feminist activist political sphere. As the Berlin project office for diversity development, Diversity Arts Culture defines, empowerment is (or should be for that matter) a process that puts "the redistribution of power" in its center as well as the recognition of discrimination. In exchange with others, barriers and insecurities through discrimination are becoming graspable (Diversity Arts Culture, 2022).

Empowerment processes thus could be a useful leverage point for unleashing anger through the revelation of common experiences as women. These emotions could be channeled into political claims and requests. In practice, however, empowerment in the context of female entrepreneurship is a container word for a neoliberal rhetoric that puts forward all kinds of content in guise of equality. This creates a self-optimization cycle that effectively does the opposite of ensuring trust-building, equal communication, and the redistribution of power, let alone the recognition of discrimination.

Campaigns promoting *female* entrepreneurship are centered around this neoliberal idea of female empowerment, highlighting the growth and learning journey of individual women. Put cynically, what is often branded as female empowerment is a collection of strategies designed to help women cope better with the patriarchy. These go way beyond the social media discourse and include tangible services and products such as mentoring programs, workshops, and trainings as well as various other formats that are specifically aimed at women. From voice training to seminars to train assertiveness or negotiation skills, it's all there.

In order to be successful in this system, the aspiring *female* entrepreneur must adapt to the structures that uphold and reproduce the status quo and pro-actively prove her value. By performing the self-optimizing practices that are promoted by programs and campaigns, she constantly works on herself. Being situated within a male-dominated system that operates on the described rules means that she must live up to the male entrepreneur who sets the benchmark. This generates an entrepreneurship environment in which the female can only ever be the "other" (Beauvoir, 2015), the *female* entrepreneur. Her narrative serves as a counterpart to the male entrepreneur which remains the norm. The identity of this new emerging subject then must be produced along the lines of masculine traits that don't question the status quo (e.g., to be successful, aspiring, risk-taking, etc.) while incorporating the sphere of the traditionally feminine. The output is a new stereotype that is presented on social media, one that has failed to unravel and deconstruct what it means to be an entrepreneur.

Most spaces in which entrepreneurship happens have so far failed at building cultures that invite people of all genders to participate. They have also not managed to move away from the stereotypical narratives about entrepreneurship. It is the persona of a (male) founder that is implicitly or explicitly the focus of funding programs as well as public discourses aimed at reinventing entrepreneurship in Germany. Current narratives fail at representing diverse entrepreneurs and thus the ecosystem does not account for the realities and the needs of those who don't match the type of what is commonly understood as a founder or entrepreneur. By being oblivious to these realities and instead reproducing ideas of founding that are rooted in masculine traits, programs are missing their goal of enhancing entrepreneurial activity and fostering innovation across different societal communities.

This is particularly striking given the fact the government as well as privately financed programs have opened a case for advancing women into entrepreneurial careers. One indicator is the investment of these stakeholders into projects that produce data on women. An increasing amount of research activities that are aimed at producing more data about gendered aspects of entrepreneurship, like the Female Founder Monitor and others have emerged in the last years. Various stakeholders obviously do understand that the numbers put forward by the research projects pose a problem. Most of Germany's innovation potential remains unlocked, clever ideas don't get financed and female perspectives are underrepresented in the development of new products and services.

The available data does not only monitor the lack of representation of females in entrepreneurship but also offers explanations for this imbalance: structural disadvantages that are linked to both, women's broader positioning within society (that result in more care responsibilities, double-burden and less resources) as well as gate-keeping mechanisms that are specific to the entrepreneurial sphere (e.g., gender bias, mostly male investors, gender gap in financing). Surprisingly, however, these findings don't seem to find their way into action plans although they hint at very specific pain points that could be addressed. Put simply, the data reveals that existing structures are not designed to cater for female entrepreneurs, they are not taking into consideration the lived realities of most women and thus posing hurdles that are hard to overcome.

One example for such a hurdle is care work and its impact on women. As of today, care work is predominantly the responsibility of women in German society any empowerment program needs to recognize this. Otherwise, empowerment, in that regard seems not at all to be about "resolving the structural contradictions that arise between the flexibility demands of caring practice in the domestic sphere and the flexibility demands of paid work" (Senghaas-Knobloch, 2015, p. 213), but about getting women to "pursue their careers as evidence of their new and independent gender identity" (McRobbie, 2010, p. 121).

Taking seriously some of these systemic hurdles would reallocate the responsibility for change to various stakeholders who have leverage over the rules of the game in contrast to the current rhetoric where change is supposed to happen through the affected group themselves. In spaces where this happening and stakeholders are starting to take on responsibility, measures are often not tackling the root of the problem. They are also not user-centric and don't acknowledge the (diverse) lived realities of women. They are based on a presumably female version of a (male) entrepreneur who has a privileged position in society that allows him to go all in. It is this persona of a fully abled, *white*, well equipped, and educated male entrepreneur that is implicitly or explicitly the focus of aid programs as well as public discourses about entrepreneurship in Germany, now sugarcoated in pink.

By being oblivious to the diverse realities of different kinds of women who are aspiring to become entrepreneurs and instead reproducing ideas of founding that are rooted in gendered ideals, programs are missing their goal of enhancing entrepreneurial activity and fostering innovation across different societal communities. Instead of acknowledging this complexity, it is seemingly easier to choose an *individualized female empowerment* approach that focuses on educating women how to better adapt to the system in place. Thus, available support programs follow suit with the rhetoric visible on social media. They make it seem like the demands of success in the spheres of entrepreneurship are inherently and exclusively linked to a specific level of hard skills along with obtaining the right mindsets, i.e., that attitude that is relevant for success. Thus, empowerment programs are touted with a strong emphasis on emotions such as insecurity and weakness as potential threats to the successful *female* entrepreneur. Women whose self-esteem is not adequate are thus encouraged to use their opportunities to eliminate potential sources of their insecurity.

While providing disadvantaged groups with a qualification offer and supporting them with customized strategies can be a helpful measure for equality, precisely because access to these resources is unequally granted, it can only ever be one side of the coin. The crux of the matter is female empowerment that solely focuses on upskilling and providing women with a new mindset can only fix some of the symptoms and not the root of the problem of gender equity. In this approach, all rules of the game remain unchallenged, and *female* entrepreneurs will always present as lacking – in contrast to men who seem to naturally be equipped with the traits that make them succeed as entrepreneurs. An *individualized empowerment rhetoric* cannot and will not break down the structural problems that arise between the sphere of entrepreneurial activity and the sphere of unpaid care work. Individualized empowerment rhetoric can also not fix gender-biased decision-making processes, unfair distribution of capital and access to knowledge and power. Instead, it blurs the inequalities and plays back the responsibility to aspiring women entrepreneurs to fix a system that was not designed for them.

Especially in the last years unconscious bias literature has found its way into the mainstream; feminist books about gendered research, medicine, and design, like Invisible Women (Criado-Perez, 2019) hit bestseller lists. The notion that our society is patriarchal in structure by now might seem like common sense and with it the idea that structural change is needed to move towards gender equity. However, this is not the case. Although there might be a lot of talk about diversity, stakeholders within the entrepreneurship field remain stuck. If there is a genuine desire to earnestly promote entrepreneurial activities among women, it is essential to establish an environment that does not perpetuate these existing disparities. Structures must be consciously and proactively dismantled and rebuilt. This touches upon bigger systemic issues such as care work but also upon context-specific issues that might be easier to tackle, such as gender bias and microaggressions against women in male-dominated spaces. Numerous studies from a wide variety of academic fields and disciplines provide findings about some of the bugs in the classical entrepreneurship process, some of which allow us to derive very specific recommendations for action. Strangely, according to my impression at work, this research apparatus is often given little to no consideration when building founder programs or other support tools. Studies show, for example, that a female first name on an application leads to her being perceived as less competent – with the same resume as her male counterpart (Moss-Racusina et al., 2012), a "foreign-sounding" name (Bertrand & Mullainathan, 2004; Kaas & Manger, 2010) will put the candidate at a disadvantage and photos on resumes (Johnson et al., 2010) matter. With this research at hand, there is a responsibility to act upon it and to take seriously the effects of patriarchy on our decision-making processes in the sphere of entrepreneurship.

To kick off this process requires system change – a change in structures and processes, the incentives and mechanisms. Unfortunately, like most working environments, entrepreneurial systems are marked by a gendered distribution of power, the ones on top are often oblivious to structural discrimination. Hence, those who have power over resources and capital – or at least the power to rethink structures and processes – do not feel the urgency to use their power accordingly. However, there are positive examples emerging, such as female-focused VCs and other stakeholders who are trying to seriously reinvent the whole game, offer alternative perspectives and approaches to entrepreneurship and who is being spotlighted. The potential of such alternative approaches should not be underestimated, making visible various kinds of entrepreneurs that currently fall under the radar does not only help women. Producing new narratives about what it means to be an entrepreneur can also uplift intersectional identities, leading to an abundance of diverse stories.

To avoid falling into the pitfall of believing that a new rhetoric about diverse kinds of entrepreneurs would solve the problem, it is important that actions follow suit. Programs catered to *female* entrepreneurs need to accommodate and put on an intersectional perspective, catering to women of color and migrations who might need different kinds of support. Governmental programs need to open to these realities, if they want to foster women. This would be a big transition to their current outline that clearly prioritizes the investment in tech-oriented, up-scalable start-up ideas. If taken seriously, this deconstruction of the current system in place would also critically assess what entrepreneurship means. As much as the term is currently married to the myth of the entrepreneur, and all its masculine traits, as much potential it could have to expand its meaning by including diverse narratives around entrepreneurship.

These narratives don't have to be invented from scratch, there are plenty of interesting cases of entrepreneurship out there – they just don't fit into a narrow-minded definition of who gets to be called an entrepreneur. Once we challenge the idea of entrepreneurship and what it means to be successful, the existing narrow idealized figure of the entrepreneur could not be upheld. It can exist only if it is granted a monopoly position among the abundance of founder narratives. If we allow complexity and question the status quo, structurally, other groups will come forward. Perhaps we would think of a founder as a female Black climate activist who runs an impactful politically influential organization, instead of a white male software developer who is seeking an early existence of his scalable tech startup.

In order to get there, the acknowledgment of the different kinds of entrepreneurial activities women are currently performing is important. Data shows that more than half of female founding teams self-associate with social entrepreneurship (Startup Verband, 2022[2]), for example. It would be important to give relevance and

[2] These sources of data show that in 2022, only 20% of all founders were women. Moreover, the gender capital gap last year showed presented male founders as having nine times as much capital on their hands as females (Start Up Verband, 2022).

recognition to this focal area. Moreover, people with less privilege and resources need different things in order to make advancements as entrepreneurs. For many, the step into entrepreneurship is and cannot not a linear one. Women and other less privileged groups need to take de-tours and build an infrastructure that allows them to move into entrepreneurship step-by-step, by having a job on the side, by stretching out their degree, or by becoming solopreneurs first. It is skewed to believe that anyone has the privilege to start off into a heart project from one day to another. Programs need to facilitate unconventional journeys that are marked by deceleration and nonlinear CVs.

References

Balachandra, L., Briggs, T., Eddleston, K., & Brush, C. (2019). Don't Pitch Like a Girl!: How Gender Stereotypes Influence Investor Decisions. *Entrepreneurship Theory and Practice, 43*(1), 116–137. https://doi.org/10.1177/1042258717728028

Bertrand, M., & Mullainathan, S. (2004). Are Emily and Greg more employable than Lakisha and Jamal? A field experiment on labor market discrimination. *The American Economic Review, 94*(3), 991–1013.

Boss Babe Brilliant. @bossbabebrilliant. (2022, February). *If you want to see change you need to get out of your comfort zone and face challenges head on*. https://www.instagram.com/p/CoHwlosuAoM/. Access 07 February 2022.

Brooks, A. W., et al. (2014). Investors prefer entrepreneurial ventures pitched by attractive men. *Proceedings of the National Academy of Sciences of the United States of America (PNAS), 111*(12), 4427–4431.

Creativewomencommunity @Creativewomencommunity. (2020, November). *I like to smile at people who don't like me*. https://www.instagram.com/creativewomencommunity/. Access 07 February 2022.

de Beauvoir, S. (2015). *The second sex*. Vintage Classics.

Diversity Arts Culture. (2022). *Wörterbuch*. https://diversity-arts-culture.berlin. Access 07 February 2022.

Elias, A. S., Gill, R., & Scharff, C. (2017). Aesthetic labour: Beauty politics in neoliberalism. In A. S. Elias, R. Gill, & C. Scharff (Eds.), *Aesthetic labour: Rethinking beauty politics in neoliberalism* (pp. 3–50). Palgrave Macmillan.

Eurostat. (2022). *Europäische Union: Hauptgründe für Frauen einer Teilzeitbeschäftigung nachzugehen, aufgeschlüsselt nach Mitgliedsstaaten im Jahr 2021*. https://de.Statista.Com/Statistik/Daten/Studie/1098786/Umfrage/Hauptgruende-Fuer-Frauen-In-Der-Eu-einer-teilzeitbeschaeftigung-nachzugehen/. Access 07 February 2022.

Gilbert, J. (2013). What kind of thing is "Neoliberalism"? *New Formations, 80*, 7–22.

Johnson, S., Podratz, K., Dipboye, R., & Gibbons, E. (2010). Physical attractiveness biases in ratings of employment suitability: Tracking down the 'beauty is beastly' effect. *The Journal of Social Psychology, 150*(3), 301–318.

Kaas, L., & Manger, C. (2010, February). *Ethnic discrimination in Germany's labour market: A field experiment*. IZA DP No. 4741.

Kanze, D., Huang, L., Conley, M. A., & Tory Higgins, E. (2017). Male and female entrepreneurs get asked different questions by VCs — and it affects how much funding they get. *Harvard Business Review, 27*.

McRobbie, A. (2009). *The aftermath of feminism: Gender, culture and social change*. SAGE.

McRobbie, Angela. (2010). Top Girls: Feminismus und der Aufstieg des neoliberalen Geschlechterregimes. Germany: VS Verlag für Sozialwissenschaften. ISBN 978-3531162720 [Book].

McRobbie, A. (2013). Feminism, the family and the new “mediated” maternalism. *75 New Formations, 80*, 119–137.

Moss-Racusina, C., Dovidio, J., Brescoll, V., Graham, M., & Handelsman, J. (2012). Science faculty’s subtle gender biases favor male students. *PNAS, 109*(41), 16474–16479.

Perez, C. C. (2019). Invisible Women. [United States], Abrams.

Senghaas-Knobloch, E. (2015). Fürsorgliche Praxis als weltweite politische Herausforderung – Perspektiven für eine nachhaltige Organisation gesellschaftlicher Arbeit, erschienen in *Feministische Studien, IMPACT FACTOR*, 0.077.

Start Up Verband. (2022). *Stepstone: Female founders monitor.*

Thon, C. (2012). Individualisierte Geschlechterordnungen? Feministische und hegemonieanalytische Kritik eines modernisierungstheoretischen Konzepts. In V. Moser, & B. Rendtorff (Hrsg.), *Riskante Leben? Geschlechterordnungen in der Reflexiven Moderne*. Budrich. S.27–S.43.

Womenempowermentcorner. @Womenempowermentcorner. (2020, November). *A strong woman never gives up. She may need a cry or a day in bed, but she will always come back stronger*. https://www.instagram.com/womenempowermentcorner/. Access 09 Feb 2022.

Chapter 5
Beyond Square Meters: Space, Gender, and the Design of Coworking Hubs

Jona Wolf and Kirsten Mikkelsen

5.1 Introduction

This chapter aims to look at the concept of inclusive entrepreneurship through the lens of architecture. Using the typology of coworking spaces as an exemplary case, it aims to contribute to a broader discussion on the relationship between space and gender. The focus of this essay is on coworking spaces. Coworking spaces have developed an image of serving as hubs for emerging startups, entrepreneurs, and freelancers. As previous chapters in this book have shown, both the concept of entrepreneurship and the person of an entrepreneur underlie rules dominated by masculinity. This raises the question to what extent or under what circumstances these spaces such as coworking spaces appear to be inclusive and provide equal opportunities for a diverse range of entrepreneurs.

Recently, voices claiming that the startup scene is sexist have become louder media reports and academic contributions support these critiques. Although this is alarming, from an academic perspective this does not come as a surprise. For more than three decades, scholars from different disciplines have criticized entrepreneurship and the entrepreneurial eco-system to be male dominated, discriminating against for example women and people of color and higher age or people with disabilities.

Hence, looking at coworking spaces from a feminist perspective combining both entrepreneurship and architecture provides an interesting field of research and

J. Wolf (✉)
Berlin, Germany
www.jo-na.xyz

K. Mikkelsen
Jackstädt-Center Flensburg, University of Flensburg, Flensburg, Germany

K. Mikkelsen, A. Wolf (eds.), *Minds, Brains, and Doxa for Inclusive Entrepreneurship*, International Studies in Entrepreneurship 47,
https://doi.org/10.1007/978-3-031-50164-7_5

discussion. Both disciplines are to date still male dominated and underlie to a large extent a connotation of masculinity.

The contribution raises two main arguments. First, it highlights the relevance that space has for builders and investors. Space is viewed as a product in the real estate market, with square meters being a measurement of value. It is a great challenge for the design of new spaces to find a balance between what serves the investors and what is beneficial for users – here entrepreneurs – of a space. Second, architectural design approaches are suggested that can support the creation of more inclusive environments in coworking spaces, addressing a diverse group of entrepreneurs, particularly those who do not match the heteronormative and hegemonic image of an entrepreneur.

Overall, this essay is intended to initiate a discussion about more equitable and accessible spaces for future entrepreneurs from diverse backgrounds.

5.2 The Architect's Dream

Architectural history takes a very one-sided view of who the creative minds behind the ideas were and whose architectural design was worth documenting. The writing of history is done repeatedly and from the same structural – masculine – point of view, denying diversity and different approaches. Visibility and popularity can be seen as indicators for relevance and acknowledgment to a broader audience within any social sphere, architecture as well. The Pritzker Prize, often referred to as the Nobel Prize of Architecture, is an international prize awarded annually to a living architect or group of architects for a significant achievement. Hence, it is an artifact representing desired design, perceptions, and preferences within architecture. It was established in 1979 and has since only awarded six women architects. Similarly, BauNetz, an online magazine for architects, has an office ranking that marks the visibility of architectural companies in Germany, Austria, and Switzerland. The ranking is based on the number of publications in the current months. By the end of 2022, of the five best-ranked architectural offices, only one had a female director (and that was in partnership with two male directors).

How can architecture actually be capable to guide new ways to inclusive spatial design strategies if the architecture firms themselves are non-inclusive? And where are the origins of this imbalance?

Although universities set goals and make efforts to assign more diverse professorships, numbers in architecture are still disappointing. If we want to create a future with equal opportunities, we also need diversity among architects who can design these spaces. The majority of architects in leadership positions or founders of financially successful architecture firms are still white men (Barker, 2022). We argue that coworking spaces that empower (among others) female-led businesses can only be designed effectively by architects from similar backgrounds or with an awareness for and openness toward topics and aspects of diversity and inclusion.

As one source for this, it is crucial to monitor equal opportunities for academic staff at universities and to ensure encouraging role models for future architects. It is time to open the discussion, rethink architectural education, and develop future design strategies that create more inclusive spaces for society. Currently, there is still a patriarchal perspective on what makes a "good" design. Doreen Massey describes in "Space, Place and Gender" (Massey, 1994), how she felt like being a space invader going to a football stadium wanting to watch a game. Not much has changed it seems since then.

In 1490, Leonardo Da Vinci created the drawing "Vitruvian Man," one of the first human-scale guidelines with many more to follow. Until now, a popular manual for architects is "Bauentwurfslehre," a book by Ernst Neufert, first published in 1936 (Neufert, 1936). It contains dimensions and drawings for various architectural typologies. It enforced gender roles onto architectural spaces by explaining routines and user cases different for men and women. As an example, activities related to household tasks, such as preparing food in the kitchen or cleaning the bathroom, were assigned to women and illustrated with drawings and measurements that reflected this division of labor. Although these books have been updated, the principles of efficient space and the corresponding dimensions remain deeply rooted in contemporary architecture. These standards are still upheld by the relevant regulations. Architectural environments replicate oppressive systems and reproduce stereotypical perceptions of gender roles.

With artificial intelligence technology at the forefront, a rethinking of design processes becomes obviously more urgent. In the near future, AI systems will take on repetitive tasks like architectural surveys of existing spaces or the production of drawings corresponding to a design, but they will also be more and more responsible for the creation of the actual design proposal and plan layout itself. Each AI system has different features but mainly the intention is to be more efficient with design solutions. AI-based parametric planning tool, Co-Designer, is developed by a manufacturer for office furniture. It aims to find the most space-efficient plan for office spaces, considering headcount, meeting spaces, and other facilities. As a result, it allows to export quantities of products and directly order the matching furniture from the manufacturer.

To what extent is the AI trained to create equal work experiences for all users and inclusive spaces or to what extent does the profit from selling large volumes of office furniture outweigh the needs of diverse groups of users? Although this chapter will not solve these challenges, it further aims to initiate a new discourse.

AI systems learn to make decisions based on training data. The data set is selected by humans with conscious and unconscious biases. AI also reflects inequities, simply by the data that is available and that does not document history and present it in a diverse way (Amaro, 2020). It is hardly traceable, which data is responsible for an AI system's output. If one asks an AI Image Generator to create an image of a "coworking space with successful entrepreneurs," the result is an interior with desaturated materials, white exposed ceilings, and people working on desks appearing mainly white and male. In the dream of the AI, not everyone is allowed to dream. It is the opposite of a vibrant and diverse space with opportunities for everyone. Independently from visual image creation, AI systems are slowly being incorporated for generative designs. Companies can carry out surveys with their employees. Preferred locations in space, lighting, or team requirements are being collected and fed into the system to create the most efficient plan configuration. AI can work with high quantities of collected data that humans could not consider in their design decisions. It gives architects the opportunity to create various options in a short time and a set of layouts to evaluate. The architects' task is consequently collecting the input data and selecting the output. Hence, they carry a lot of responsibility.

Joys Boys, an architect, activist, and founder member of Matrix, starts spatial design from a minority's point of view and creative potential with "The DisOrdinary Architecture Project." In collaborative projects, they challenge ableist attitudes and practices and aim for alternative interventions (Boys, 2014).

Architectural education in universities still celebrates the iconic mastermind and portrays primarily the white, never-sleeping genius who will shape the future of architecture. It promotes a hierarchical approach to the creation of space without appreciating the efforts and opinions of collaborators. The ideas of other professions or individuals with diverse perspectives are not considered worthy for design development. As one result architecture frequently fails to capture demographic diversity.

5.3 History of Office Design

Architecture is a tool for translating certain social structures into a built environment. As part of architecture, office design is a powerful instrument for reinforcing patriarchal structures in a workplace. Consequently, office design has always represented hierarchical power structures and still translates a patriarchal vision of society into a space.

Architecturally, such power relationships are evident in the arrangement and quality of certain spaces. In office buildings, for example, people in leadership positions of whom the majority are men, often had individual offices where they enjoyed privacy. Women, on the other hand, worked mainly in open desk arrangements in lower positions and were monitored (Weisman, 1992).

Office design is also a way to ensure an efficient workforce. Inventions of new technologies had an impact on the way of working and opened up possibilities for even more efficient uses of space. In the early twentieth century, office design was inspired by processes in factories. The goal was to transfer the organization of fabrication processes into office layouts. The Larkin Building by Frank Lloyd Wright, which was built in 1903, was an open office floor plan with desks organized like a production line. The managers could oversee a large number of workers through the organization of the floorplan. In the 1950s, air-conditioning became popular in the USA and allowed to organize a space independently from windows that could be opened and would let enough fresh air into the building. Work desks could be arranged tightly at every location. The workspace inside and the environment outside were completely detached. Health conditions of the workers were not prioritized or even ignored. Often there was a lack of daylight, almost no privacy, and exposure to noise. Starting in the 1990s, the Internet, mobile phones, and laptops allowed working independently from a dedicated desk or space. Employees could explore new ways of flexible working and would spend only part of their time in the office space. Through sharing work desks, the number of workplaces could be reduced and as a consequence the total areas for office buildings. Companies from Silicon Valley (which are known to be male dominated) shaped the image of an office and are still today. Casual clothing at work, informal activities, and casual events became part of a new office culture, in which social- and professional life would fluidly merge together. Coworking was the new catalyst for startups and entrepreneurs that would ultimately shape certain industries in the future. It is critical to recognize the importance of masculinity in architectural design and entrepreneurship when interpreting the role of coworking spaces in this context.

5.4 (Office) Space is a Product

Space is a product like any other. It is an investment and a good for speculation on the market (Doderer, 2022). Square meters are a currency. The architecture related to those square meters represents the importance of a brand (MacCormac, 1992). Buildings are not simply constructed to meet the demand for space but to demonstrate power and success of a company and the people navigating this space. To translate the values of a brand into a design, star architects are commissioned to create monument-like buildings with the companies' logos decorating the facades.

Coworking spaces are one typology in the space range. While the building and its design represents the coworking company's brand, the users of that space, e.g., entrepreneurs, are another interest group who might have different preferences and needs than the coworking provider. In a coworking space, entrepreneurs share a space and operate within the architecture of the providing company.

In general, architectural design cannot meet the diverse needs of an entire society. It is targeted at certain groups and attracts some people more than others. In fact, there are so many different qualities that influence who feels comfortable in a space. It could be the light settings, size, or circulation in a particular space. Materials, signage, and colors can affect who feels represented and empowered to express their personality. Spatial design affects how individuals use a space in relation to other people. Accessibility is another crucial factor for creating inclusive spaces. Hence, the design of coworking architecture ultimately affects who feels attracted to renting parts of the workspace. It can also influence how people interact, engage, and collaborate with others in the space.

Just like with any other subscription, users of coworking spaces pay monthly for a service that provides a work environment – they are members. The more memberships, the better the revenue for the coworking company.

In order to recruit more members, the online presence highlights people and stories that take place within that space. The architecture and design of that space act as a stage for the users' stories. Successful start-ups that already rent workspace are essential for the coworking's PR strategy. Consequently, the members of coworking spaces are not only paying clients but also sales representatives and creators of that space.

The interior design of coworking spaces aims to leave space for imagination. With slogans like "[…] members and partners collaborate to build the world of tomorrow" (The Factory Berlin, 2023), members imagine not only their own future, but also they ultimately become part of a bigger collective vision.

The architectural design is supposed to support the visionary mind and intentionally gives an unfinished, sometimes industrial, look. Exposed pipes on the ceiling or raw concrete walls give the impression that even the architecture is just a structural support in the background and open for the members' imagination of how it might shine one day. Individual users are invited to envision themselves and their startup's identity. It is a minimal environment where supposedly everything is possible.

The architectural design emphasizes the arrangement of spaces for communal activities. Ultimately, the vision that a coworking space sells is the community itself.

The architectural planning supports the creation of a community and spaces that are designed to spend plenty of time for socializing. The floorplan is not a mere arrangement of desks and different meeting rooms but social activities are in the center: table tennis, big coffee kitchens, hang-out spaces, etc.

Any program and spaces additional to the working areas become a main part of the identity that a coworking represents. And even if one does not use table tennis in the end, it makes them at least think about fun. They are not being sold a workplace but a holistic lifestyle and a work–life balance that will make them part of a bigger collective (Mörtenböck, 2020).

While this architecture may appear democratic, this chapter questions whether an architecture designed around certain activities provides equal access to everyone. Against the background of the previous paragraphs on hegemonic structures within architecture and entrepreneurship, it is thrilling to discuss whether an architecture, where anything seems possible, truly allows for equal representation of individuals from diverse backgrounds.

One of the world's biggest coworking providers, from a feminist perspective, represents little diversity within their own structure. The company's board of six added its first female director in 2019. From 2018–2020 the company appointed their first chief architect, selecting a white male architect who is known for building monuments with financial success and high representation on social media. His designs propagate the discourse that success in architecture is determined by the scale or size of buildings, effectively translating capitalist ideals into tangible structures. He was confronted with allegations of misogynistic behavior in 2017 (Mairs, 2017) but was still assigned with the position of the coworking's chief architect a year later. Looking at the people who design and lead these coworking spaces, one sees predominantly white, heterosexual men at the forefront. The environment built translates social structures and the pre-dominantly masculine sphere of entrepreneurship and startup scene (intentionally or not) and reinforces as well reproduces hierarchies shaped by patriarchy. It may not be surprising that in spaces created from such a one-sided perspective and additionally being driven by performative reasons for activities in a space, an all-inclusive work environment that facilitates equal access seems difficult. Considering the financial goals and pressure that some coworking providers have and the goal of being relevant in the real estate market, new memberships that rent more square meters are more important than the experience and success of an individual member itself.

According to these thoughts, coworking spaces potentially reproduce dominant cultural norms and lack diversity of design, leaving individuals who do not identify with those norms un(der)represented. As a result, these spaces may become less inviting and more difficult to navigate for those who do not identify with the spatial environment. Spaces have the potential to tell stories and provide a platform for diverse experiences; as of yet, big coworking providers predominantly represent white, cis-men who benefit from this representation. The architecture of coworking spaces does have a responsibility for representing diversity and creating an inclusive environment that invites individuals from diverse backgrounds to use and contribute to the space.

5.5 Conclusion

In summary, the challenge of developing inclusive architectural workspaces that provide equal opportunity is multifaceted. Architecture is an entanglement of real estate investment, a rigid architectural education, and top-down design strategies. In view of these aspects, architectural design projects power dynamics and gender roles from the dominant culture into a physical space – the coworking space. If we want to create inclusive spaces, the complex interrelationships need to be dismantled and radically reimagined.

Also, using AI systems to create new spaces, architects who aim to create inclusive spaces are to host a setting where everyone can share their experiences and spatial challenges. Additionally, architects are responsible for taking actions in developing new collaborative design practices for co-creation. If they employ a survey to capture needs, they could provide questions that allow to understand the needs of underrepresented groups. Furthermore, creating spaces is not simply a task to represent people of all genders, ages, social- or cultural background but to recognize their expertise as a valuable resource for developing more inclusive design. It is about acknowledging users as producers and creators of their very own environment.

This chapter sought to give an impulse for the issue of inclusivity in coworking spaces and to highlight possible solutions. Through a deeper understanding of the complexities involved, coworking can take steps from different directions to create more inclusive spaces.

References

Amaro, R. (2020). More-than-Human. *The empirical reality of AI and a racialised future*. Het Nieuwe Instituut.

Barker, N. (2022). Dezeen. *Women make up just one in five top positions at biggest architecture firms despite "huge jump"*. https://www.dezeen.com/2022/03/08/women-top-positions-biggest-architecture-firms/

Boys, J. (2014). *Doing disability differently: An alternative handbook on architecture, dis/ability and designing for everyday life*. Routledge

Da Vinci, L. (c. 1490). *Vitruvian man*.

Doderer, Y. (2022). Arch+ 246. Zeitgenössische feministische Raumpraxis. *Queer-feministische Städte für ein anderes Leben!?*

Factory Works GmbH. (2023). https://factoryberlin.com

MacCormac, R. (1992). The architectural review. *There is no reason why the office as a building type should not re-invest itself with a sense of belonging*. Emap Business Publishing Ltd.

Mairs, J. (2017). Dezeen. *"If I was misogynist would I hire a woman as my CEO?" says Bjarke Ingels*. https://www.dezeen.com/2017/06/16/bjarke-ingels-hits-back-claims-sexism-big-interview/

Massey, D. (1994). *Space, place and gender*. University of Minnesota Press.

Mörtenböck, P. (2020). *Live-Work-Play und die neoliberale Utopie der Wohlfühl-Gemeinschaft*. https://www.youtube.com/watch?v=AMCxW1egDAA&ab_channel=EmergingFieldsinArchitecture

Neufert, E. (1936). *Bau- Entwurfslehre*. Bauwelt-Verlag.

Weisman, L. (1992). *Discrimination by design: A feminist critique of the man-made environment*. University of Illinois Press.

Chapter 6
Challenges in Entrepreneurship: A Practical View from a Closed Society to Diversity, Equality, and Inclusion

Ann-Carolin Helmreich

I am a woman.
I am a queer woman.
I am a queer neurodiverse woman.
I am a queer neurodiverse multi-weight woman.
I am a queer neurodiverse multi-weight woman from a working-class family.
I am a queer neurodiverse multi-weight woman from a working-class family who dropped out of university.

So much for labels.
There's a lot to include.
Welcome to my story.

When I thought about contributing a chapter about my experiences in the Berlin startup bubble, two feelings came to me. I wanted to come to terms with that time, and I doubted that this unscientific chapter could be included in such a book. This field report is one-dimensional, very personal, and radically open. It describes what I have experienced in the Berlin startup bubble over the past 16 years. My perspectives are those of a (serial) founder. Sometimes I have failed; sometimes I have succeeded. My experiences expanded further when I decided to advise other entrepreneurs as a mentor and coach, and finally as a therapist. It was only retrospectively through this work that I began to understand what my years in the entrepreneurial sphere have done to me internally, mentally, and psychologically.

A.-C. Helmreich (✉)
Tatsinn, Berlin, Germany
e-mail: perspektiven@tatsinn.com

K. Mikkelsen, A. Wolf (eds.), *Minds, Brains, and Doxa for Inclusive Entrepreneurship*, International Studies in Entrepreneurship 47,
https://doi.org/10.1007/978-3-031-50164-7_6

6.1 A Closed Society, Sexism, and Big Ambitions

When I started working in the Berlin startup scene in 2008, it was one thing above all: male, white, mainly from the educated middle class and hetero. Nobody questioned this; it was normal! It was standard and had sharp but invisible edges. I was given a lot of responsibility right from the start. Be brave and try. Nobody could have imagined the events that would take place: a hacker attack with password theft and the founder being intoxicated with investors. This founder was male and straight, but he was the child of immigrant parents. His good education and his eccentric nature legitimized him as a CEO. I learned a lot from him. Not everything was good, but everything was experience. His origins were less of an issue than his sexist abuse and comments. It came up, but it was mostly played down. It was joked about and appeased. In the 2000s, there wasn't the sensibility of today after the "Me too" movement. While at the time I tried to laugh off the sexual assaults in embarrassment, I would react differently today. More important for the corporate world was the CEO's ability to think entrepreneurially from big to crazy and to dare to do things that others did not. But this eccentricity had two sides.

Many successful startups in Berlin in the 2000s involved graduates from self-proclaimed elite universities. Investors also emerged from these cadre schools and at that time people liked to distribute the money for startup ideas among themselves. The homogeneity of these often-elitist structures was laughed at rather than criticized: the same university, the same style of clothing, the same gender, the same circle of friends that connected us and allowed cliques that like to form in such microcosms. Women in this scene were so rare that I couldn't name any right off my head. That has since changed, but the industry is still male-dominated.

The following picture emerges from the German Startup Monitor (Deutscher Startup Verband, 2022):

Gender The proportion of female founders is 20.3%, which is an increase of 2.6% compared to the previous year (17.7%). Although there have been constant increases in the proportion of female startup founders since 2017 (14.6%), the number remains low. Regarding the founding teams, it is also clear that almost two-thirds of the teams were exclusively men (62.2%). A closer look at the female founders shows that the proportion of women under 30 years of age (27.6%) is slightly higher than that of men (24.1%). There is also a growing number of networks, events, and initiatives specifically aimed at women in the startup scene, such as Women in Tech, Women Who Tech, and Female Founders.

Nationality and migration background The majority of the founders only have German citizenship (84.1%). In total, 4.2% have both German and one other foreign citizenship and 11.7% have one or two foreign citizenships. In total, 21.1% of the founders have a migration background, which is only slightly below the value in the general working population (25.9%, cf. Statistisches Bundesamt, 2023).

Educational qualifications and subjects of study Overall, 87.2% of the founders have a university degree. More than one in two have a master's degree (37.1%) or a diploma (17.1%). The highest degree of 17.8% of those surveyed is a bachelor's, while 15.1% have a doctorate. In total, 4.7% state their highest level of education is the Abitur, and 4.1% have completed vocational training. Among the degrees, STEM subjects (46.6%) and economics (38.0%) are the most relevant courses for founders, and just 15.3% of those surveyed graduated in another field.

I did not perceive the lack of diversity at the time. I found it exciting to let the pull of the scene flow over me and to be asked in the elevator what I would like to find one day. The reason is that it was so natural and self-evident. Employees went into positions that offered them little sleep and money, but plenty of inspiration, steep learning curves, and good networks. Many of my former colleagues have themselves founded after their time in a startup or are in management positions in well-known unicorns. They have produced Oscar-winning films, worked on digitizing banks, and became investors.

It was less about who you were than what you wanted to find. The aims for this were as different as the people who came up with the ideas. Sometimes it was a quick exit and the promise of being wealthy; sometimes the chance to digitize or disrupt markets with one's own idea. The prerequisites for being successful were a mixture of daring, innovation, and privilege. Few knew that they were privileged.

6.2 Co-founding My Own Startup

After leaving a startup, a male colleague and I met a well-known German entrepreneur and investor who founded his first company at the age of 21. He has also been an active business angel and has invested in several successful companies. He is a well-known face on the German startup scene and is actively involved in promoting founders and entrepreneurship. But in 2008 he was above all looking for the next big idea. At one meeting, three young men came to our table as if on cue waiting to be assigned. This was followed by a 10-min pitch of their business idea and the question of whether I wanted to be part of it. On impulse, I said yes because I thought the idea was pretty cool. That is how I became a co-founder of a startup. Of course, I was the only woman and it stayed that way for the first few months. I signed a contract stating that we would exit the company within 3 years and received a single-digit percentage in the form of virtual shares. Most importantly, I was given a fantasy. A fantasy of working on a smart technology that could disrupt a market.

The founding team consisted of four white men and myself. I felt much pressure to live up to my role as a woman without knowing how to be the only woman to embody that role. There were hardly any role models I could look up to. Therefore, I decided to do what many women still see as the solution today: to be the woman among men who is particularly tough and hard-working. Who laughs at all dirty jokes and doesn't take herself too seriously. I was toxic to myself with that; I just didn't know it at the time.

Within the setup of my role, there were quickly conflicts of competence and preferential treatment. I had to fight harder for the same sales pitches and argue for them better than my male colleagues. Also, informal get-togethers such as playing soccer together or drinking in the evening were often not the right occasions for me to negotiate sales strategies or my shares in a company. But these were exactly when negotiations, discussions, and politics took place.

We were all in our early-to-mid-20s and most of us weren't in a committed relationship, let alone with a family of our own. We only used our apartments to sleep. When I partied, I partied hard. After all, the message this conveyed was "Work hard, play hard." I neglected my body, my health, and my psyche. It was like a rush that didn't want to end. This rush changed me and made me harder on myself and others. I lost friends because I subordinated everything to the company. Our CEO coined the term "work-life choice" and said that there should be no balance – it was a conscious choice to choose business over life. The company became my life and remained so for many years.

Issues such as intersectionality, feminism, discrimination, and inclusion had not yet reached the startup bubble, and therefore there was a diminished-to-atrophied awareness of them. I tried to change things, i.e.

Recruiting Inclusivity was an important issue for me. Therefore, we soon had a more diverse team with people from different cultural and ethnic backgrounds as well as age diversity, but still not enough women. It took some time before I was not the only queer person in the company, and we occasionally hired more people from the LGBTIQ+ world.

Maternity leave When the first employee announced her pregnancy exactly 2 days after the end of her probationary period, we were all overwhelmed. What was the legal situation, how could we replace her and would she even come back? Children were not part of our concept at the time, and I remember talks behind closed doors that would lead to scandals today. Accordingly, the employee was not returned to her old job after her maternity leave but was put in an unattractive position, which she then quickly left in return for a severance payment and a termination agreement. As the organization matured, it became more normal for employees to have children and there was a growing understanding that it couldn't all be about the startup, but that there were people who just came to us to do a job.

Looking back at that time, I didn't see myself as a feminist, I wasn't openly queer, and I wasn't diagnosed as a neurodiverse person. What was apparent is that I was a multi-weight cis woman. I wasn't aware that because of my structural disadvantage, I had to fight for my points of view more than others. My own experiences of discrimination relate almost exclusively to the management level. There, my qualities such as empathy and a desire for gender equality were not only smiled at but also partially attacked and suppressed. In our team, I experienced above all verbal discrimination against team members, violent and unreflective language, and exposure of individuals. This was mostly wrapped in a humorous context, which didn't make it any better. The management style was based on these same principles, and therefore often appeared unfair and ill-considered.

6.3 A Turning Point in My Consciousness

After I was transferred from sales to people development by my management colleagues, my job was to coach employees and advise the organization on further training. Without a budget, it went without saying that I would continue to take care of my major customers in sales, i.e., do two jobs in one. What initially felt like powerlessness soon turned out to be a decision that would shape my further professional path. In my dual role as an internal coach and management member, I had the opportunity for the first time to develop a deep understanding of the employees' needs.

In confidential coaching sessions, I developed a new perspective on management and became aware of the shortcomings in our leadership. These new multi-perspectives opened up new ways of thinking for me. For the first time, I felt how a lack of opportunities for further training or advancement, a lack of attention to the needs of employees, and an immature management style led to our most important performers wanting to leave the organization. I tried to raise awareness of this in discussions with the CEO and the management team, but I didn't succeed. The focus of my coaching should instead be on increasing performance in sales and I was presented with additional KPIs. My coaching was assigned a sales growth target that I should achieve, and I could not avert this misguided decision even with a lot of argumentations. My intention was to establish emotional leadership in the company and thus promote a cultural change in management style.

Emotional leadership means a leadership skill based on the ability to purposefully recognize, understand, and use emotions to motivate, inspire, and influence people. It is about viewing emotions not just as personal or private matters but as important factors in job performance, satisfaction, and employee engagement.

Emotional leaders are able to recognize and understand the needs, desires, and emotions of employees. They can influence emotions positively by creating an atmosphere of trust, openness, and appreciation. They communicate clearly and empathetically and show empathy for the concerns and challenges of their employees.

Through emotional leadership, employees can be motivated to improve their performance, achieve their aims, and identify with the company and its vision. This type of leadership can also help to create a positive working atmosphere and promote cohesion and cooperation in the team. However, it is important to emphasize that emotional leadership does not mean that a leader should express their emotions uncontrollably. Instead, it is about regulating one's own emotions and using them in a targeted manner to promote the well-being and performance of employees.

The prerequisites for emotional leadership were established, and it was also partially applied in individual teams, albeit intuitively and not learned. Transferring this leadership style to the entire company, especially to the sales department, which was exposed to much fluctuation and uncertainty, failed.

6.4 An Involuntary Farewell

Insights into a leadership style that was increasingly having a negative impact on team retention in certain areas led to tensions between me and some of the management team. Similar to my transfer to a new department, my departure from the organization I co-founded was executed over my head. My multiple perspectives and my naming of grievances with the management were interpreted as a loss of loyalty and trust in me was withdrawn.

At the same time, we were planning to sell the company to a large publishing house and were in the middle of due diligence and final negotiations with a large established company. In this context, my anti-sales attitude became dangerous and I needed to be minimized as a risk factor and leave the company. This hit me at a time when my motivation to drive a change process in the organization had reached a low point. We agreed on a severance package and they cancelled my contract.

My strong identification with the company unfolded into many disadvantages:

Revision Over-identifying with the company can result in taking on too much responsibility, which can lead to overwork and burnout.

Lack of work–life balance Strong identification with the company can lead to putting work and career ahead of other important things in life, such as family, friends, and leisure activities, which can lead to a lack of work-life balance.

Disappointment and frustration When the company is doing poorly or there are problems, strong identification with the company can result in feelings of personal concern and disappointment, which can lead to frustration and dissatisfaction.

Ultimately, my burnout, which had been brewing for many months, broke the path. I had two nervous breakdowns and was faced with a major crisis of purpose.

Finding purpose When our company was bought by another company in 2015, I was on the other side of the world, sitting on a terrace with a beer in heavy rain. I imagined the exit party. Champagne corks, dancing on the tables and reeling with happiness after all the hardships. I had imagined the party differently. And suddenly I realized that it didn't matter that everything I drew my self-worth from for 7 years was a story. A bubble that burst. It was painful and liberating at the same time. It began the journey on the way to me.

There was only me.
There I finally was.

During that time, I had an experience that would change my life forever. I was in Nepal during the earthquake of the century that killed nearly 9000 people. Everything that I previously took for granted was destroyed in a minute. There was no more security, no roof over my head. Buildings started to collapse one after the other. There was no more electricity, no money, and no food. How small my problems in Berlin seemed to me in the face of this experience.

After a few hours and aftershocks of the earthquake, I was able to push aside my instincts of survival and to reflect. What could I do? How could I help? With years of focusing on quick pragmatic solutions and with a can-do attitude, I couldn't just sit around doing nothing. Who would have thought that my mind would fall back on the knowledge I had from my startup days at precisely such a moment? Activate a network, write press releases, process inquiries, and collect donations. Without knowing it, I founded an NGO in the middle of a natural disaster. No bureaucracy, no bank account, no previous experience. My head was spinning over how we could collect more money so that we could leave for the mountain villages that were cut off from supplies as soon as possible. My decision to stay in Nepal and help on site brought me back to myself. I finally felt self-efficacy again.

I asked myself what I wanted to do professionally in the future. Due to my burn-out and the post-traumatic stress disorder caused by the earthquake, I did not feel myself able to return to the Berlin startup scene. That is how I became an investor by investing in disadvantaged women in Nepal who survived by selling cashmere scarves and colorful woolen scarves in the markets in Nepal after there were no more tourists. I sold those items in Berlin. Later followed self-designed bags and backpacks made from hand-woven fabrics in Nepal's oldest fair-trade weaving mill, which specialized in empowering women who were excluded from society. Divorce, disability, and adultery are existentially threatening for many women in Nepal. They are rejected by their families and usually no longer find employment. In the weaving mill, they received training, health insurance, and the opportunity to take out microcredit.

After years of being in a male-dominated environment, I made a conscious decision to promote women and only hired female interns, who accompanied me on my travels and whom I supported. Running a business with women for women was liberating for me and I felt my leadership style change. Working in an Asian country, transport and communication with producers were challenging and often tedious because I couldn't always be on site. I donated 20% of my sales to our NGO and thus promoted its continued existence, since willingness to donate rapidly decreases only a few months after a natural disaster.

Old customers from my time in Berlin contacted me, wanted to know how I was doing, and kept in touch. When a customer asked me if I could support him and his recruiting business with a workshop and advice, I quickly founded a second company. This would survive. The other would not.

The independence of the opinions and strategies of the management team inspired me and I took courage to be able to run both companies in parallel.

Therefore, I invested the remaining proceeds from the sale of the company, half of which went into setting up the NGO in Nepal, in my two companies.

It went well for 2 years. My nervous system was used to high tension, constant availability, and problem-solving. The fact that I could only afford two interns at the fashion company and that my parents supported me in shipping the goods increasingly became a bottleneck. Raising capital was out of the question for me and I ended up back where I was before – self-exploitation!

Another challenge was around the corner. In a mixture of daring and naivety, I had not registered the brand, and a French company with the same name insisted on their trademark rights. A change of name did not seem worthwhile to me, the brand and domain were based on the name, and it would have taken a lot of money and time to change the name. A good friend and advisor asked me at the time whether I still had enough power on a scale of 1–10 to continue. I gave myself a four and realized the chapter was over. After winding up the company, I reflected on the past 3 years and came to the conclusion that I had not indeed failed. As an entrepreneur, it was always important for me to gain different experiences and less to write a one-off success story. With my own label, I seized the opportunity to bring my ideas and creativity out into the world. My main learning was that I am much more of a business midwife than a keeper. It was time to devote myself to just one thing and to no longer be two-pronged.

6.5 A New Horizon Ahead

Founding a management consultancy without knowledge of spreadsheets or a degree in business administration no longer seemed absurd to me. My experiences in Nepal and my tendency to implement and try things out no matter how adverse the circumstances are benefited me enormously. My first contracts with companies in the recruiting sector showed how much I had learned in my seven intensive years in management. My knowledge was transferrable. I was able to recognize mistakes made in good time with the customer and my workshops on a human-centered sales approach met with positive responses.

From the start, my company was without one thing – market positioning. A vision, mission, and brand identity would have been counterintuitive for me. Throwing everything I had learned upside down suddenly became very easy after I had learned in Nepal that entrepreneurship can be done differently. Being clear about what you want to change or support is more important than conforming to external regulations.

For the first 2 or 3 years, I let whatever came pouring in on me. Workshop requests for sales teams, coaching with managers and team leaders, and questions about application processes, I was very open to everything that resonated. At the same time, doubts arose when I looked at others in my sector who seemed crystal clear and had defined customer segments. The proportion of freelance workers in Berlin is almost ten percentage points higher than at the national level. This results in more opportunities for comparison but also more pressure. While my colleagues from the past were either still in the same business or had careers in startups or corporations, I was one of the few who became self-employed after their startup time.

6.6 A Startup Mindset and a Self-Employment Mindset

In order to work successfully in a startup, a special mindset is required that differs from that in established companies. Here are some qualities that can be important for success in a startup:

- Flexibility: Startups change quickly, and it is important for employees to be flexible and able to quickly adapt to new circumstances.
- Risk-taking: Startups tend to be riskier than incumbent businesses because they are still in the development phase. It is important for employees to be willing to take risks and learn from their mistakes.
- Creativity: Startups often need to find innovative solutions to complex problems, so creativity is an important trait in employees.
- Proactivity: Employees in a startup should be proactive and not wait to be told what to do. You should be able to take initiative and take responsibility.
- Team orientation: Startups are often small and every employee has an important role to play. It is important for the employees to work well in a team and be able to coordinate their work with others.
- Passion: Startups often face many challenges and setbacks, therefore, it is important for employees to have a strong passion for the company and the vision it is pursuing.

It is important to note that these characteristics are not set in stone and may vary according to the industry and company. Over the years, I have found that flexibility in thinking and acting has become an important action value for me, and my professional environment has strengthened this quality.

The same applies to proactivity, passion, and creativity. In terms of willingness to take risks, I am a bit more conservative than the benchmark for other entrepreneurs and have often taken on the role of the doubter in teams. This is important in order to not make headless hasty decisions or allow oneself to be carried away by hubris, which can quickly happen in this bubble.

These partly learned, partly inherited, qualities made it much easier for me to switch to solo self-employment. In order to become self-employed, you need an entrepreneurial and proactive mindset. Here are some properties that can be useful:

- Risk-taking: Self-employment often comes with uncertainty and risk, so it is important to be willing to take risks and also deal with potential failures.
- Flexibility: As a self-employed person, one must be able to quickly adapt to changes and learn new skills to meet the changing needs of the market.

- Creativity and innovative ability: Self-employment often requires innovative solutions to stand out from the competition. It is important to generate and implement creative ideas.
- Goal orientation: Self-employment requires a clear vision and goals in order to successfully shape one's own path. It is important to focus on the most important goals and work hard to achieve success.
- Self-motivation: As a self-employed person you have to be able to motivate and drive yourself. You have to be willing to work hard and persevere even in difficult times.
- Willingness to learn: Self-employment requires continual training and constant striving for improvement. It is important to be open to new knowledge and ready to continually develop.
- Customer orientation: As a self-employed person, you have to understand and respond to the needs and wishes of customers in order to build long-term customer relationships.

However, these characteristics are not all-inclusive and may vary depending on the type of self-employment and industry. There is much overlap between these lists, although they are not all-inclusive or always accurate. My startup mindset helped me to start my own business and to be sure to have a good base of qualities and values.

6.7 Further Development for Social Entrepreneurship

I see the future of entrepreneurship in the area of social innovation and social entrepreneurship, in the development of solutions to social problems and in networking with other actors toward social change. Over a weekend that turned out to be a think tank for people from the private sector with a penchant for social projects, I delved deeper and deeper into the world of social entrepreneurship. In informal rounds and in fireside chats, I got to know the founders and managing directors of large foundations, and also well-known investors in the Berlin startup world.

At lunch, I sat opposite one of the most well-known investors from my bubble, who coyly explained to me that no one should know that he was here today. It is ridiculed when an investor like him, who has successfully accompanied many well-known companies to their exit, is interested in social entrepreneurship. That bothered and fascinated me at the same time. What exactly is unpopular about dedicating yourself to the common good as a successful entrepreneur and investor? What unwritten laws and biases ensured that he secretly visited such think tanks at that time?

In one session, he revealed his idea of a neighborhood network in which he wanted to create more neighborly proximity in urban areas and asked me if I would be interested in managing the company. In short, I didn't become the managing director of this startup, but I'm happy to see that this idea materialized and a few years later there shouldn't be any more shame in turning such ideas into reality.

As a coach, I have been accompanying social entrepreneurs in their challenges for over 6 years now, and I offer them a safe place where they can spar with me about challenges, being overwhelmed, and their well-being.

These insights have shown me how related entrepreneurship and social entrepreneurship are, and also what differentiates them at their core. Some are chasing after the next round of financing and the exit, while others apply for tenders and must constantly ensure that their impact unfolds. The challenges may play out in different sectors but the psychological challenges are very similar. I am able to identify an even stronger tendency toward self-abandonment and overspending in social entrepreneurship, which I see as being mainly due to the fact that this group of entrepreneurs is committed to a goal that is far bigger than the pockets of investors or even filling one's own. The psychological challenges and aspirations are great. I accompany these people and it fascinates me to see how much these committed social entrepreneurs appreciate having a space in which they can express themselves and develop and it is all about themselves. Keeping these spaces and promoting authentic self-expression in my clients touches me again and again.

There are now a number of organizations that want to establish the basic idea of steward ownership in Germany. Steward ownership is a concept of corporate ownership that aims to promote long-term sustainable orientation of companies and to achieve a more equitable distribution of corporate profits.

Unlike the traditional ownership model in which a company is usually controlled by investors or owners who are primarily focused on short-term returns and profits, the concept of steward ownership is to hand the management and control over the company to people who have a long-term interest in its development and want to ensure sustainable management.

Steward ownership can be implemented in different ways. One option is to turn the company into a foundation or nonprofit organization that acts as the owner of the company and has control over the management. Another possibility is to transform the company into a cooperative, in which the employees act as members and thus participate directly in the management and profits. As a rule, steward ownership goes hand in hand with a long-term orientation of the company, which is based on social and ecological aims and economic success. This enables long-term investments and innovations that are in line with the goals of society and the environment. In addition, steward ownership can contribute to achieving a fairer distribution of profits and greater employee participation in the company's success.

The idea is not new, so business people have long built such constructs in order to ensure that their companies are owned in part or in full by the employees. These constructs are often awkward to build, since the legal forms in Germany currently only allow foundations to reflect such intentions. There is a nonprofit cooperative based in Berlin that specializes in supporting social startups and companies that want to have a positive impact on society and the environment. The cooperative offers financing, advice, and support to social startups and companies active in the fields of the environment, education, health, and social justice. This cooperative invests in companies that have a clear social purpose and want to be economically successful at the same time. It is not primarily about achieving a maximum return but about creating sustainable effects in society. The cooperative also offers an extensive network of consultants and mentors who support companies in the development and implementation of their business models and in the strategic orientation of their activities. The focus here is on topics such as sustainability, social impact, and steward ownership.

Another aim of the cooperative is to set up a new financing system based on the idea of "investing for the common good." The aim is to bring together investors and companies that have a common vision of a sustainable and fair future. This model is intended to help transform the traditional financial system and establish new sustainable forms of financing. Overall, it can be said that the cooperative plays an important role in promoting social startups and companies that want to have a positive impact on society and the environment. With its financing and advice, the cooperative supports companies in achieving their goals and at the same time making a positive contribution to society. The establishment of a new legal form for this type of company is one of the items in the current coalition agreement of the German federal government (Koalitionsvertrag, 2021–2023):

> A modern corporate culture also includes new forms such as social enterprises, or companies with tied assets. We are developing a national strategy for social enterprises in order to provide greater support for public welfare-oriented companies and social innovations. We are improving the legal framework for public welfare-oriented business, such as cooperatives, social enterprises and integration companies. For companies with tied assets, we want to create a new appropriate legal basis that excludes tax-saving structures. We will remove obstacles to access to financing and funding. We will create the legal framework to enable assets in orphaned accounts to be used to promote the common good.

The German government also recognized the role of diversity in the startup world:

> We are removing obstacles for women and people with a migration background in accessing financing and funding; we are ensuring better access to venture capital for female founders. […] We want to significantly strengthen the participation of women on investment committees of state funds and investment companies.

It is interesting to recognize that the coalition agreement in considering women and migrants in their strategy, however, not bearing to recognize that this is still limiting, not recognizing other gender groups in their approach.

6.8 The Turning Point in Entrepreneurship: New Longings

Considering diversity, equality, and inclusion is so much more than participation. It also recognizes the individual and their needs. There are hardly any offers for employment that are holistically oriented, go in depth, and offer psychological security in order to be able to reflect and experience oneself. Our greatest longing is to be seen, heard, and felt. We need open spaces for this.

The Corona crisis shook the Berlin startup bubble and presented it with new psychological challenges. Working remotely was not standard in many companies and the changeover went smoothly due to the high degree of digitization in the companies that I supported, but that was the smallest problem. The double burden of childcare, loneliness, and fear increased. What was mostly bubbling under the surface suddenly came into the everyday life of companies. Fears, trauma, insecurity, and the feeling of losing control. As work was the only space for social exchange for many, these things became more apparent.

For the first time, this opened up the possibility of providing companies with holistic support and opening up space for discussion not only for CEOs but for all employees who need it. Therefore, trauma and nervous system-sensitive rooms are needed to meet people. If they experience slowness, mindfulness, and need orientation, they can feel safe to look at and redeem parts of their traumatization – and they can redevelop a purpose. These rooms are far too rare in the business context. Quite the opposite is the case. It's about performance, speed, and perfection. This can be very triggering for traumatized people, causing them to constantly act with a deregulated nervous system. It follows that the constantly felt (often subliminal) stress in us makes us physically and mentally ill. Preventing burnout means becoming aware of these mechanisms, especially as an entrepreneur if you want to lead people responsibly.

6.9 A Practical View

We have come a long way from a closed, male-dominated society – and we have even a longer way to go to ensure diversity, equality, and inclusion on an individual level as well as on a societal level. Even though there is a political will, it is on each and every individual to tackle this issue consciously.

While writing these words about my journey, I realized how I was also strengthening the closed system in my early years. Becoming conscious about my experiences as well as about myself and who I am (and want to be) made me realize that – as part of the system – I can also challenge it, improving it for the better. Diversity, equality, and inclusion in the startup world are and will remain a challenge – one I am willing to take on!

References

Deutscher Startup Verband. (2022). *Deutscher Startup Monitor 2022*. Available at https://startupverband.de/fileadmin/startupverband/mediaarchiv/research/dsm/DSM_2022.pdf. Accessed 12 August 2023.

Koalitionsvertrag. (2021—2025). *zwischen der Sozialdemokratischen Partei Deutschland (SPD), Bündnis 90/Die Grünen und den Freuden Demokraten (FDP)*. Available at https://www.spd.de/fileadmin/Dokumente/Koalitionsvertrag/Koalitionsvertrag_2021-2025.pdf. Accessed 23 August 2023.

Statistisches Bundesamt (2023). *Mikrozensus – Arbeitsmarkt 2022 (Erstergebnis)*. https://www.destatis.de/DE/Themen/Arbeit/Arbeitsmarkt/Erwerbstaetigkeit/Publikationen/Downloads-Erwerbstaetigkeit/statistischer-bericht-mikrozensus-arbeitsmarkt-2010410227005-erstergebnisse.html. Accessed 17 August 2023.

Chapter 7
Inclusive Policy-Making in Social Entrepreneurial Ecosystems: The Role of Local Policy Frameworks in Cultivating Inclusive Social Entrepreneurship

Sandra de Boer

7.1 Introduction

> Every country is a developing country if looked at through the lens of the Sustainable Development Goals (Aromar Revi, 2022[1]).

While the Sustainable Development Goals themselves can be criticized (e.g., that targets overlook fundamental inequalities in the global system), this thought-provoking quote by Aromar Revi illustrates an ongoing debate on the development of an inclusive and sustainable economy. It indicates that the path or even the shape of an inclusive economy is still the subject of discussion and development. In this context, the role and potential of social entrepreneurship [SE] in terms of inclusion, diversity, and empowerment is a nascent subject of debate in academia and practice. Tackling social challenges through economic activities has become a widespread objective (Lundström & Zhou, 2014a) and in the face of increasing societal and environmental challenges, SE is also receiving policy-maker's attention. This can be illustrated by the way the concept of SE itself is increasingly discussed in economic and political discourse. In this debate, SE is considered to be an element that is expected to contribute to achieving a more inclusive economy (OECD, European Union, 2017).

Studies indicate that SE is a growing part of the economy underlying rapid development and transformation (e.g., Martin & Osberg, 2007; Liger et al., 2016; OECD,

[1] Taken from: Aroma Revi (2022)

S. de Boer (✉)
Europe-University Flensburg, FAC III, Flensburg, Germany
e-mail: sandra.de.boer@uni-flensburg.de

K. Mikkelsen, A. Wolf (eds.), *Minds, Brains, and Doxa for Inclusive Entrepreneurship*, International Studies in Entrepreneurship 47,
https://doi.org/10.1007/978-3-031-50164-7_7

European Union, 2017; European Commission, 2020). As a result, SE is receiving greater attention from public authorities, as well as from stakeholders in the private sector (Volkmann et al., 2012: 6). The importance of promoting and enabling SE is emphasized by institutions and government: "Social enterprises can only meet their full potential if an enabling environment is in place to allow them to start-up, scale-up and flourish" (OECD, European Union, 2017: 3).

On these grounds, it can be argued that policy-making is of high relevance as it directly and indirectly shapes the entrepreneurial ecosystem with the government's role as "feeder" (Stam, 2015: 1759). Research and theoretical debates on policies fostering SE are still in their infancy; however, several researchers emphasize the important role played by municipalities. These highlight their relevance in enhancing SE and, thus, enabling inclusive growth, e.g., by strengthening the distribution of capital toward Social Entrepreneurs that place social value creation at the core of their business model but tend to be marginalized by investors. As a reaction to this discourse, an increasing number of countries have created policy frameworks and adapted their legislation to support the development of SE (European Economic and Social Committee, 2018: 7). The European Union has been conducting a mapping series of social entrepreneurial ecosystems in European countries since 2011 (European Commission, 2020: 134) and states that "Against the uncertainty and, sometimes, scant effectiveness of national public policies, the role of municipalities in supporting social enterprise in their local contexts has in-creased in many EU Member States over the last five years" (European Commission, 2020: 138).

It can therefore be argued that local forms of support are of great importance. Access to finance is argued to be one of the "most important elements" for social entrepreneurs in order to operate their enterprise successfully while accomplishing their social mission (Spiess-Knafl & Achleitner, 2012: 158). In fact, a solid financing structure appears to be one of the main challenges for social enterprises (e.g., Scott & Teasdale, 2012; López-de-Alba et al., 2017). The access to capital is often inequitably distributed, albeit in varying degrees and forms. Hence, the area of finance is one where policy-makers can apply their power resources to nurture local ecosystems and leverage the potential of SE.

Based on this preliminary knowledge, this study examines approaches developed by municipalities to support SE in general and in finance in particular. The chapter begins with an introduction to the concept "social entrepreneurship" and its potential for a more inclusive economy. The nature of policy-based design approaches is examined. Accordingly, the research field focuses on the specific topic "access to finance." Based on a multi-case study approach, links between theory and practice are drawn. The case studies are analyzed regarding three research questions:

R1. How are municipalities approaching the topic of SE?
R2. How do policy-makers experience finance markets for social entrepreneurs?
R3. How are policy-makers developing mechanisms to stimulate access to finance for social entrepreneurs and, thus, elevating inclusivity?

While illustrating how policy-makers face normative and practical issues in implementation, this study outlines the ways policy-makers respond differently to these issues. Ultimately, this chapter offers four key characteristics for inclusive policy-making in social entrepreneurial ecosystems.

7.2 Methodology

This study pursues the progressive case study approach described by Steenhuis and Bruijn (2006). Its approach, which combines an inductive procedure with deductive elements, corresponds to the relatively new research field addressed in this study, allowing the researcher to openly explore the research field embedded in a theoretical foundation. In this way, it is possible to develop a detailed understanding of the role played by local public support schemes in fostering SE. Ultimately, this enables new insights and relevant elements to be identified in the context of policy-making to boost access to finance for SE, its practical challenges, and critical factors of success.

Steenhuis and Bruijn (2006) developed the progressive case study approach to merge the advantages of both the deductive, *theory based,* case study approach (Yin, 1994) and the inductive, *theory developing,* Grounded Theory approach (Glaser & Strauss, 1967). The methodological approach utilizes a deductive, *theory based,* case study approach (Yin, 1994) and an inductive, *theory developing,* Grounded Theory approach (Glaser & Strauss, 1967) simultaneously.

The research design of this study was developed accordingly: First, theoretical insights in the field of SE and their relevance for policy-making are elaborated. After a focus on the specific policy field of "finance," concrete case studies of cities that foster SE are assembled and analyzed in the empirical part of this study. This is achieved by conducting narrative guideline interviews with policy-makers implementing policies at local government level. The interviewees are either policy-makers or executing project managers of the policies in the respective cities. In the second step, the practical implementation and experience of local policy-making is linked back to theoretic debate to generate a comparison of both and to identify possible deviations. Finally, results from the theoretical and practical analysis are combined and key findings are presented.

Table 7.1 offers an overview of the cases and the respective cities. While the results of research question one are based on four interviews, the results of research questions two and three consist of two interviews

Table 7.1 Data sample of case studies

	Research question/policy field	City
Case 1	R1	Edinburgh
Case 2	R1	Hannover
Case 3	R1, R2, R3/Finance	Amsterdam
Case 4	R1, R2, R3/Finance	Parramatta

This chapter extracts result from a larger study, which also investigated policies promoting business development for social enterprises. Due to the size of this chapter, these findings are only discussed regarding R1. Thanks to a comparative content analysis, the data obtained will be processed. The overlaps and discrepancies in these approaches, as well as relevant insights, will be analyzed. Based on these results, the research questions will be answered by formulating significant elements and characteristics for local policy-making for SE.

7.3 The Role of Finance for Social Entrepreneurship and Entrepreneurial Ecosystems

Theoretical classification of social entrepreneurship In academic publications, the notion of SE is often connected with the concept of multiple value creation: the economic theory of creating multiple forms of value through entrepreneurial activity (Lundström & Zhou, 2014b: 346). Based on this understanding, the potential of SE for an inclusive form of entrepreneurial activity becomes evident. The following section takes a closer look at the opportunities and challenges of SE in terms of inclusion.

Some scholars connect socioeconomic changes with their effects on SE (Nicholls, 2006: 2). In this context, Nicholls identified two aspects differentiating current approaches of SE from previous forms: "What is different today is the scale and reach of the new social impact being generated (often at a systemic level), as well as the extraordinary variety of approaches being employed" (Nicholls, 2006: 2). Several scholars argue that the reason for this growth and diversity of SE can be seen in a global request for innovative solutions to pressing global challenges, combined with new possibilities and tools for creating solutions (e.g., Nicholls, 2006; Lundström & Zhou, 2014a). While a large heterogeneity of social entrepreneurs is desirable, the vast variation in (mainly nonprofit oriented) value creation also complicates identifying suitable forms of financing in the ecosystem. Investors want a return on investments. The increasing recognition of SE in various academic disciplines (political sciences, social sciences, and economics) underlines its potential in terms of inclusive economic activity. Inclusive business empowers economically disadvantaged individuals, for instance, through business models aimed at tackling obstacles to inclusion. An example of inclusive entrepreneurship is Elle La, a company that produces sustainable textiles made by tailors who had to flee their country and values the potential of craftsmanship (Elle La, 2023). To illustrate, Lundström and Zhou offer a characteristic example of how SE is treated in a socio-political context: "With its combination of social goals and commercial means, social entrepreneurship is increasingly considered a viable approach to creating new ideas for the evolution of existing social systems" (Lundström & Zhou, 2014a: 6). Looking at its definition, the overarching potential for SE for different forms of inclusivity can be concretized (Table 7.2).

Table 7.2 Definitions of SE

Source	Definition
Lundström and Zhou (2014b: 345)	"Social entrepreneurship is best understood as an organizing process in which true social entrepreneurs seek to increase social value and sustainably solve problems often neglected by the market and government"
Portales (2019: 55 f.)	"The elements that define the nature of social entrepreneurship are four: (1) Social mission and the creation of social value as a central element. (2) Motivation focused on the change of the structural conditions that generate the problem that wishes to address — visualized by the entrepreneur as an opportunity for social change. (3) Model for the generation of social and economic value. (4) Success based on indicators of social impact and not financial performance"

Based on these definitions, it appears that elements and characteristics of SE offer key potentials for addressing inclusivity. For example, in the sense of the capabilities approach, when considering its motivation of changing structural conditions and increasing social value generation (Lundström & Zhou, 2014b; Portales, 2019). SE aims at motivating and facilitating transformation on a citizen entrepreneurial level.

A critical academic discussion on the contribution of SE to achieving the mentioned objectives is valuable. However, measuring and evaluating social impact generated through entrepreneurial activity is difficult (Martin & Osberg, 2007; Then et al., 2017: 35). Various models and approaches of measuring social impact were developed over time (Maas & Liket, 2011). Since social value creation outweighs financial aspiration in SE, traditional investments are hard to get and attract.

Focus on specific policy area: Finance In order to generate in-depth knowledge about how policies can promote inclusive business forms, a focus is placed on the specific policy field "finance" to understand financing options for SE.

Finance instruments for social entrepreneurs The following brief overview on financing structures for social enterprises helps to review policies aimed at the accessibility of sources of finance for social enterprises.

Spiess-Knafl and Achleitner (2012) developed an overview of possible financing forms and tools for social enterprises (Fig. 7.1). They distinguish between internal and external financing forms. One source of internal financing concerns the generation of capital by offering products or services to target groups, which generates income. This source of financing is widespread. However, there are some social enterprises for which this option is not feasible, such as in the area of human rights (Spiess-Knafl & Achleitner, 2012: 158). Another source of internal financing can be acquired via the public sector. Here, policy-makers can have direct influence: "Public authorities are often legally obliged to fund the services and products provided by social organizations or can use their discretionary power to fund projects on a cost base" (Spiess-Knafl & Achleitner, 2012: 158).

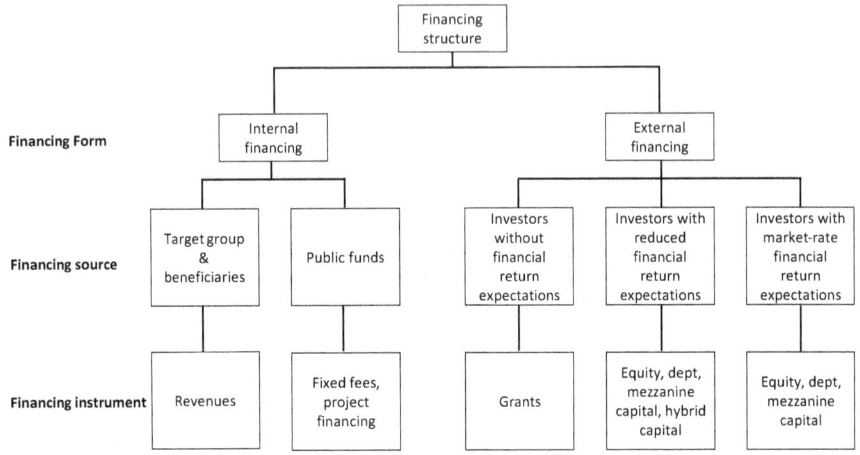

Fig. 7.1 Internal and external financing (Spiess-Knafl & Achleitner, 2012: 158)

This overview of financing forms, sources, and instruments is an important reference point for analyzing a local entrepreneurial ecosystem, identifying opportunities or gaps, and developing appropriate measures.

Depending on their stage of development, SEs have different access to capital. Studies have shown that raising capital is easier in the start-up phase – attracting investors for business ideas – and for financially established companies wanting to expand their business – attracting investors for business development (Wonglimpiyarat, 2014; Ganju & Heyman, 2018). In contrast, it is difficult to find investors for the phase in between which is why this financing gap is sometimes referred to as the "valley of death" for enterprises (Wonglimpiyarat, 2014; Ganju & Heyman, 2018).

7.4 Theoretical Approach of Clustering Policies

In order to investigate which practices are applied in specific ecosystems, a methodological approach to the clustering of different policies is needed. Different classification types are combined resulting in four different policy measures in total. To begin with, relational and transactional policy instruments are differentiated. Mason and Brown describe relational policy instruments as follows: "Main forms of assistance are 'relational' forms of support such as network building, developing connections between entrepreneurial actors, institutional alignment of priorities, fostering peer-based interactions" (Mason & Brown, 2014: 4).

In contrast to relational policy instruments, transactional policies concern primarily monetary policy instruments: "Main forms of assistance are 'transactional' forms of support such as grants, tax incentives, subsidies etc." (Mason & Brown,

2014: 4). Mason and Brown argue transactional policy instruments[2] to be particularly effective in young entrepreneurial ecosystems with many enterprises in the phase of starting up (Mason & Brown, 2014: 5). Ecosystems in advanced stages of development are expected to benefit more from relational policy instruments, i.e., the promotion of favorable conditions through networks and legal frameworks (ibid.). Mason and Brown conclude: "Accordingly, policy makers are now beginning to recognize the merit of a more systems-based form of support for high growth entrepreneurship" (Mason & Brown, 2014: 5). Consequently, a movement toward holistic policy measures is described (ibid). At the end of the qualitative study, the case studies will be categorized and analyzed according to the framework presented. As a result, conclusions can be made about the type of policies used in the case studies and thus about the focus of policy-makers to promote finance for SE.

Approaches of supporting access to finance through policies Having outlined different forms of financing structures and their relevance for SE, this section discusses policies that aim at optimizing accessibility of finance for social enterprises.

While considering the small sample size of former studies and their high dependency on regional frameworks, three main causes for challenges regarding finance for social enterprises can be abstracted:

1. Structural environment: e.g., a lack of investors, support funds, and networks; a dynamic and changing framework (Scott & Teasdale, 2012: 24; López-de-Alba et al., 2017: 44).
2. Context: "difficulty and slowness in getting financial support from government" (López-de-Alba et al., 2017: 46), "distrust and resistance, both public and private, in the participation with and investment in social enterprises" (ibid.).
3. Internal organization of social enterprises: e.g., a lack of skills and knowledge (López-de-Alba et al., 2017: 48; Scott & Teasdale, 2012: 17).

These results demonstrate that the reasons why social enterprises experience difficulties in acquiring finance are complex and concern the political and structural conditions as much as the internal management of a social enterprise. These issues can be addressed by local governments.

The European Commission and the OECD (2020; online source) have developed a helpful policy guidance note around supporting access to finance for SE. In this note, five general steps for building an ecosystem with favorable conditions are formulated:

1. The financing market has been mapped.
2. Social Enterprises have access to the appropriate type of financing for their stage of development.
3. Social enterprises are supported by a number of specialized service providers.

[2] Relational policy instruments can be differentiated into soft policies (aiming at creating a conductive environment) and hard policies (improving the effective execution of business operations) (European Economic and Social Committee, 2018).

4. Sufficient number of specialized private funders actively target social enterprises as an investment opportunity.
5. Policy-makers actively reach out to mainstream funders to raise awareness about social enterprises.

However, each entrepreneurial ecosystem consists of individual sets of characteristics and resources. Political decision makers are dealing with these specific conditions and challenges when implementing policies.

7.5 Results and Analysis

The theoretical examination of the research field illustrated a mixed portrait on SE and policy-making. The presented methods for schematizing and analyzing SE are essential steps for establishing a transparent scientific field. Yet, research on policy-making at local government level is still in its infancy. This study is based on a more extensive research project (see Table 7.1) that included further analysis of interviews.

Strategies for enhancing access to finance Two case studies concerning the support of access to finance were examined by qualitative interviews. While both cities have larger programs for enhancing SE, two specific policies were identified as particularly instructive regarding finance for social enterprises (Table 7.3).

Case Study 1 Integrated Capital Network, Amsterdam In order to support SE, the initiative "Amsterdam Impact" was established in the Department of Economic Affairs. The program consists of six pillars and 18 measures designed to strengthen the ecosystem for SE and socially responsible businesses in Amsterdam (Amsterdam Impact, 2020). One pillar focuses specifically on the topic of capital with three measures (ibid.). One measure, the Integrated Capital Network, is briefly illustrated in the following[3, 4]

Table 7.3 Case studies regarding access to finance

	Policy	City
Case 1	Integrated Capital Network	Amsterdam
Case 2	Pitch for Good	Parramatta

[3] The interview was carried out with the program manager Ellen Oetelmans.

[4] The Integrated Capital Network members are: DOEN Foundation, OnePlanet-Crowd, SI2 Fund, Heroes & Friends, ABN AMRO Social Impact Fund, ABN Sustainable Finance Desk, Triodos Business Credit, Rabobank Foundation, City of Amsterdam, Impact Hub Amsterdam, and Generous Minds (City of Amsterdam, 2019, online source)

The City of Amsterdam connected financiers and jointly developed the Integrated Capital Network in 2017: a growing group of impact-driven financial providers, including private investors, banks, foundations and venture capital firms. The design of the network was co-created with the project partners Impact Hub Amsterdam and Generous Minds as well as with twelve network members. The financiers conduct assessments of social enterprises during monthly labs. In these labs, they discuss the case of a selected social entrepreneur. Since the financiers provide expertise on different growth phases, it is evaluated, in which way the social entrepreneur can be supported with a mix of appropriate financial resources, business expertise and networking opportunities. In this way, the aim is to reduce risks, increase the chances of success and maximize the impact of the social enterprise.

Case Study 2 Pitch for Good, Parramatta In order to support access to finance for social enterprises, the City of Parramatta (2018) developed a Social Investment Action Plan in which two grants are offered: "Social enterprise business plan grants" aiming at stimulating the creation of social enterprises, and "Growing Social Enterprise in Parramatta" aiming at expanding social entrepreneurial activity in Parramatta (City of Parramatta, 2018)

The Social Investment Action Plan focuses on three areas: Driving Innovation, Education & Engagement and Leadership (City of Parramatta, 2018: 7). One specific measure of promoting access to finance was formulated under the area "Driving Innovation": "Run/support 'Pitch' events, which enable social entrepreneurs to pitch a proposal to an audience and seek support and seed-funding to establish their venture" (City of Parramatta, 2018: 9).

Pitch for Good Parramatta is executed by the council of Parramatta in partnership with the crowd funding platform "Start Some Good". It combines a live pitch event with an online crowd funding campaign for 4-5 local social enterprises. During the pitch event, social enterprises present their products. The pitch event serves as the launch of an online crowd funding campaign by each of the featured social enterprises. The special nature of the event lies in the fact that the audience -the local community- decides about who they invest in: Entry tickets serve as tokens (3x10 dollars) that the audience can distribute among the pitching social enterprises. The council of Parramatta will match the value of the funds raised during the pitch event: The amount of money that each social enterprise collected, will be doubled and serves as the start of their online crowd funding

7.6 Comparison and Recommendations

The research questions will be used to present and interpret key findings. The contents of the qualitative research and the corresponding theoretical considerations are compiled and linked together to ensure that meaningful results are obtained to answer the research questions.

R1. How are municipalities approaching the topic of social entrepreneurship? (Normative)

A consensus on the importance of the political environment and politicians' perception of SE emerged: General political interest was described as a foundation for enhancing SE. Therefore, political openness to the subject can be identified as a central precondition for policy-makers to develop support structures. The interviewees described the role of the political environment as that of a connector or linker, with an emphasis on the importance of a local government's knowledge of its community. The benefit of local government and its proximity is also described in the theoretical analysis (Scott & Teasdale, 2012: 450). The interviewees addressed a disadvantage of this closeness, which can lead to friction between social entrepreneurs and policy-makers as described by Scott and Teasdale (2012): policy-makers were identified, among other things, as service providers. The interviewees reported that this position could cause difficulties in the process of understanding the ecosystem and its needs, since it often raises social entrepreneurs' hopes and expectations. It is not possible to meet all needs, which means that political decision makers have to weigh up the measures' urgency and feasibility.

A further problem regards political cycles which are short in comparison to the time it takes to capture the effects of SE, leading to less political interest. The interviewees described ways of approaching this problem: Using political sensitivity when managing expectations and pointing to the positive effects of SE, which could cover several types of political agenda (education, elderly care, etc.). A second method of attracting political attention is to pick up on changes in society and current sustainability debates, to introduce SE. The creation of community awareness was, thus, identified as a lever for receiving political attention and support. Community awareness was enhanced, e.g., through companies' good practices which create social impact or through a campaign for SE.

Another insight from the interviews is that no strict, overarching definition of SE exists, which is in accordance with the theoretical findings (Martin & Osberg, 2007; Volkmann et al., 2012). However, the qualitative research showed that in practice, a distinction is made between a definition used for granting subsidies (strict criteria, often aligned with the European Commission's definition) and that used in the wider field of work (broader interpretation, focused on the impact created). In this context, there is a connection to literature, which distinguishes between SE as an institution and SE as a function (Lundström & Zhou, 2014b). The definition determines access to and exclusion from programs, networks, and advisory services. Therefore, in practice, policy-makers have developed approaches for defining SE to be either inclusive (enhancing social impact created through their programs) or exclusive (when distributing grants), depending on the context in which they use the expression and the objectives of the programs they refer to. The terms used to describe SE as a concept were *social investment, social impact business,* or *socially responsible business*.

The normative evaluation of the policy-maker's approaches revealed a mindset comparable to that of a start-up. Policies are often written from scratch by utilizing and combining elements of the entrepreneurial ecosystem and following an iterative approach. The description of the methodical approach was often accompanied by terms such as *trying out* and *testing*.

R2. How do policy-makers experience finance markets for social entrepreneurs? (two interviews)

The literature analysis revealed three aspects as being particularly challenging when creating an ecosystem to enable social enterprises to match their financial needs: The structural environment (number of financiers), context (distrust, resistance), and internal organization of social enterprises (lack of knowledge) (Scott & Teasdale, 2012; López-de-Alba et al., 2017). These factors are compared with the results of the qualitative analysis. Both interviewees stated that, generally, the capital available for social enterprises in their specific ecosystems was increasing. However, the developmental stages were identified in which social enterprises experience greater difficulties in obtaining finance. These stages varied depending on the ecosystems they exist in. The interviewee of Amsterdam described a trend of increasing interest from investors in SE in the Netherlands and Amsterdam specifically. However, a lack of exchange and collaboration between impact investors and social enterprises made the matching of these stakeholders a hurdle. Some financiers struggled with finding the right social enterprises among which they can distribute their capital. In addition, financiers tended to target social enterprises that are financially well established which resulted in difficulties of connecting social enterprises in the start-up phase with suitable investors. These insights set the foundation for the development of the Integrated Capital Network.

In Parramatta, another critical period for attracting investors was identified: the phase between starting up and being well-established as a social enterprise.[5] The City of Parramatta awards grant money for starting up as well as scaling capital, but it was found that capital for the phase in-between was limited for social entrepreneurs. These circumstances were considered in the development of the Pitch for Good events. In summary, empirical research has revealed two different financing gaps in the *structural environment*; during the growth phase (Parramatta) and when starting a business (Amsterdam).

The qualitative analysis also provides insights on the aspect of *context* which was identified as being critically important, in the theory (cf. López-de-Alba et al., 2017: 46). The interviewee from Amsterdam described that investors were reluctant to

[5] In theory referred to as valley of death (Ganju & Heyman, 2018).

social enterprises in the start-up phase due to financial risks. However, a general openness toward the concept of SE, as well as willingness to collaborate and provide business support for SE was experienced. The interviewee from Parramatta mentioned that investors had less interest in investing in social start-ups. The reason given here was that investors were mainly interested in generating financial and not social profits. To counteract this, the council awards start-up grants for social enterprises. From these specific findings, it can generally be deduced that it is necessary to understand the financial context and state of an entrepreneurial ecosystem, in order to be able to develop appropriate policies. Depending on the stage of development of the ecosystem, corresponding measures can be taken.

The *internal organization* and knowledge about finance in social enterprises were identified as limiting factors (e.g., López-de-Alba et al., 2017: 48; Scott & Teasdale, 2012: 17). Since social entrepreneurs often do not come from a business background, they usually do not have extensive knowledge in this area. This circumstance is reflected in the empirical findings: for example, the policy-maker in Parramatta stated that part of their task was to support social enterprises to establish their enterprise in an economically sustainable way. A high level of linkage between the areas of corporate planning and finance was noted. A solid business case is essential for attracting investors. Thus, the theoretical conclusions regarding *internal organization* as a limiting factor are reflected in the qualitative findings. In order to address the challenges presented, tailored approaches have been developed, which are discussed in the following sections.

R3. How are policy-makers developing mechanisms to stimulate access to finance for social entrepreneurs? (two interviews)

The policy-makers interviewed had each developed different policies for improving access to finance for social enterprises. Their distinct approaches can be explained by the diverse preconditions of the entrepreneurial ecosystems. Even though the policies and their method of implementation vary, it was possible to identify some commonalities. The qualitative research revealed that understanding the impact finance sector and its stakeholders was the starting point for the policies' development. In order to do so, research was carried out in the form of interviews and surveys. Collaboration and co-creation were fundamental elements for enabling the policy developed in Parramatta: the online crowdfunding platform "Start Some Good" is the project partner of the Pitch for Good events. Another essential element of Pitch for Good is the involvement of the local community and, in this way, informing about the concept of SE. The interviewee describes the engagement of the audience as positive for the promotion of SE through participation. An important conclusion is to keep the event affordable so that low entry barriers arise. Co-creation also played a significant role in developing the Integrated Capital Network in Amsterdam. The impact and knowledge of the project partners Impact Hub Amsterdam and Generous Minds were utilized as leverage. It can be concluded that a crucial part of the process was the investigation and connection of ideas and stakeholders within the ecosystem. The interviewee stated that while developing the policy, many conversations were held with investors. During one of these conversations, an idea emerged and set the course of the project: "*...in half a sentence he* *[investor] said, 'I would like to have more contact with my peers and other investors'. I think the city, as an objective outside party – because they [investors] are peers but also competitors- the city can play a role in this*" (Amsterdam l. 198). These two elements (examination of the ecosystem and collaboration) formed the objectives of the policies: Parramatta: Creating capital for social entrepreneurs in the finance gap (pitch event, crowdfunding campaign), creating knowledge about raising capital (master class) and raising awareness of SE (involvement of the local community). Amsterdam: Establishing co-creation and cooperation between finance providers and social entrepreneurs in all developmental stages, enabling financial and consultative forms of support and disseminating the SE concept. In this regard, the interviewee explained that it is crucial to understand not only the needs and roles of investors but also those of social enterprises: "*we connected them [Investors] not only together but also with social enterprises in order for them to also be able to understand each other*" (Amsterdam l. 212).

In theory, the role of cities is described as *feeders* of ecosystems (Stam, 2015). The empirical survey points to how policy-makers perceive their own role and the challenges that come with it. Essential aspects of the role of the city were described: "*as a city, we are an objective outsider and this enables us to stimulate collaboration between financiers, who normally would be competitors*" (Amsterdam l.238). This process can be challenging, which is why leadership and moderating skills are relevant characteristics for policy-making. In order to influence the atmosphere and mindset toward exchange and co-creation, the interviewee remarked it as helpful to emphasize the purpose of the project and having strong alleys among the investors during this process: "*We want to make impact together so it means that we have to solve these issues*" (Amsterdam l.232).

According to the analysis, both policies were developed in an iterative process building on existing projects, examples from other cities, and experience gained over years: "*it was about picking what was kind of... looked interesting and might work in Parramatta*" (Parramatta l. 117); "*the strategy that we have got now is based very much on the trial and errors of the first one*" (Parramatta l. 119). The results of the qualitative analysis show that an examination of the ecosystem and collaboration are central elements for developing policies. Both policies address the respective financing gaps and foster awareness and exchange about the concept of SE. The outcomes and indicators of success are similar in several respects. These are increased visibility of SE, more external capital for social entrepreneurs, and additional skills in finance. These outcomes result in an increased survival rate for social entrepreneurs and a more inclusive ecosystem. In Parramatta, these effects are measured by three indicators: A local survey, the crowdfunding success rate, and the return on contribution for council to community activity. The survey found that the crowdfunding success rate of the program is above average in respect to traditional crowdfunding campaigns (Clifford, 2016). In addition, soft factors are also of importance: A strengthened community and a feeling of connectedness. Such a reinforced ecosystem can contribute to recurrent funding in the long term. It also provides a rationale for the existence of SE-supporting policies at the political level. This is especially enhanced by the local community's participation in the decision about which social enterprise should receive financial support. The money provided by the community is prolonged because it is matched by council money. The interviewee in Amsterdam stated that important factors of success were the creation of a functioning, growing, and sustainable design for the Integrated Capital Network and the proportion of social enterprises that have successfully raised finance. Accordingly, one aim was to create a self-sustaining network so that the city can withdraw as a sponsor. This aim was achieved.

Both policy-makers described the challenge of finding social enterprises that were at the right stage for their programs "*you need to have prospects, propositions, you need social enterprises that want to pitch*" (Amsterdam l. 273). Project-specific issues were on the one hand, being dependent on the participants' commitment and attracting an audience (Parramatta) and on the other hand, coordinating and aligning investors and their perspectives (Amsterdam). Furthermore, the interviewee expressed an issue regarding the topic of impact investing in general: the system of business reporting. If not only financial but also ecological and social forms of value creation are reported, it is easier to enhance investments in social enterprises: "*because it is sometimes difficult for impact investors themselves to break open the environment they are in*" (Amsterdam l. 297).

General considerations In order to provide an overview of the types of measures applied, this section classifies policies according to the classification explained in the theoretical part. First, it is noticeable that a mixture of hard and soft policy instruments was used in all the case studies. Accordingly, the measures aim to directly enhance the entrepreneurial ecosystem, in addition to improving the effective execution of social enterprises' business operations. The analysis reveals a slightly stronger focus on soft policies. This mixed approach can be explained by the role of municipalities, which the interviewees described as linker, connector, and accelerator of SE. Transactional policy instruments are used less often than relational ones, with the city often acting as an intermediary in dealings with external partners. However, there is also an academic debate around whether transactional or relational forms of support are more effective. According to one theoretical perspective, the ecosystem's developmental stage is a decisive factor, since it is argued that younger ecosystems profit more from transactional and older ecosystems from relational, policy instruments (Mason & Brown, 2014). In this regard, a comparison of the theory and practice would be an interesting research question for further studies (Table 7.4).

When comparing the theoretical and practical results of this study, characteristics and elements for developing local policy instruments, which can be applied regardless of the field of action and the ecosystem's preconditions, emerged. As indicated, these results are of a universal nature and were recognized as additions to the specific approaches of supporting access to finance. A recurring insight is that those making policy for SE, are moving in a comparatively young field, which requires

Table 7.4 Overview of policy types (own illustration)

		Access to finance	
		Pitch for good	Integrated capital network
Relational policy instruments	Hard policies (business process)	Training in pitching for investors and leading a crowdfunding campaign	Experience and knowledge in pitching and attracting financiers
	Soft policies (favorable environment)	Creating awareness of social entrepreneurship in the local community	Awareness of social entrepreneurship and impact investing
			Creation of a capital network
Transactional policy instruments	Grant Voucher Loans Etc.	Capital from audience of pitch event	Different forms of capital (donations, loans, equity) are provided by investors of the capital network
		Council matches the value of the funds raised during the pitch event	
		Capital from online crowdfunding campaign	

them to develop new approaches for designing effective policies. As discussed, policy-makers are similar to their target group in this respect. This may explain why the analysis shows that policy-makers have, in part, adopted the behavior and methodological approaches of entrepreneurs, such as iterative approaches or design thinking. It can further be argued that participative approaches are utilized in order to improve the inclusion of various social entrepreneurs. The characteristics and elements are connected and influence the process-related development and refinement of policy instruments. They support the policy-makers' empirically observed, result-driven approach. They will each be described and the methodical tools that shape the application of the characteristics will be presented (see Table 7.5).

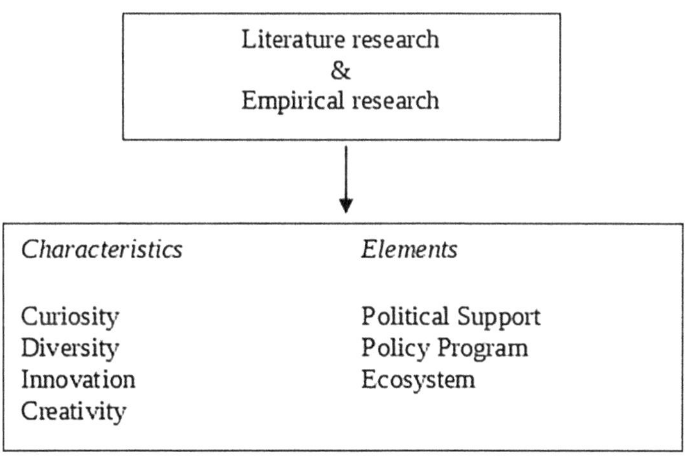

Table 7.5 Key characteristics and tools for policy-making (own illustration)

Characteristic	Description	Tools
Curiosity	Understanding the ecosystem Why: Curiosity is fundamental for understanding the entrepreneurial ecosystem and for analyzing, which role the city can play in strengthening the ecosystem	Research, interviews, surveys, network meetings Exploring ideas, networks, and projects in the ecosystem
Diversity	Comprehending and enabling diversity in terms of community and in terms of social entrepreneurship Why: Diversity is a key driver for expanding the reach of policies and multiplying the impact. It also supports in expanding a program, reaching various people and offers arguments for maintaining a policy strategy	Connecting key stakeholders in an ecosystem; Platform Economy Approach Designing inclusive policies
Innovation	Developing strategies from scratch and adapting iterative, entrepreneurial approaches Why: Including new methods and approaches in public administration is a key component for developing suitable, effective, and lasting policies	Design thinking, Platform Economy Approach Lean start-up Co-creation
Creativity	Change, Leadership Why: Developing new policies has to do with change and rethinking the current system. Creativity is a basic element for enabling change. It can be facilitated through leadership and a trusted environment	Passionate and charismatic leaders Enabling a trusted environment Building a shared language and having a space to co-create

Curiosity particularly determines the beginning of policy development. An understanding of the ecosystem surrounding SE provides the foundation for potential policies. This includes identifying the needs of relevant stakeholders and exploring the role that local government can play in specific areas. Relevant methods for achieving these objectives are studies and surveys, together with mapping and understanding the ideas, networks, and projects within the ecosystem. Being open to *diversity* is a key feature in this process; investigating the community and its social offerings and being open to actively encouraging diversity in policy-making. This factor was observed several times in the empirical analysis. Policy-makers stressed the importance of embracing the diversity of ideas and considerations in an ecosystem. It was emphasized that disadvantaged districts should be included, as they have a high potential for amplifying the impact of policies and should be valued. The projects, ideas, and stakeholders identified in the first step can be connected through policy-making. This approach has the advantage of increasing the program's reach, which is a significant prerequisite for justifying and continuing SE policy programs. O*penness toward innovation* is another essential feature for designing policies in the field of SE. As was shown in the theoretical and empirical parts, including new methods and approaches in public administration is a key component for developing effective policies. Methods, such as design thinking and the platform economy approach, as well as trust and co-creation were identified as supporting elements for enabling innovation. To facilitate these, local governments could form partnerships with networks and stakeholders on the basis of open communication and managed expectations. As a final aspect, *creativity* emerged as an enhancing component. This includes curating space for ideas, even though it is not possible to execute everyone. According to the analysis, creativity can be facilitated by leadership: Two interviewees mentioned passionate, charismatic, and trusted leaders, as important levers for enhancing SE ecosystems. Having leaders in the areas of council, community, and among social entrepreneurs was therefore stressed as an important factor. Having a place in which leadership can take place to enable co-creation, and networking is an advantage. Creativity is crucial for facilitating the change in systems and public administration which is often needed to enhance the conditions for SE: creativity is particularly necessary for stretching (bureaucratic) rules without exceeding their legal limitations. It was found that these characteristics not only enhance policy-making in the field of SE, but they can also motivate policy-makers, making their work more interesting.

These characteristics can be applied by developing three elements, which were identified as relevant for facilitating the implementation of policies: *Political support*, a *policy program,* and a nurtured *entrepreneurial ecosystem*. These elements can be enhanced by using the characteristics presented, i.e., exploring, including, co-creating, and leading a process toward a politically supportive ecosystem. The analysis showed that policy-makers promote SE within the municipality and among colleagues in order to achieve *political support*. Creating a shared language is a way to strengthen the recognition of SE, for example, by communicating and encouraging the implementation of the Sustainable Development Goals. An important element for enhancing social entrepreneurial ecosystems is having a suitable *policy program*, to which policy-makers can refer while carrying out their work. The interviews stated relevant parts of a policy program. The most important was to have clear objectives tailored to the needs of the social entrepreneurial ecosystem. Furthermore, the policy program should be based on credibility and strong arguments (acquired through research, surveys, and social entrepreneurs' best practices). Credibility and having arguments to fall back on provide the foundation for negotiating a budget to enable the implementation of policies. Finally, the city's role was identified as that of a link, with the function of facilitating the connection and networking of the relevant stakeholders in the ecosystem.

7.7 Conclusion

The analysis showed that SE is itself a complex concept touching on the most diverse areas of local policy frameworks. SE affects not only politics, economics, and law but also ecology, health care, and society as a whole. The answer to how social entrepreneurial ecosystems can be enhanced through local policy frameworks is, therefore, complex and requires individual, local approaches. The theoretical analysis, as well as the results of qualitative research, demonstrated that there is still vagueness surrounding the definition of SE. While the practical analysis showed that some policy-makers follow the European Commission's definition, it was also observed that different ways of extending this definition were developed in order to broaden the scope of the policies. The qualitative analysis identified the generation of social added value through economic activity, as the guiding motivation of policy-makers. An extended definition is used in order to achieve this goal, as well as a formal definition, which is necessary for the allocation of grant money.

The literature review showed that several policy recommendations exist. However, these are mostly formulated broadly and are aimed at national government level. It should be noted that many practical approaches for designing policy frameworks are currently being investigated by institutes and international research missions. So, while it is possible to observe a discrepancy between theory and practice, further in-depth results, including at local government level, can and should be expected in the future.

This study has drawn on literature to identify key elements for promoting finance for social entrepreneurs, as finance has been identified as a critical success factor for diverse social entrepreneurs, since not all have access to funding of different kinds. Elements enhancing access to capital can be summarized as the structural environment, context, and knowledge of social entrepreneurs. The literature proposes a braided policy support system. When comparing these results with the conclusions of the study, all these elements proved to be significant in the case studies analyzed. In particular, a mixture of hard and soft policy types was identified. The qualitative results indicated that this approach allows policy-makers to target multiple objectives from their respective SE agendas. There was a particular focus on soft policies aimed at enhancing a favorable entrepreneurial ecosystem. This finding can be seen in connection with the role with which policy-makers identify: as connectors, objective outsiders, and facilitators. This self-perception is also consistent with the role of cities as feeders of entrepreneurial ecosystems, as described by Stam (2015).

The qualitative research has shown that measures should be selected according to the state of development of the ecosystem. The collaboration with stakeholders in the social entrepreneurial ecosystem was identified as a crucial factor. Furthermore, the analysis revealed a special element relating to public authorities, namely, the benefit of broad networks as well as access to the various city departments touched by SE. This position was utilized by approaching and connecting stakeholders and their services when designing policies. Social entrepreneurs see the city's role as not only being an objective outsider but also as a service provider. Policy-makers describe this role as challenging for developing policies, because not all the requirements and needs in an ecosystem can be met. Weighing the urgency and feasibility of measures was described as a critical factor for understanding the ecosystem and designing policies. The practical analysis revealed two significant challenges in developing local policies: The recognition of SE in political contexts and policy-makers' dependence on the commitment of social entrepreneurs in programs and crowdfunding projects. Methods for promoting SE in political contexts were described.

In addition to these specific approaches, four key characteristics were deduced: Curiosity, diversity, openness toward innovation, and creativity. Specific tools were described for each characteristic. These can be implemented in every context, allowing individual policies to be developed which are specialized for the conditions in each entrepreneurial ecosystem. It was found that policy-makers often adopt their target group's entrepreneurial mindset and methods, such as an iterative approach or design thinking. This can be explained by the fact that policy-makers themselves are moving in the rapidly changing and still developing, field of local policies for SE. Further elements that enhance policies at local government level are the development of a policy program tailored to the social entrepreneurial ecosystem's needs, political support and the integration of ideas, projects, and citizens into the ecosystem.

This study has shown that each social entrepreneurial ecosystem is a transforming entity with its own conditions, advantages, and shortcomings. Therefore, it is essential to understand a city's local ecosystem and to derive suitable approaches and strategies. The policy development process is itself critical for the success and impact of the designed policies. At best, it is characterized by the horizontal involvement of municipal departments and representatives of the ecosystem, by means of interdisciplinary cooperation. Vertically, policies should be designed inclusive and across social levels, since the practical analysis showed that SE unfolds its potential when different ideas and ways of thinking are involved. The fact that such a cooperation can be successful and lead to positive synergy effects for ecosystems, such as reduced transaction costs and increased social value generation, was demonstrated several times in the case studies presented.

Finally, this study should be positioned as a preliminary study of local policy frameworks for enhancing SE in general and in the field of finance. Relevant research steps such as validation and reliability are not feasible due to the small sample size. Due to the nature of inductive research approaches, further studies are needed to extend the results obtained. In addition, other policy fields, such as market access or legislation, offer opportunities for generating further knowledge about public support schemes for SE.

References

Amsterdam Impact. (2020). *Impact entrepreneurship action programme*. Retrieved 27.12.2022, from: https://www.iamsterdam.com/en/business/amsterdam-impact/who-we-are/action-programme-2019-2022

Aromar Revi. (2022). *Sustainable development solutions network. A global initiative for the United Nations*. Retrieved 11.12.2022, from: https://www.unsdsn.org/cities

City of Amsterdam. (2019). *Impact financiers and experts join forces in the integrated capital network*. 29.05.2019. Retrieved on 05.11.2022, from: https://www.iamsterdam.com/en/business/amsterdam-impact/news-and-insights/news/integrated-capital-network

City of Parramatta. (2018). *Social investment action plan 2018–2021*. Retrieved 11.11.2022, from: https://www.cityofparramatta.nsw.gov.au/sites/council/files/inline-files/Social%20Investment%20Action%20Plan%202018-2021.pdf

Clifford, C. (2016). *Less than a third of crowdfunding campaigns reach their goals. Crowd-funding*. 18.01.2016. Retrieved 15.11.2022, from: https://www.entrepreneur.com/article/269663
Elle La. (2023). *About*. Retrieved 10.05.2023, from: https://elle-la.com/pages/about
European Commission. (2020). *Social enterprises and their ecosystems in Europe. Comparative synthesis report*. Publications Office of the European Union.
European Commission, OECD. (2020). *Guidance note: Access to finance. The better entrepreneurship policy tool*. Retrieved 01.12.2022, from: https://betterentrepreneurship.eu/en/node/51
European Economic and Social Committee. (2018). *Best practices in public policies regarding the European social economy post the economic crisis*. Publications Office of the European Union.
Ganju, E., & Heyman, C. (2018). *Scaling global change: A social entrepreneur's guide to surviving the start-up phase and driving impact*. Wiley.
Glaser, B. G., & Strauss, A. L. (1967). *The discovery of grounded theory. Strategies for qualitative research*. Aldine Publishing Company.
Liger, Q., Stefan, M., & Britton, J. (2016). *Social economy. Policy department A: Economic and scientific policy*. European Parliament. Retrieved 27.11.2022, from: https://base.socioeco.org/docs/ipol_stu_2016_578969_en.pdf
López-de-Alba, P. L., Zavala Berbena, M. A., de la Garza-Carranza, T., Lopez Lemus, J. A., Ramos, C., Vázquez, M., Alatorre, D. (2017). *Causes of failure in Mexican social enterprises*. The failure institute. Retrieved 05.11.2022, from: https://thefailureinstitute.com/wp-content/uploads/2017/04/Causes-of-failure-in-social-enterprises-low-res.pdf
Lundström, A., & Zhou, C. (2014a). Introduction. In A. Lundström, C. Zhou, Y. von Friedrichs, & E. Sundin (Eds.), *Social entrepreneurship. Leveraging economic, political, and cultural dimensions* (pp. 3–22). Springer International Publishing.
Lundström, A., & Zhou, C. (2014b). The policy strategy of supporting social entrepreneurship. Based on a three-dimensional approach. In A. Lundström, C. Zhou, Y. von Friedrichs, & E. Sundin (Eds.), *Social entrepreneurship. Leveraging economic, political, and cultural dimensions* (pp. 343–356). Springer International Publishing.
Maas, K., & Liket, K. (2011). Social impact measurement: Classification of methods. In R. Burritt, S. Schaltegger, M. Bennett, T. Pohjola, & M. Csutora (Eds.), *Environmental management accounting and supply chain management* (Vol. 27, pp. 171–202). Springer.
Martin, R. L., & Osberg, S. R. (2007). Social entrepreneurship: The case for definition. *Stanford Social Innovation Review, 2007*, 29–39.
Mason, C., & Brown, R. (2014). *Entrepreneurial ecosystems and growth-oriented entrepreneurship*. OECD. Retrieved 16.11.2022, from: https://www.oecd.org/cfe/leed/Entrepreneurial-ecosystems.pdf
Nicholls, A. (2006). Introduction. In A. Nicholls (Ed.), *Social entrepreneurship. New models of sustainable social change* (pp. 1–35). Oxford University Press.
OECD, European Union. (2017). *Boosting social enterprise development: Good practice compendium*. OECD Publishing.
Portales, L. (2019). *Social innovation and social entrepreneurship. Fundamentals, concepts, and tools*. Palgrave Macmillan.
Scott, D., & Teasdale, S. (2012). Whose failure? Learning from the financial collapse of a social enterprise in 'Steeltown'. *Voluntary Sector Review, 3*(2), 139–155.
Spiess-Knafl, W., & Achleitner, A. (2012). Financing of social entrepreneurship. In C. K. Volkmann, K. O. Tokarski, & K. Ernst (Eds.), *Social entrepreneurship and social business: An introduction and discussion with case studies* (pp. 157–174). Springer Gabler.
Stam, E. (2015). Entrepreneurial ecosystems and regional policy: A sympathetic critique. *European Planning Studies, 23*(9), 1759–1769.
Steenhuis, H. J., Bruijn, E. J. (2006). Building theories from case study research: The progres-sive case study. OM in the new world uncertainties. In *Proceedings of the 17th Annual Conference of POMS*, 28 April–1 May 2006 (pp. 1–13).

Then, V., Schober, C., Rauscher, O., & Kehl, K. (2017). Introduction: What is an SROI analysis? How does it relate to other forms of analysis? Why is impact key? In *Social return on investment analysis. Palgrave studies in impact finance* (pp. 1–42). Palgrave Macmillan.
Volkmann, C. K., Tokarski, K. O., & Ernst, K. (2012). Background, characteristics and context of social entrepreneurship. In C. K. Volkmann, K. O. Tokarski, & K. Ernst (Eds.), *Social entrepreneurship and social business. An introduction and discussion with case studies* (pp. 3–30). Springer.
Wonglimpiyarat, J. (2014). *Technology financing and commercialization. Exploring the challenges and how nations can build innovative capacity*. Palgrave Macmillan.
Yin, R. K. (1994). *Case study research, Design and methods* (2nd ed.). Sage Publications.

Chapter 8
Financing Entrepreneurial Ventures

Heidrun Twesten

Financing a startup is one of the greatest challenges for founders – as startups focus on fast growth rather than on break-even in their first years, they need external funds to survive. On the other hand, today more so than in the past decades, money is the most influential change driver. In order to raise startup ecosystems' diversity, addressing the investment angle is one of the biggest levers – investing can create opportunities to build a better world when done wisely.

Raising money is incredibly more difficult for women founders (and for all underrepresented groups). While their share has risen, e.g., in Germany by 7.5% since 2013 (from 12.8% to 20.3% in 2023, (German Startup Monitor, 2022), the share of worldwide venture capital invested in all-women teams dropped from an already low 2.4% (2021) to 1.9% in 2022 – the lowest figure since 2016. Mixed-gender teams got 17.2% of the 2022 VC cake, whereas the lion's share went to all-male teams (TechCrunch, 2023).

In order to generate a more inclusive startup ecosystem we need to tackle this systemic disadvantage hindering women to exploit their full entrepreneurial potential. Even more so given the fact that (not only) gender-diverse founder teams start more sustainable businesses and are more successful. According to a study by Boston Consulting Group, "startups founded and cofounded by women actually performed better over time, generating 10% more in cumulative revenue over a five-year period," and what is even more impressive, they generated 78 cents on every dollar invested by VCs – their male counterparts only achieved half the return on investment (ROI): 31 cents on the dollar (BCG, 2018). The same mechanisms are true for all other types of diversity – as startups tackling wicked problems in unknown environments can only profit from as many different perspectives on the

H. Twesten (✉)
IMPACCT GmbH, Hamburg, Germany
e-mail: twesten@impacct.de

K. Mikkelsen, A. Wolf (eds.), *Minds, Brains, and Doxa for Inclusive Entrepreneurship*, International Studies in Entrepreneurship 47,
https://doi.org/10.1007/978-3-031-50164-7_8

best path to success as possible. Let's have a look on how startup funding works in general and at the implications for women founders.

What's important? In order to start their own company, founders need external capital in addition to their own money, depending on the business model and growth perspective. One of the most important questions when founding a company is: What should it be? A fast-expanding, VC-funded start-up with unicorn potential and an expected million-dollar exit or an organically growing, long-term existing company that may be passed on to the next generation? This decision defines the financing path - whether "bootstrapping," in which the founders initially finance their company out of their own funds and later from their own cash flow, acquiring outside capital from "family, friends and fools," government funding agencies or banks, acquiring a strategic partner or pursuing the "classic VC model."

Either way, it is important to plan the path well and soundly. Some mistakes made at the beginning of the (VC track) journey can hardly be corrected later: e.g., giving away too many shares "early stage," getting the next best investor on board under pressure or having a nondiverse cap table. Handing over 20% of the shares to a business angel in the seed phase for €10,000 almost always destroys the cap table (written list of what belongs to whom in the company) because too much of the company was given away too cheaply too early – which on the one hand sets the valuation very low and on the other hand restricts the scope for later financing rounds too much.

Timing is also immensely important – there should always be enough "runway" (time until the next financing requirement) to avoid coming under pressure and, in the worst case, having to take money from an investor who is not a good fit. Because: This partnership is like a marriage – both in terms of intensity and duration of the union. If there is no dream honeymoon at the beginning, the relationship will certainly not become more harmonious over time.

Who's in the game? Business angels are private early stage investors who usually not only aim to grow their fortune but rather also want to participate in exciting new topics and do something meaningful. Many are (former) founders themselves with successful exits and the desire to contribute their experience to the startup ecosystem in addition to money. They usually get in early at comparatively low valuations (investments in the five- to six-figure range, often between €50 and €250 k per startup and financing round) and get actively involved in building the startup, usually in the "pre-seed" or "seed" phase.

In contrast to VC funds, business angels are usually looking for another form of return besides money: satisfaction and purpose resulting from their startup engagements. Often, they are already "fully financed" and no longer have to work for their own living, but they do not feel ready for any kind of retirement. Instead, they want to stay in the loop, learn about new technologies and business models, share their knowledge, meet exciting people, and expand their network. To achieve these goals, they are often willing to accept lower financial returns.

Good angels have two wings: in addition to money, they bring relevant nonmonetary capital – active engagement, know how, and contacts. Because they are involved so early on and thus have a significant influence on the further success of the start-up, it is extremely important to catch the right ones. It helps to consider a few criteria: Ideally, angels have relevant industry know-how and contacts in addition to their own entrepreneurial experience. Good angels offer added value without being annoying and are very well connected in the start-up ecosystem.

As there are historically much more male exited founders with deep pockets to invest into startups, they also form the majority of the angel landscape. In early stages though, the nonmonetary contribution of angels is often more important than the amount invested. Only in the past few years, smaller ticket sizes (from €5 k) have become more common, especially with women angels (who historically are less likely to own big fortunes) – opening up the space for more of them in the game.

For female founders, it is advisable to attract female angels – with the respective women supporting bias – on board early: they often not only understand "female" business models such as femtech better but also think more alike and offer personal support in a still very much male-dominated business. Moreover, in the past few years, female investor networks have been growing, and using them actively will probably lead to more successful funding attempts in later stages.

Venture capital (VC) funds are still very much male-dominated investment funds that in turn invest the money their limited partners (LPs, e.g., pension funds, insurance companies, universities, foundations, family offices, wealthy individuals) trust them with in startups. How this capital is used and where is decided in the VC funds by the so-called general partners (GPs), who – unlike business angels – only invest their own money to a certain extent (usually 1–2% of the fund volume). Important to know, because this construction explains how VC funds behave: They have to meet the performance targets of their investors – and, if necessary, put corresponding pressure on the start-ups in which they are invested.

VC funds classically have an "investment focus," i.e., a clear orientation toward certain start-up phases from the seed round onwards, and often also toward certain thematic areas. There are dedicated pre-seed and seed funds that enter very early (ticket sizes from €250,000), but most get involved from the "start-up phase" (proof of concept for the first product has been provided, market entry phase, company set-up, first KPIs are available), i.e., in "Series A" and B rounds. Many VCs – if they are not "agnostic" – focus on specific industries, topics, and/or technologies in which they have expertise and see great growth potential for certain business models – very few of them tackling women topics such as femtech.

VCs want to make a lot of money. As simple as that. All VCs are looking for the next "unicorn," i.e., a start-up with the potential to reach a valuation of at least 1 billion US dollars even before going public. Each individual portfolio company should theoretically be able to increase the capital invested tenfold over the duration of the VC investment (usually 5–7 years). VCs invest without receiving collateral – their basis for decision making is the probability that a start-up will develop successfully. How do they assess this at a stage where quantitative data is scarce? For this purpose, VCs use a set of essential qualitative criteria:

1. Does the *market* for the product have a volume of at least 10 billion US dollars and continues to grow, so that the start-up is "hyperscalable"?
2. Is the *team* so good that it can "roll up" this market with a high probability, i.e., are all the skills necessary for the business model available, do the founders have the potential to act very successfully in the market, how well have the founders managed to implement things in the past – did they know each other beforehand? Top degrees from excellent universities also help, of course.
3. Will this *product* solve a fundamental market need, i.e., will it be ten times better or ten times cheaper than the current leading product?
4. *Unfair Advantage:* This is, for example, a special market access that the product opens up or a disruptive technology that makes it possible to solve a specific market problem significantly faster or more efficiently.
5. Fortunately, there are more and more VCs who also value *impact* – that is, they not only want to see top financial returns, but at the same time that start-ups also have a quantifiable, sustainable positive impact on society or the environment.

In addition, certain "hygiene factors" are important: Is the cap table still intact – i.e., the question of the shareholder structure. There should not be too many with too small investments in the early phases, and above all: the right ones! In other words, investors who, in addition to relevant "tickets," also bring relevant expertise and/or a network.

At some point, VCs want to exit – i.e., realize the greatly increased valuation of their portfolio companies through a sale, to another fund, a large corporation (trade sale), or through an initial public offering (IPO), in order to be able to distribute the promised proceeds to their financiers (LPs). In this context, it is important to know that VC funds classically run for a period of ten years and usually invest in the first three to four of these. Why is this important for founders? A fund invests a certain amount of money in a number of start-ups. In the early stages, its managers still have a lot of money at their disposal and do not know how the investments they have made will perform. The later in the fund cycle the investment is made, the higher the risk of having to compensate for underperformers and being pushed to grow quickly.

As indicated above, "image" also plays a big role in the VC business – a significant part of a startup's reputation is determined by the reputation of its investors. So, just like with angels, it is extremely important to make a very well-informed decision when choosing and to back it up with sound due diligence.

How to acquire Angels and VC? VCs are difficult to acquire "cold" – getting in touch with them works through "warm intros," i.e., a recommendation from someone who knows both of you. Or they will approach you if you are visible and exciting enough for them. Experienced angels are very good introducers – you can research which angels which VC fund has already done a lot with. Renowned law firms, corporate and tax advisors, or auditors active in the start-up ecosystem are also good intro sources: They get to know the founders much earlier than VCs and are highly motivated to help their startup clients get good financing, which they can in turn spend with them in the following years.

When it comes to successful networking, kindness, sales talent and a really good (and well-told) story help immensely – and of course that little bit of luck to meet the right person at the right moment. Important to know: It is often more useful to network "informally" and to talk to VCs "without obligation" than to write to them directly with a pitch deck. Founders should be well prepared for this: find out in advance who they could potentially meet and where, and do specific research on what questions they should ask and to whom. It has to fit!

The first – and totally important – step in the search for investors is to draw up a "long list" of theoretically suitable partners. In addition to the structural information (topics, phases, tickets), it should also contain possible points of contact, i.e.: Who do I know who could give me a warm intro to this person (these can also be founders of portfolio companies)? Where could I myself meet one or more of these suitable investors and start a conversation with them? Experience shows that everyone in this ecosystem is willing to make contacts – provided the approach is right. Once this list has been created, it should be meticulously maintained: Who did you meet and when, what did you discuss, what was the feedback, what's next, etc. – there is nothing more embarrassing than not knowing what you discussed 18 months ago with an investor who might later be relevant. And: follow-ups! You should have a plan for when and on which topics it is appropriate to address certain contacts again or to pick up the thread.

It makes sense to get in touch early on with VCs whose investment focus only fits your own development later on – e.g., by asking them for advice – and to keep them in the loop. This way they can follow you early on and get a better impression of your performance over time. It is important to actively network with supportive people – so as a female founder, join groups with female investors.

VCs are also actively scouting themselves and are now using AI tools to do so – so it is advisable to be as present as possible on the relevant platforms such as Product Hunt or GitHub, as well as at the relevant events and in the industry media, etc. This increases the chance of being seen and possibly even approached directly by investors – this is, of course, the ideal way to acquire capital: being found by investors.

Structural gaps and how to address them Gender gap One of the main reasons for the low share of global VC flowing to all-women teams is male bias. Like any human group, being defined by gender, class, country of origin, age, etc., they feel more secure in their own comfort zone: "Ultimately, venture capital at the early stages is a people thing, I'm betting on you. People are just more comfortable betting on somebody that is more like them, looks like them, talks like them, went to the same schools, eats the same food, goes to the same restaurant, drinks the same wine, goes to the same country club, all these little things. They're not overtly racist or overtly discriminatory, it's just comfort. Ultimately, it's a comfort thing" (Interview with a male investor, August 2015, in Solal/Snellman, 2023). When investing into high-risk startups, likeness creates security.

"The guys" (unfortunately, at least 84% of all US VC "checkwriters") are still mostly "old white males," 63% of US VCs have no female checkwriters at all (All

Raise, 2021)) don't understand "women's language." Women founders can get angry about this, send their male co-founders to pitch or simply use less "would have, could have, maybe wanted to" – VCs want to know what founders are specifically confident about today and why, where their rocket should take off and where it should land, and when. It is especially important for women to make it VERY clear that they are not afraid of risk, because many men generally deny them that instinctively. And the questions: male founders usually are being asked about the "potentials" of their business case while female founders are very often asked "prevention" questions focusing on possible pitfalls. A very useful technique to handle this is to focus answers on potentials.

Even among business angels, women are still underrepresented: In the U.S. their share has grown to 33.6% in 2021, according to the Angel Capital Association, in Germany it is still only 15% (Business Angel Report, 2023) – for female founders, it is worth the effort to find them: According to a study by the University of New Hampshire, for example, the share of invited start-ups with female founders was 30% in angel groups with more than 25% female members, while it was only 12–13% on average in more male-dominated angel groups (Robb, 2015). In Germany, only 16% of male angels invested in teams with female founders, whereas 26% of female angels did (Business Angel Report, 2023).

For angels as well as VCs, if female decision makers are on board, women founders stand a better chance – even if many men now address the issue and are aware of their bias, similar people are simply more likely to understand their group's specific issues and are better able to assess their value.

Social gap Unfortunately, another important hurdle in the "VC game" is still origin – and all that it entails: It is much easier for "white" graduates of top international business schools and top-class universities to found start-ups and acquire funding, as they gain access to the relevant networks during their studies at the latest. Often, they already bring them "from home" because their parents are well-connected accordingly.

In view of the fact that the probability of studying as a German nonacademic child has been decreasing since the 1970s, this is first and foremost a challenge for politics. The same applies to migrant founders, who are structurally disadvantaged in Germany, Europe, and the USA, both in their studies and in setting up and acquiring capital.

In the meantime, there are some initiatives that support founders in overcoming these gaps. Beyond that, it also helps here: be bold, go the extra mile, and donate to Karma – it will return the favor eventually!

8.1 Conclusion

So, what is needed to close gaps like the gender funding gap? First and foremost, more female and underrepresented investors, while at the same time training everyone on recognizing and addressing his or her biases.

At the moment, there is no sufficient pipeline from which to promote female or otherwise diverse checkwriters, many male VC GPs say. So obviously they need to employ more women and underrepresented people to generate a bigger pool from which later more diverse GPs can be promoted. Therefore, employment criteria might need to be more flexible as there are, e.g., less women meeting the "classic" ones – but can surely add comparable value.

Political initiatives are helping, e.g., Germany's Federal Ministry for Economic Affairs and Climate Action in 2023 expanded its startup funding for female entrepreneurs and founders from scientific backgrounds with the new "EXIST Women" funding line.

KfW Capital, a subsidiary of the German KfW Development Bank, a major limited partner (LP, institutional investors in VC funds) in European VC funds assesses funds based on their risk return profile as well as on the diversity of their team – driving VCs to put more effort into team diversity. KfW Capital also initiated the awards: "Best Female Investor" and "Best Impact Investor," giving the topic a lot of visibility. IfB (Investitions- und Förderbank) Hamburg backed a pitch event series "FemaleStartAperitivo" initiated by Hamburg Investors Network and WEstartupSH. This is a yearly and nationwide pitch event for female founders. Besides they run the Female StartAperitivo Academy for female founders and aspiring angels.

Many networks and organizations supporting the female part of the startup ecosystem were founded in the last few years, more and more women raise their own VC funds – and together, they are having a huge impact internationally.

Not big enough so far – also due to another gap: the relevant business media don't feature female founders proportionally. On top of that investing in startups is still a "bubble" game – it's still a relatively small circle of people active from angels to VCs, and it needs some knowhow. Hence another angle to work on is giving the topic more media coverage, explaining how it works, who can play the game how.

I think it is unlikely to take bias out of the equation – but it's totally possible to raise awareness for it and act accordingly: invest in diverse teams building impact startups to change the world for the better!

In the long run, a lot of other things need to be addressed and changed:

- Starting from early ages more gender-independent and socially inclusive education.
- Better cooperation and more exchange between the educational systems and entrepreneurs.
- A structural change in the STEM education model so that it attracts more female students.
- Better childcare conditions, enabling all genders to pursue their careers and at the same time raise families.
- Active political support for women and underrepresented groups (through appropriate means, such as quota and special funding programs) in the startup ecosystem until satisfactory diversity is implemented.
- More role models promoting change.

Let me close with a quote from the World Economic Forum Annual Meeting in 2019: "Innovation has always been about generating good ideas by challenging the status quo with new viewpoints. That is why diversity is fundamental to the sustained success of any innovation ecosystem. Promoting diversity in entrepreneurship and technological innovation can deliver greater economic and societal value" (Krishnamurthy, 2019).

References

All Raise x Crunchbase VC checkwriter dashboard. (2021). https://allraise-data-dashboard.s3-us-west-2.amazonaws.com/center/html/index.html, seen 19.7.2023.

Business Angel Report (2023). Google for Startups/AddedVal.io.

German Startup Monitor (2022). https://startupverband.de/fileadmin/startupverband/mediaarchiv/research/dsm/dsm_2022_English_Summary.pdf, seen 19.7.2023.

Krishnamurthy, D. (2019). *Here's how to improve diversity in startups, World Economic Forum Annual Meeting.*

Robb, A. (2015). *Women: The next wave of angel investors?* https://www.forbes.com/sites/kauffman/2015/04/21/women-the-next-wave-of-angel-investors/?sh=247b9eab333c, seen 26.2.2023.

Solal, I., & Snellman, K. (2023). *For female founders, fundraising only from female VCs comes at a cost.* Harvard Business Review Feb 01 2023.

TechChrunch. (2023). *Women-founded startups raised 1.9% of all VC funds in 2022, a drop from 2021.* https://techcrunch.com/2023/01/18/women-founded-startups-raised-1-9-of-all-vc-funds-in-2022-a-drop-from-2021/?guccounter=1&guce_referrer=aHR0cHM6Ly93d3cuZ29vZ2xlLmNvbS8&guce_referrer_sig=AQAAAAYCGBUkFUnxqCguqHdyHUxjL30VGLN0r_6nBeSwwESBHD0o46p1qKJiwYTURLOcghR9TKT-ln1wqSb7fid_uESMR-gVip1z_pQFummhwM-D3ZKOX4LlV3v4V_JZ1IUmKrcvtBPwmsgk4C19o2NjO0MEgq2mYWVNOS5jVrhENuVc, seen 19.7.2023.

Chapter 9
Senior Entrepreneurship Economy on the Rise: Every Age Counts

Annika Wolf

9.1 Introduction

There is a challenge for sustainable economic growth and innovation with a decline of an active skilled labor force and an aging population with older people retiring from the labor market. In Germany and throughout the European Union, the aging population has let senior entrepreneurs to become an important driver for innovation in achieving sustainable economic growth. This chapter analyzes the opportunities and challenges for seniors engaging in entrepreneurship. The theoretical lens discusses the broad definition of senior entrepreneurship, focusing on the motivation for seniors to start entrepreneurial activities as well as their educational background, showcasing the importance for inclusivity of this group in the entrepreneurial ecosystem. The practical lens focuses on senior entrepreneurship stories. Those stories highlight the challenges of seniors and sets forth specific recommendations for creating opportunities that are more inviting for senior entrepreneurs to participate in the entrepreneurial ventures.

9.2 Senior Entrepreneurship

Definition There are different definitions for the older generation engaging in entrepreneurship. Senior entrepreneurship has been a widely used term by the research studies conducted by the OECD and the European Commission (OECD and European Commission, 2022). The European Commission also refers to the

A. Wolf (✉)
University of Applied Sciences Emden/Leer, Emden, Germany
e-mail: annika.wolf@hs-emden-leer.de

K. Mikkelsen, A. Wolf (eds.), *Minds, Brains, and Doxa for Inclusive Entrepreneurship*, International Studies in Entrepreneurship 47,
https://doi.org/10.1007/978-3-031-50164-7_9

"Silver Economy" as "a balancing factor, and one that will be profitable to businesses as well as connected to a positive and socially inclusive identity for older adults in Europe" (European Commission, 2018), recognizing that the "Third Age" is nowadays an extended period of time for the older generation with "a high quality of life and the desire to remain active" (European Commission, 2016). A policy framework focusing on "olderpreneurs" ought to enhance the "social-economic contribution of older people in the European Union." The World Bank (World Bank, 2015) refers to "Golden Aging," arguing that a demographic shift due to "ageing societies are not pre-destined to experience stagnation or a decline in living standards."

According to the Gründungsmonitor (KfW, 2023), 25.1% of German founders are already 45 or older (45–54 years of age: 15.7%/55–64 years of age: 9.4%) – and that percentage is rising. This means that the aging population will have an even greater impact on the German startup scene in the future. The populations of European Union Member States and OECD countries are also aging. The proportion of the EU population over the age of 65 years old will increase from 21% in 2020 to nearly 30% in 2050. One of the major reasons for this increase is the long-term decline in fertility rates and an increase in life expectancy (OECD and European Commission, 2022). On a global scale, however, Europeans do not find becoming an entrepreneur as attractive as those in North America and China (European Commission, 2016).

Considering the demographics, the Gründungsmonitor (KfW, 2023) refers to the startup activities of people aged 45 and older in two specific categories age groups (a) from 45 to 54 years old and (b) from 55 to 64 years old. The OECD and European Commission, however, defines senior entrepreneurship for the age group (a) from 50 to 64 years old, (b) from 65 to 69 years, and (c) from 70 to 74 years old. Senior individuals actively engage in self-employment, with the proportion of self-employed seniors rising with age. In 2020, seniors aged 50–64 were more likely to be self-employed than the overall adult population aged 15–64 in the EU (18% vs. 14%). This percentage further increased to 39% for those aged 65–69 and 52% for those aged 70–74 during the same year (OECD and European Commission, 2022).

Engaging seniors in entrepreneurship also offers socioeconomic benefits by relieving pressure on social security and pension payments by keeping older people active and contributing to the economy. Promoting senior entrepreneurship also allows older people to flexibly manage their work schedules, improve their quality of life, and reduce the risk of poverty. Independence, freedom, and flexibility, as well as self-actualization or career fulfillment, are key drivers of self-employment. These attributes are socially respected and important values that should not be neglected in the context of promoting senior entrepreneurship (Frerichs und Fachinger, 2020).

Activities In Germany, there are two factors for seniors to engage in entrepreneurship activities: pull and push. The pull factor refers to senior founders (65%) that have taken the opportunity to realize a business idea and specifically founded their company for that endeavor; the push factor drives senior (23%) into self-employment due to a lack of employment alternatives (RKW Kompetenzzentrum, 2019).

Considering the opportunity (pull factor), the motivations for senior entrepreneur can differ significantly from one individual to another. Some common reasons to start a business (for 55+ years old) include, among others, the following: (1) independence and flexibility (73%) – for seniors, entrepreneurship offers a level of independence and autonomy that traditional employment often lacks. Starting a business allows individuals to be their own boss, make their own decisions, and set their own schedules in terms of work hours and location; (2) passion (59%) – senior entrepreneurs are driven by a deep passion for a particular product, service, or industry. They want to turn their interests and hobbies into a livelihood and create something they genuinely care about; (3) work-life balance and family (33%) – seniors value a work-life balance and/or have personal commitments or health conditions that require adaptability; and (4) problem-solving/innovation (26%) – after a traditional professional career, some senior entrepreneurs are driven by a desire to solve specific problems or address unmet needs in society and/or can disrupt existing industries or improve upon current offerings. They want to pass on their experience in this context. Entrepreneurs overall often have the goal of owning and running a business (RKW Kompetenzzentrum, 2019).

Within the European Union, there is a relatively low engagement of seniors for self-employment: Only 2% of seniors aged 50–64 were engaged in starting a business between 2016 and 2020, in contrast to 4% of the overall population aged 18–64. The OECD average for seniors during the same period stood at 5%. Overall, seniors were pushed into self-employment out of necessity whereas roughly 25% of new senior entrepreneurs within the European Union began their ventures between 2016 and 2020 driven by a lack to secure traditional employment, compared to approximately 18% of the total population aged 18–64 (RKW Kompetenzzentrum, 2019).

Education In Germany, most senior founders are formally educated. Almost half of all founders in their middle age and older have either a university degree (49%) or completed a vocational training (46%). Almost all of the founders surveyed (76%) were previously employed before switching to self-employment. Looking more closely, 52% were employees and 24% were in a managerial or executive position. On the other hand, only 20% had already been self-employed, 2% percent were in school, and 2% were unemployed (RKW Kompetenzzentrum, 2019). There is one limitation with the survey: the economic situation in Germany, at the time of the survey, was excellent, as displayed in the low unemployment of the survey respondents, with many opportunities for older employees on the labor market. Self-employment was a minor alternative in such a market environment.

The study also shows that there has been a shift in the labor force by age group in Germany in favor of older people. Even more important for the further development of the labor market is the following fact: while employment has declined in all other age groups, older people have made strong gains in employment. In Germany,

48% of those aged 55–65 years old were in employment in 2006; 10 years later, more than two-thirds of this age group were still employed (68.6%). In the age group 65–70 years old, 15.4% were in employment in 2016 compared with only 6.6% ten years earlier. Accordingly, Germany had the strongest growth in employment of older people among European Union countries, followed by the Netherlands, Italy, Austria, and Poland (RKW Kompetenzzentrum, 2019).

Within the European Union, there has been a notable shift in the educational profiles of self-employed seniors between 2002 and 2022. In 2002, approximately 19% of self-employed seniors (aged 50–64) held a tertiary education, climbing to 33% by 2020. Similarly, the proportion of self-employed seniors with an upper secondary and non-tertiary education increased from 33% to 44% over this same period. These advancements were counterbalanced by a decline in the percentage of self-employed seniors who possessed less than an upper secondary education, dropping from 49% to 23%. The rise in the percentage of self-employed seniors with tertiary education credentials mirrors the overall population trend, driven by a growing proportion of the population attaining tertiary education qualifications and the aging of this population cohort (OECD and European Commission, 2022).

9.3 Senior Entrepreneurship in Practice

The following three examples are only a snippet for senior entrepreneurship activities, however, it needs to be recognized that there is not much diversity. Although there is no statistical evidence about diversity in senior entrepreneurship, there is an assumption that the diversity factor within senior entrepreneurship is very low, proving even more the necessity for inclusive entrepreneurship with a focus on gender diversity.

The first two examples of Professors Richard Meier and Michael Schlaak show the spirit of research. Both professors identified many implementable projects from their research and, afterward they stopped working, these projects disappeared into an archive. The transfer from (university) research activities to startup ventures is an important factor to drive innovation. The coalition agreement of the current German government is recognizing the importance of theory into practice to foster innovation. It is manifested as part of the future strategy for Germany as a business location in the coalition agreement in order to spark new technological, digital, social, and sustainable innovation (Koalitionsvertrag, 2021–2025).

It is not just professors who start their own business. The third example highlights another perspective of senior entrepreneurship. With the experience gained in business, Thomas Laux decided to get off the corporate train and fulfill his dream later in life.

Research-Focused Senior Entrepreneurs: Seaweed Ideas often arise in everyday life. While walking on the beach, Richard Meier discovered brown seaweed balls lying around by the thousands. He learned that this grass is not flammable. It made Meier sit up and take notice, because that sounded extraordinary. It was the intellectual nucleus for Meier's idea: the seaweed balls could be used to make a natural insulating material, without chemicals. Richard Meier quit his job as an architecture professor and devoted himself to his business idea. It was a long road until production ran smoothly. After all, no one before Meier had any experience with this seaweed. At first, his wife tried chopping up the seaweed balls with her food processor. In the end, Meier bought a professional chopper. Meier describes setting up production as an extreme learning-by-doing.

Workers in Tunisia and Albania collect the seaweed balls for him. On the outskirts of Karlsruhe, Meier then has the sand shaken out of the seaweed balls in a production hall, chops them up into insulating wool, and finally fills them into waterproof plastic bags. This seaweed based insulation currently insulates the roofs of schools, guesthouses, and the homes of many private individuals who do not want chemicals in their insulation material.

Meier has won nearly a dozen prizes for his business idea. The fact that Meier became successful within a short time is likely also due to his professional experience and in-depth knowledge of the industry, as well as life experience and the resulting composure to deal with frustrations and setbacks. While he is thinking about quitting, he also has his next business idea: he wants to mix the sand that falls out of the seaweed balls during production with some seaweed fibers, because this mixture is a good braking material for icy surfaces in winter (Gojdka, 2015).

Research-Focused Senior Entrepreneurs: Chitosan Professor Michael Schlaak also had a sustainable idea. For years, the professor of environmental engineering researched chitosan, a recyclable substance in crab shells. The crabs were caught and shelled on the North Sea coast, the latter mostly in Morocco. Schlaak and colleagues considered how a new sustainable product could be developed from the waste product of crab shells. Among other things, they developed a coating for inkjet printers in which the ink was sprayed onto transparencies and showed good durability. However, since overhead transparencies are no longer current, this application was dropped. In Japan, there was already a toothpaste made from chitosan. After the Japanese patent expired, the formulation was modified and a proprietary toothpaste was developed. A separate company was founded to market it, a Ltd. To avoid investment, production was contracted out to an outside company. Distribution also proved difficult. As an expensive niche product, there was no demand for the toothpaste in supermarkets, so distribution ended up being through pharmacies. After Schlaak decided to quit, he began looking for successors.

Schlaak did not want to continue to bear the financial risk that the development of the toothpaste had already entailed over the years and contacted a well-known toothpaste manufacturer who was interested in the antibacterial effect of chitosan. The toothpaste manufacturer declined to cooperate, but shortly thereafter came out with its own product that also contained chitosan; Schlaak terminated the production. The toothpaste manufacturer contacted also subsequently ceased production of its chitosan toothpaste: From the point of view of the well-known toothpaste manufacturer, the competing product had thus been successfully driven off the market.

In another research project, a skin cream containing chitosan (with an effect similar to artificial skin) was also developed. The cream was again produced by an outside company. The cream also had a wound-healing effect, e.g., on poorly healing wounds (such as those caused by diabetes or burns). However, this was not allowed to be marketed in this way, as it would be a medical effect. Medical products can only be marketed by very large companies because of the effort required for approval. Cooperation with a company was not realized, because not enough people get burned in Germany, so that an economic marketing is not profitable for the contacted. Since the product was not accepted by the market as a pure hand cream, the production of this product was also discontinued over time. The quantity sold was too small.

Senior Entrepreneurship: Living the Dream Thomas Laux has implemented a change of a different kind. For decades, Laux had worked at various banks and financial service providers. However, when his employer was to be bought out by another bank, Laux took the opportunity to jump ship. He wanted to fulfill his dream and rent out a houseboat on the river Lahn as a vacation home. Equipped with a business plan, he went to the bank, which did not take his idea seriously. But Laux stuck to his idea, bought the houseboat in Brandenburg, and launched it on the river Lahn. The workload is different than it used to be. Today, he is responsible for everything from marketing, controlling, and finance to explaining how to steer a houseboat and clean the holding tank.

9.4 Challenges for Seniorpreneurs

The above examples clearly highlight some of the challenges for senior entrepreneurship which includes: (a) stereotypes, (b) access to finance, (c) energy and perseverance, (d) technology skills, (e) social network, and (f) market understanding.

Stereotypes Older founders often face ageism and, thus, prejudice and stereotypes are applied to ventures by seniors. These stereotypes are often personal, showcased in the belief that older people are not as resilient as younger people, notwithstanding their experiences in life, dealing with the life cycle of ups and downs. Stereotypes can also be technological driven, i.e., when the senior applies for a loan and the credit score model recognizes the age and the applicant would have to pay a premium for additional risk or will be denied directly due to a shorter life expectancy or retirement payments as the means to repay the debt, which will also refer to the next point.

Access to Finance Access to finance is limited for seniors when starting a business, because in competition with younger founders, investors prefer younger founders. Seniors usually bear the financial risk themselves in getting their startup off the ground. The preference of investors to provide capital to young founders is not understandable in view of the statistics. That is because the success of a business, founded by older people, is more promising than can be assumed. For example, only 28% of the companies founded by younger people survive more than 3 years, while 70% of businesses created by seniors last longer than 3 years (European Commission, 2016).

Energy and Perseverance Starting a business often requires long hours, a lot of energy, and perseverance. Older founders may have less energy and stamina to keep up with the pace and demands of a startup. In addition, health limitations, lack of self-confidence, and family obligations can be hindering.

Technology Skills Technological innovations play a crucial role in many business areas today. Older people may have difficulty learning new technologies, which could make it difficult to adapt to modern business practices.

Social Network Younger founders often have a broader network of colleagues, mentors, and investors. Older people may have had fewer opportunities to build such a network within the startup scene, which can make it more difficult to access resources and support. However, due to their professional network of prior contacts, they can inquire assistance when and where needed (European Commission, 2016).

Market Understanding Older founders may have difficulty understanding the preferences and needs of a younger target group if their own living environment and experiences are different.

Despite these challenges, there are many successful examples of older entrepreneurs who have turned their life and work experiences into successful businesses. It is important to recognize these challenges and develop strategies to deal with them, such as collaborating with younger partners, seeking advice and support, and carefully weighing risks and opportunities. Governments on national levels as well as policy makers at the supranational level can provide frameworks that are engaging seniors in entrepreneurship.

9.5 Recommendations for Action

Based on the previously mentioned challenges for senior entrepreneurship, the following recommendations for action can support and promote senior entrepreneurship effectively: (a) promote entrepreneurship among people over the age of 45, (b) raise awareness of the benefits of senior entrepreneurship, (c) overcome barriers, (d) create a supportive environment, (e) combat age discrimination, (f) government promotion, and (g) invest in education and research.

Promote Entrepreneurship Among People Over the Age of 45 Develop programs and initiatives tailored to older individuals, enhancing their interest and skills in entrepreneurship. The European Commission's Senior Entrepreneurship Good Practices Manual lays out various types of sources and information for seniors supporting businesses depending on the expertise needed, the preferred scope and objective of the business endeavor.

Raise Awareness of the Benefits of Senior Entrepreneurship Highlight the advantages, such as improved work-life balance and income opportunities, to change perceptions about older entrepreneurs.

Overcome Barriers Identify and address barriers that deter older individuals from entrepreneurship, including providing financial support, boosting self-confidence, and helping balance family responsibilities.

Create a Supportive Environment Establish networks, mentorship programs, and community support systems for senior entrepreneurs to share knowledge and experiences.

Combat Age Discrimination Promote age-friendly work environments and equal opportunities for older individuals in society.

Government Promotion Implement government initiatives such as financial support, tax incentives, and reduced bureaucracy to encourage senior entrepreneurship.

Invest in Education and Research Continuously study and educate on senior entrepreneurship, encompassing cognitive training, and personality development.

By taking these actions, societies can harness the untapped potential of senior entrepreneurs, not only contributing to economic growth but also fostering a culture of inclusivity and equal opportunity for all age groups. Senior entrepreneurship offers a path to a more diverse and sustainable entrepreneurial landscape.

9.6 Conclusion

In conclusion, fostering inclusive entrepreneurship, particularly among seniors, is crucial for building a diverse and vibrant society that will ensure economic welfare on a national level as well as the European integrated market with a growing aging population. The examples of Richard Meier, Michael Schlaak, and Thomas Laux showcase the diverse avenues that senior entrepreneurs can explore, leveraging their experience and expertise. Although not always successful these examples demonstrate how individuals in their "golden age" can continue to stay active and maintain a high quality in life in their "silver years."

References

European Commission. (2016). *Senior entrepreneurship good practices manual*. Available https://op.europa.eu/en/publication-detail/-/publication/8fdadabd-9ac8-11e6-868c-01aa75ed71a1/language-en. Accessed March 28, 2023.

European Commission. (2018). *The silver generation*. http://publications.europa.eu/resource/cellar/2dca9276-3ec5-11e8-b5fe-01aa75ed71a1.0002.01/DOC_1. Accessed August 24, 2023.

Frerichs, F., & Fachinger, U. (2020). *Selbstständige Erwerbstätigkeit und Erwerbskarrieren in späteren Lebensphasen*. Springer VS.

Gojdka, V. (2015). *Senioren als Unternehmensgründer – Alt, Dynamisch, Erfolgreich*. Available at https://www.spiegel.de/wirtschaft/unternehmen/senioren-als-unternehmer-wenn-alte-menschen-gruenden-a-1026844.html, 07.04.2015. Accessed August 1, 2023.

Koalitionsvertrag. (2021— 2025). *zwischen der Sozialdemokratischen Partei Deutschland (SPD), Bündnis 90/Die Grünen und den Freuden Demokraten (FDP)*. Available at https://www.spd.de/fileadmin/Dokumente/Koalitionsvertrag/Koalitionsvertrag_2021–2025.pdf. Accessed August 23, 2023.

Kreditanstalt für Wiederaufbau (KfW). (2023). *KfW Gründungsmonitor 2023 – Gründungstätigkeit in Deutschland: im Spannungsfeld zwischen Fachkräftemangel und Corona-Blues*. Available at https://www.kfw.de/PDF/Download-Center/Konzernthemen/Research/PDF-Dokumente-Gr%C3%BCndungsmonitor/KfW-Gr%C3%BCndungsmonitor-2023.pdf. Accessed April 23, 2023.

OECD and European Commission. (2022). *The missing entrepreneurs 2021 – Policies for inclusive entrepreneurship and self-employment*. Available at https://www.oecd-ilibrary.org/docserver/71b7a9bb-en.pdf?expires=1694324887&id=id&accname=guest&checksum=A39B861B9FE4020E6443016AB7CEE6CC. Accessed July 23, 2023.

RKW Kompetenzzentrum. (2019). *Studie "Senior Entrepreneurship"2018 – Gründerinnen und Gründer 45plus:Senior Entrepreneure folgen dem Trend*. https://www.rkw-kompetenzzentrum.de/fileadmin/media/Produkte/2019/Studie/20190116-Aeltere-Gruender.pdf. Accessed April 1, 2023.

World Bank. (2015). *Golden aging: Prospects for healthy, active and prosperous aging in Europe and central Asia*. Available at: http://www.worldbank.org/en/region/eca/publication/golden-aging. Accessed August 24, 2023.

Chapter 10
The Inclusivity Tax for Migrant Entrepreneurs

Alexandra David, Judith Terstriep, and Laila Zohaib

10.1 Introduction

Inclusive entrepreneurship aims to qualify marginalised groups for employment or empower them to create their own business (Krüger & David, 2020). The groups of entrepreneurs being addressed by the concept of inclusive entrepreneurship include, amongst others, women, people with disabilities, and migrants. While inclusive entrepreneurship is supposed to provide support for these target groups to accelerate and ease self-employment, our studies have shown that in the case of migrant entrepreneurs, they often act themselves inclusively. In that line, the authors of the chapter argue that inclusive entrepreneurship also means that migrant business owners, often located in local spatial entities such as neighbourhoods, overtake the raw models of inclusion in a manifold manner. This seems to be the case, especially in deprived regions or *'left behind places'* (MacKinnon et al., 2022), often characterised by the erosion of general interest services and high brain drain (David 2015). From the regional perspective, the status quo in most local entrepreneurial ecosystems (EE) reveals the absence of an inclusive design and execution (David et al., 2019). This leads entrepreneurs explicitly to overcompensate and fill in the blanks, calling it an *inclusivity tax*, which entrepreneurs of super-diverse, underrepresented communities pay during their venturing activities.

While most of the literature proposes inclusive approaches and guidelines for self-employment training of migrants (David & Terstriep, 2023; Hello Europe Ashoka, 2022), this chapter focuses on the fact that those migrants who are already

A. David (✉) · J. Terstriep · L. Zohaib
Research Department Innovation, Space & Culture, Westphalian University, Institute for Work & Technology, Gelsenkirchen, Germany
e-mail: david@iat.de

K. Mikkelsen, A. Wolf (eds.), *Minds, Brains, and Doxa for Inclusive Entrepreneurship*, International Studies in Entrepreneurship 47,
https://doi.org/10.1007/978-3-031-50164-7_10

self-employed and running a business[1] are often considered inclusive and integrated themselves – whilst overtaking the role of a facilitator and ambassador for their own communities or co-ethnic groups. Hence, we ask:

Are migrant businesses inclusivity agents in entrepreneurial ecosystems, and if so, in what way?

In answering the above research question, using own and secondary data (David et al., 2019), the following topics are considered as categories for inclusivity for migrant entrepreneurs venturing activities: (1) local labour markets, (2) regional development, (3) social mobility, and (4) diasporic and ethnic communities. In so doing, we assume that migrant entrepreneurs make up for the lack of inclusiveness in broader entrepreneurship education and start-up mentoring programmes by actively executing inclusivity and intersectionality in their venturing efforts. This includes contributing to society with a cosmopolitan mindset by hiring staff from underrepresented, marginalised communities, driving regional innovation activities, and stepping into emerging transnational markets by leveraging diasporic structures. Migrant entrepreneurs are levelling the playing field by taking the role of game changers and trailblazers, becoming advocates for aspiring entrepreneurs while current EEs fail to design and implement inclusive entrepreneurship policies, principles, and programmes.

Due to the underrepresentation of migrants in established institutions such as chambers of commerce or business associations, from an EE perspective, it can be argued that migrant entrepreneurs overtake the role of public agents, providing these services for their communities. In addition, often migrant entrepreneurs offer youth services based on trust and closeness, which still is lacking on the part of the authorities regarding migrants in these localities.

In what follows, we start with a literature review to position our study in the scientific discourse and to explain whom we regard as migrant entrepreneurs. Next, we introduce our mixed-method research design and introduce our data collection procedure. In the next section, we present our results. Finally, the chapter concludes with a discussion of the findings. By linking results to current debates, we formulate suggestions for future research.

Revisiting Migrant Entrepreneurship and Entrepreneurial Ecosystems

Migrant Entrepreneurs in Germany

In recent years, migrant entrepreneurship has been discussed more in the context of labour market integration. Here, it became prominent through the so-called 'long summer of migration' between 2015 and 2017 and the immigration of Syrian

[1] These businesses are mainly established by first- and second-generation migrants rather than newcomers.

refugees at that time. In the wake of the Ukrainian war and the migration movements to Eastern and Western Europe starting in 2022, this debate has now been reignited (OECD, 2022). Self-employment is a way for migrants to enter economic life while facing less severe layers of discrimination and biases associated with their heritage, gender, sexual orientation, or social class (David et al., 2022; David, 2017; David & Coenen, 2017). The newest International Migration Outlook reports that in February 2022, the number of newcomers from Ukraine exceeded that of the remaining non-Germans who had moved to Germany by almost four times and that of those who arrived from Syria in December 2015 by as much as 6.5 times (OECD, 2022). Thus, Germany counts the highest number of incoming refugees since the reunification. Against this backdrop, migrant entrepreneurship is experiencing a revival, bringing about needs and calls to action to the existing infrastructure and support system. Research on migrant entrepreneurship also shows that it can be integrative and inclusive per se by ensuring that inclusive structures are built that cannot be granted by the state or other intermediaries in terms of speed and scope. It is, therefore, worth looking at the group of migrant entrepreneurs to understand the phenomenon and, from there, to be able to follow the assumptions we make in the chapter.

To draw a more detailed picture of migrant entrepreneurship in Germany, David et al. (2022) suggest revisiting the current and former migration cohorts and bundling them into the three most prominent groups of migrant entrepreneurs. In so doing, *ethnic entrepreneurship*, being the first group, refers to the entrepreneurial activities of actors with a common identity of origin and culture (Aldrich & Waldinger, 1990; Wilson & Portes, 1980). Zhou (2004) concretises this understanding by defining ethnic entrepreneurs as owners and managers of their own businesses whose group membership is linked to a common cultural heritage or origin. Ethnic entrepreneurs may or may not have experienced a migration process themselves.

The second group is *migrant entrepreneurs*, also known as immigrant entrepreneurs (Kloosterman et al., 1999), referring to companies founded and/or managed by people with a migration background, which offer products and services for different target groups. Immigrant basically stands for first-generation migrants, entailing many newcomers and a small number of refugees. Migrant entrepreneurship is a kind of umbrella term and can include migrant entrepreneurs in the second (or even third) generation, which means founders who do not have their own migration experience (Aliagla-Isla & Rialp, 2013). Today, this is the most common term used in the literature on migrants who lead or start businesses in their countries of residence.

Refugee entrepreneurship, as the third group, refers to the entrepreneurial activities of people with their own experience of flight (Stoewe, 2022; Heilbrunn et al., 2019; David & Coenen, 2017). Here the focus is placed on those entrepreneurs who have crossed a national border (Desai et al., 2021) and are thus based outside their country of origin and are active as entrepreneurs there. This new stream of research emerged in the wake of the increased refugee migration to Europe around 2015 and is now well-established (Heilbrunn et al., 2019; David & Coenen, 2017; Stoewe, 2022).

In addition to this subdivision, migrant entrepreneurship can be characterised by the features of the entrepreneur and the business itself when sticking to the umbrella term. David et al. (2022) suggest a further classification of migrant entrepreneurship tied to business models, sectoral affiliation, a transnational field of activities, development status of the company, as well as gender differences, generations, diaspora connections, qualification, resources and migration motives.

In consideration of the above, this chapter refers to migrant entrepreneurship as the totality of businesses founded [and] or run by people with a migration background (David et al., 2022). This includes people who have lived in Germany for several decades (with or without a German passport), their descendants, and recent immigrants. This includes groups of people from EU countries, non-EU countries, and the new arrivals of refugees.

In- or Exclusive Entrepreneurial Ecosystems? An entrepreneurial ecosystem (EE) is an environment consisting of actors organised in informal and formal networks and interested in the success and successful development of regional/ local-based business (Stam, 2015). In so doing, they directly contribute to regional wealth and innovativeness (Ancona et al., 2023). In essence, an EE is a complex system of interrelated factors and actors that create an environment conducive to entrepreneurship and innovation. The success of entrepreneurship in a particular location depends on the availability and accessibility of various assets, including human capital, financial resources, social networks, and institutional support (Malecki, 2018). The EE approach recognises that entrepreneurship is not solely a result of individual action or characteristics, but is also influenced by broader societal, cultural, and economic factors.

Moreover, an EE is not a fixed or static entity; rather, it is a dynamic and evolving system that requires continuous attention and adaptation. As such, policymakers and stakeholders must actively work to foster an environment that encourages and supports entrepreneurship and innovation, through initiatives such as education and training programmes, investment incentives, and regulatory frameworks that facilitate business creation and growth. By recognising the importance of a diverse range of assets and support mechanisms and by promoting a culture of entrepreneurship, policymakers and stakeholders can work to create a dynamic and thriving entrepreneurial ecosystem that supports economic growth and resilience.

In that vein, focussing on the actors' constellation in an EE, scholars discuss EEs' inclusivity (Krueger, 2021). The understanding of an inclusive EE is one that supports all kinds of entrepreneurs regardless of their background and history (Powell et al., 2021). Equal opportunities can be created by providing access to all needed resources may they be financial or social, and developing a culture of cooperation, openness, and inclusivity (ibid.). Thus, an inclusive EE can help build more equitable and innovative societies, as the creativity in such localities reflects the diversity of the whole community.

But still, EEs are not as inclusive as they could be. Especially official authorities or intermediary organisations (e.g., chambers of commerce) continue to ignore the needs of diverse types of entrepreneurs such as migrants or women (David et al.,

2019). Interviews conducted in the German municipality of Essen reveal that in times of challenges related to financing, finding a shop location, or accessing organisations, migrants' informal networks often are more effective than official authorities. Reasons for that are manifold such as little interest, not seeing eye-to-eye, discrimination, and not being taken seriously. Into this void of absence, it seems even more so that minority and discriminated groups, who fall outside the grid of the EE and its support, organise themselves and take over the tasks of the official bodies. In so doing, they become the actors of inclusiveness.

10.2 Methodology

This chapter is based on a mix of qualitative and quantitative analyses. Initially, a broad literature review of relevant studies on the topic of migrant businesses was conducted to identify fields in which these entrepreneurs act inclusive and why. Subsequently, a theoretically informed quantitative analysis of secondary data was conducted and substantiated by 11 narrative interviews with first- and second-generation migrant entrepreneurs in Germany in September and October 2019. Interviewees were selected by means of hearsay on a random basis. The interviews served as a source for practice-oriented explication of the results from the secondary analyses. The data used for the quantitative secondary data analysis comprises surveys on the topics of start-ups and self-employment. These include (a) the German microcensus for the survey years 2014 to 2016 of the Federal Statistical Office and (b) the IAB/ZEW Start-up Panel for the start-up cohorts 2009 to 2015. The microcensus is a representative annual household survey of the German Federal Statistics Office, gathering data on population characteristics including employment status and citizenship ('migration background'). Every year, around 830,000 people in around 370,000 private households and shared accommodation, almost 1% of the population in Germany, are questioned about their working and living conditions (Federal Statistical Office).

The IAB/ZEW Start-up Panel surveys present the general conditions of start-ups by following the development of newly founded enterprises over several years. Around 6000 enterprises are surveyed annually for this purpose. The sample's stratification enables sector-specific analyses for the small but economically significant group of high-tech start-ups and for newly founded companies from non-technology-intensive sectors.

Qualitative data was collected through narrative interviews, creating an open storytelling space. Placing people at the heart of the study, interviewees are encouraged to tell their stories rather than asking interviewees about facts or opinions (Erlach & Mueller, 2020). To elicit stories of experiences, the interviewees were given the narrative stimulus, 'What was your path to self-employment like, and what role did your migration background or that of your family play?'. In total, 11 interviews were conducted. Table 10.1 summarises migrant businesses and business owners' core characteristics.

10.3 The Inclusivity of Migrant Entrepreneurs – Results

In the following, we show the results from the available data, which demonstrate how migrant entrepreneurs venture activities regarding (1) local labour markets, (2) regional development, (3) social mobility, and (4) diasporic and ethnic communities and in so doing contribute to local EEs.

Local Labour Markets According to the estimation model (Leicht & Langhauser, 2014), the total number of jobs created by migrant entrepreneurs since the beginning of the 1990s is about 2.2 million, which corresponds to a share of about 18% of all jobs in owner-managed SMEs. Metzger (2016) also identifies the group of migrants as those who create more jobs more frequently after their start-up, which reinforces the positive impulses of start-up activity for the German economy. The direct gross employment effect (GEE) of migrant start-up activity from 2011 to 2014 amounted to 611,000 full-time equivalent jobs annually (ibid.). This includes 400,000 jobs for the new entrepreneurs themselves and 211,000 jobs for their employees. The share of migrants in the GEE thus amounted to 21%. According to Metzger (2016), this is above average in view of their 19% share of start-ups (i.e., excluding takeovers and active participation).

At the same time, migrant businesses in Germany, especially Turkish businesses, are making a growing contribution to training and are also approaching the qualification behaviour of German self-employed people without a migration background in this respect (Leicht & Langhauser, 2014). Migrant businesses are not only of interest to migrant workers as potential employers but increasingly address all those

Table 10.1 Core characteristics of migrant businesses and business owners

Business	Place of residence	Gender	Generation/Family background	Place of birth/Time of migration
Greek restaurant	Gelsenkirchen	Male	1st/Greek	Greece/as a child
Dental practice	Gelsenkirchen	Male	1st/Serbo-Croatian	Croatia/as a child
Advertising agency	Gelsenkirchen	Male	1st/Turkish	Turkey/as a child
Consultancy	Hamburg	Male	1st/Congolese	Congo/as a young adult
Catering	Hamburg	Male	2nd/Jordanian	Germany
Start-up	Duisburg	Male	1st/Syrian	Syria/as an adult refugee
Fashion shop	Hannover	Female	2nd/Greek	Germany
Furniture shop	Hamburg	Female	1st/Turkish	Turkey/as a child
Car dealer	Gelsenkirchen/ Katowice	Male	1st/polish	Poland/as a child
Grocery shop	Recklinghausen	Male	1st/polish	Poland/as an adult
Magazine founder	Hamburg	Male	1st/Syrian	Syria/as an adult refugee

who prefer working in intercultural structures (see own interviews). This is where multiple language skills, multiculturalism, and diversity come together and open new avenues of entrepreneurship (David et al., 2019). Sometimes the success of many migrant business models is due to the interconnections of trans/international with the regional networks of migrant entrepreneurs, where social, intellectual, and monetary capital is exchanged (see David et al., 2019b; David, 2015; Schmiz, 2014; Saxenian, 2007 and 2012). Already in 1999, Kloosterman et al. reflect the employers' behaviour of migrant entrepreneurs open and positive towards co-ethnic groups. This means that, for instance, Turkish entrepreneurs often employ Arabic or Moroccan workers (co-ethnic social capital) who share religious and cultural values and norms. This is a great achievement as many of these companies provide multicultural working environments (Edin et al., 2003) even if this is not a constant rule (Gërxhani & Kosyakova, 2022).

Examples from the Interviews

The topic of co-ethnic employees was also subject to our interviews. Four of the ten interviewees reported that they are even actively looking for other co-ethnic employees or at least with a migrant background. The reasons were different, on the one hand, so that multilingualism is given, and the customers can be better served and on the other hand so that one has someone who understands what it is like to be a migrant. Trust and culture also played a big role. One dentist entrepreneur stated: *'The more dentists, I employ, are speaking different languages, the broader my client base is, and everyone is satisfied'.*

The next aspect of the inclusive contribution to EEs labour markets is that migrant founders have a higher level of education compared to dependent employees. The level of education among migrant entrepreneurs themselves appears to be high. The share of academics with a migrant background among all founders is as high as the share of academics among founders without a migrant background (Metzger, 2016). Leicht et al. (2017) state that it can be generally recognised that the self-employed in most origin groups have on average enjoyed a better education than their counterparts in the dependent workforce. Overall, 28% of the self-employed have a university degree or a comparable professional qualification. Following Leicht et al. (2017), this only applies to 17% of dependent employees (ibid.). This trend is confirmed in the start-up cohorts surveyed from 2009 to 2015 in the IAB/ZEW Start-up Panel (2016). The share of migrant founders with a university degree is 39% there but remains significantly behind the founders of German origin (51%). Leicht et al. (2017) also share this observation. The share of self-employed migrants with a degree comparable to that of a master craftsman/civil servant/professional academy rose by 9% from 2014 to 2018.

For 2014, Leicht et al. (2017) show a much lower proportion of migrants with a qualification comparable to that of a master craftsman or technician (8%) compared to Germans of origin (18%). In contrast, the evaluation of the IAB/ZEW Start-up Panel (2016) (see chart 10 in the appendix) shows a clear increase in these qualifications. Thus, 17% of the 2009–2015 start-up cohorts with a migrant background had a qualification comparable to a master craftsman/civil servant/vocational academy qualification (+9% compared to 2014). German-born entrepreneurs account for around 20%. The Mikrozensus for 2016 clearly shows that migrant self-employed persons report *Abitur* (high school graduation) as their highest school-leaving qualification (45%), which means a slight lead over self-employed persons without a migration background (40.4%). Regarding the female self-employed in the same survey year, as many as 55.7% of them have the *Abitur* as their highest school-leaving qualification, whereas only 45.9% of self-employed women without a migration background have the Abitur. The male self-employed with a migrant background and A-levels, on the other hand, are behind their female counterparts at 39.4%, but slightly ahead of the male self-employed without a migrant background (37.6%).

In addition, a direct comparison of the Mikrozensus of 2014 and 2016 shows that the proportion of self-employed persons with a high school diploma and a migration background has risen by 2 percentage points. According to the IAB/ZEW Start-up Panel (2016), the two sectors in which most migrants with a university degree start-up are technology-intensive services, followed by trade (analysis of the IAB/ZEW Start-up Panel 2016). German entrepreneurs with a university degree often start up in technology- and knowledge-intensive services (IAB/ZEW Start-up Panel, 2016).

Regional Development It is popular that the intensity and the number of entrepreneurial activities and businesses are part of regional growth and development. These effects are most visible in local EEs. The KfW Start-up Monitor (Metzger, 2019) registers a stabilisation of start-up activity in 2018, which has been declining for years. Eight out of ten entrepreneurs set up their own businesses for the first time in entrepreneurial structures (Metzger, 2019). Despite these developments, Kriegesmann et al. (2015) point out that cultural and labour market-specific path dependencies in Germany continue to support a cautious attitude towards start-ups in certain regions. In contrast, groups of migrants among founders in Germany seem to be particularly active in setting up a company (Leifels & Metzger, 2019; Leicht et al., 2017; Metzger, 2016).

In 2014, a total of 915,000 people became self-employed in Germany, including around 179,000 migrants (Metzger, 2016), who can be subsumed under the label migrant economists/migrant entrepreneurs. The Mikrozensus 2019 shows that in 2018 the number of self-employed in Germany was around four million. This is 300,000 lower than in 2012, the year with the highest number of self-employed in the last two decades (Mikrozensus, 2019). On average over many years, around one in five start-ups is carried out by people with a migrant background (Metzger, 2016). Leicht et al. (2017) show that the number of migrant self-employed increased by one-third (33%) in the period from 2005 to 2016. In contrast, the number of self-employed without a migrant background declined over the same period (3%). At 21%, the share of migrants among the founders on average in 2013/2014 exceeds the share of migrants among those of working age (18%) by 3% points (Metzger, 2016). This again reinforces the picture of a higher propensity to start a business among migrants. In the period from 2009 to 2016, the annual start-up rate of migrants was 1.86%, while the overall start-up rate was 1.68% (also available). Also, based on own calculations of Mikrozensus data between 2005 and 2019 shows an increase of migrant self-employed of 61.7% (from 532,000 to 860,000).

A special analysis of the KfW Start-up Monitor 2018 (Leifels & Metzger, 2019) also shows that regardless of their actual employment situation, around 38% of migrants in Germany generally prefer to be self-employed rather than employed. If one compares this with the proportion of the total labour force, it shows that this is significantly lower at 29% (ibid.). The desire for self-employment is thus significantly higher among migrants.

Examples from the Interviews

Among the interviewees, very few can imagine working permanently in a dependent employment relationship. This is mainly due to their family employment histories. Many of the interviewees come from entrepreneurial families in which self-employment is more the rule. Some of them have already taken over a business in the family context. A high propensity for self-employment was reported to the IAT above all by 'newcomers' (period 2015–2017).

Contrary to the myth that migrant businesses usually arise out of pure necessity, Leicht et al. (2017) show that in many cases they are also deliberate career decisions. For example, evaluations of the IAB/ZEW Start-up Panel (2016) showed that only 9.6% of start-up cohorts with a migration background from 2009 to 2015 had previously been unemployed and thus had lower shares than founders without a migration background. This makes clear that only a small proportion of migrants started out of a supposed necessity situation. Although Leifels and Metzger (2019) illustrate that the average proportion of migrants who started in an emergency was 38% between 2013 and 2017, which is significantly higher than the overall average of 31%, the 47% share of migrants who started because out of opportunities is the majority.

The primary motives for founding a business are autonomy, implementation of business ideas and better earning opportunities. Leicht et al. (2017) conclude that the spectrum of start-up motives is a combination of push and pull factors, with the latter predominating. They include those motives that describe entrepreneurship as an attractive and desirable position (ibid.). Opportunity founders, whose founding is shaped by pull factors, are characterised by a striving for independence, a high willingness to perform, the ability to recognise market opportunities, and a positive essential attitude towards feasibility (ibid.). Although founders also describe these characteristics without a migration background, they are slightly more pronounced in the migrant group. Based on the evaluations of the 2009 to 2015 start-up cohorts of the IAB/ZEW Start-up Panel (2016), three main motives for migrants to start a business can be identified: self-determined work, the implementation of a concrete business idea (each with 32% of the mentions), followed by better earning opportunities with around 22% of the mentions.

One indicator of the relevance of a start-up is the full-time start-up. The share of self-employed migrants in the German start-up scene in full-time employment in the average of the years 2013/2014 was 43%, around 4 percentage points higher than the share of full-time entrepreneurs in the overall analysis (Metzger, 2016). In the context of their evaluation, Leicht et al. (2017) also conclude that migrants are more likely to start up as full-time entrepreneurs. In 2018, around 18.4% of full-time entrepreneurs in Germany came from non-EU-27 countries. Compared to the previous year, this corresponds to an increase of 11.2% (Metzger, 2019b). A high full-time equivalent is a good indicator of regional development options. Hereby, migrant entrepreneurs seem to contribute appropriately.

Migrant entrepreneurs and migrant self-employed persons are younger on average. An examination of the age structure of founders and self-employed persons reveals differences between persons with and without a migration background. Migrants who have become self-employed since 2009 are on average 36 years old (Metzger, 2016) and, thus, one and a half years younger than German entrepreneurs. This is due to the lower proportion of older people among migrants who can work. 'Overall, 29% of those capable of working are over 50 years old - among migrants only under one in five' (Metzger, 2016: 1). The lower age of the potential founders thus lowers the average age of the general age of the actual founders. Evaluations of the 2009–2015 start-up cohorts have also shown that migrants start-up on average at the age of around 39. In contrast, founders of German origin are on average about 4 years older, at around 43 years (IAB/ZEW Start-up Panel 2016).

The analyses of the Mikrozensus (2016) also show that migrant self-employed persons are on average 46 years old, about 5 years younger than German self-employed persons, whose average age is about 51. In terms of age, however, there is no difference between female and male self-employed persons with a migration background. Here, both are on average 46 years old (see Table 3 in the appendix). Leicht et al. (2017) also show that this applies to the age at the time of founding as well as to the self-employed population. While the average age of founding migrants is around 35 years overall and 36 years in the first generation, Germans of origin found businesses at 38 years on average (Leicht et al., 2017). For the second generation, Leicht et al. (2017) identify an even earlier start-up tendency with an average of 31 years. Overall, the average age of persons with a migration background is lower, both among the founders and among existing self-employed persons.

The next indicator to look at in the regional context is the innovativeness of migrant entrepreneurs. Access to transnational knowledge flows is thus also central for migrant entrepreneurs. This requires a knowledge base at the institutional, entrepreneurial, and individual levels, as well as knowledge brokers who contribute to a continuous renewal of the knowledge base (David, 2015; Boshuizen, 2009; Growe, 2009; Lichtenthaler, 2009; Saxenian, 2007, Trippl & Maier, 2007). The more diverse the regional knowledge base, the more likely it is that external knowledge can be absorbed, and new knowledge is generated and combined with existing knowledge (Terstriep & Lüthje, 2018). People with a migration background, with their specific behavioural patterns and cultural backgrounds, contribute significantly to the diversity of the regional knowledge base (David, 2015). The use of their transnational networks enables them as knowledge brokers to contribute to a continuous influx of new knowledge, to generate new knowledge with local actors (David & Coenen, 2019; Schmiz, 2014; Pries, 2011; Stockhorst, 2011) and to disseminate innovative ideas (Rabadjieva & Butzin, 2019). Transnationality thus becomes a regional resource anchored in persons of different cultures (David & Coenen, 2017; Asheim & Gertler, 2005) and an element of regional innovation systems (Schmiz, 2014).

Examples from the Interviews

The second generation of migrant entrepreneurs also confirmed in the interviews that they still make use of networks in their countries of origin. They hope to gain new knowledge and inspiring ideas that they can implement in their own companies in Germany. Although the exchange also takes place digitally, many are on-site several times a year and consciously look for inspiration. Some even revive family networks with which there has been no contact for some time to establish an anchor point of exchange with the country of origin. Most respondents confirmed that they consciously exploit the resource of *transnationality* and use it in a controlled way in their company in Germany.

David et al. (2019b) see integration into international networks and the use of knowledge stocks generated in an international context as prerequisites for the innovative capacity of migrant businesses. Leicht et al. (2017) consider these characteristics to be advantageous for migrants in their start-up projects. The authors observe that the business models of migrant companies are more often than average based on international networks embedded in diverse ecosystems (ibid.). Founders who have acquired their knowledge and skills abroad are more likely to develop innovative products and market novelties (ibid.; see also David et al., 2019). Metzger (2016) also confirms that migrants offer regional market innovations slightly more often (20% compared to 18% of Germans). The author sees the strong tendency to start businesses in the trade as an explanation for this. Among the market novelties, he identifies products and services that are new to the relevant market. He considers it irrelevant whether the offers are technologically innovative (ibid.). The evaluation of the IAB/ZEW Start-up Panel (2016) with the cohorts 2009 to 2015 confirms that although entrepreneurs with a migration background introduce fewer national/

global market novelties compared to entrepreneurs without a migration background, they are slightly ahead of the German-born founders in introducing regional market novelties with an average share of 5% since the founding.

Examples from the Interviews
The trend to actively use transnationality or transnational networks for business activities is also evident in the interviews. Some of the interviewees, for example, are using the knowledge brought from their countries of origin, which they also acquire through travel and/or networks. In the sense of a brain exchange (David, 2015, David et al., 2012), some of them returned to their country of origin to study and then set up a business in Germany.

But not only the country of origin seems to be relevant in this context. Some of the interviewees reported that they went abroad to work or study – Regardless of their country of origin – To gain international experience. The USA, Australia, and European countries are popular to do so.

Social Mobility Just as start-ups are an important component and a measuring instrument of an economy, going into self-employment also holds opportunities at the individual level. Among them is the social advancement that leads many migrants to start their own businesses (Leicht et al., 2017) and the associated attainment of a higher status, also in terms of social integration (David & Terstriep, 2018; David & Coenen, 2017), as well as better earning opportunities.

Examples from the Interviews
In the interviews, it was reported that when migrants become self-employed, they are more highly regarded in both the society of origin and the society of arrival. *'If you tell people that you are an entrepreneur, they know that you have made it economically and socially – You are completely integrated'*. The possibility of a better income was also mentioned in the interviews as a main motive for becoming a businessman, which in many countries of origin stands for specific character traits of a person as a pars pro toto: Punctual, educated, business-minded, motivated, strong, resilient, ambitious – All characteristics that correlate with the capitalist idea of the market economy in many countries of origin.

Whereas in the past it was assumed that the mobilisation of ethnic resources was a unique selling point for migrant self-employment, today people with a migration background increasingly rely on education as social capital, especially when they decide to become self-employed. 28% of the self-employed have a university education or comparable vocational training. In contrast to dependent employees

(17%), 28% of migrant self-employed persons in 2014 had higher education or comparable vocational training (Leicht et al., 2017). Based on analyses of the Mikrozensus, Leicht et al. (2017) show that the likelihood of self-employment is related to the level of education and that education and professional qualifications are also key determinants of entrepreneurial self-employment among migrants. There is a positive correlation between the level of education and professional self-employment. At the same time, the authors point out that it is not only the level of education that counts but also the proximity to the profession (ibid.). Leicht et al. (2017), for example, find no differences in the propensity to become self-employed between people without a school-leaving certificate and those with a higher education entrance qualification, while the probability of professional self-employment is 1.3 times higher for people who have a higher education entrance qualification with in-company training than for those without a degree. Migrants with a doctorate are twice as likely as the unqualified to enter self-employment (Leicht et al., 2017). Migrants with a master craftsman's or technician's diploma as well as vocational academic training are four times more likely to become self-employed than the reference group (ibid.).

The figures of Leicht et al. (2017), who observed an increase in the proportion of highly qualified people among migrant and German self-employed up to 2010, but which then stagnated among self-employed migrants, give pause for thought. In contrast, the proportion of highly qualified self-employed people in the group of ethnic Germans continues to rise. One possible explanation given by the authors is that members of the younger immigration cohorts are more likely to take up dependent employment. In the medium term, a continuation of this development is likely to weaken the start-up potential of migrants in both quantitative and qualitative terms, as higher-value start-ups are dependent on the supply of new knowledge (Leicht et al., 2017).

As shown above, the level of income is not only a pull factor into self-employment for migrants but is also understood as an indicator of integration in the labour market and in society in general. For many migrants, especially those of the first generation, who are confronted with possible difficulties in the recognition of their qualifications in Germany, labour policy measures initially do not lead to the local labour market at all or only under more difficult conditions (David et al., 2019). In addition to social advancement, the path to self-employment is also an instrument of integration (David & Coenen, 2017). Leicht et al. (2017) show that self-employed migrants have on average a 40% higher net income than employees. The higher income also improves the opportunities for social participation (compare own interviews).

Earning an income that is even higher than the average not only boosts the migrants' self-esteem, but also means social integration in the countries of residence. For the country of origin, it is also a sign that migrants have successfully completed the migration process, which in turn has a positive effect on the target group's self-perception and increases the ability and willingness to integrate into the society of arrival (David, 2015; Cassarino, 2004).

Diasporic and Ethnic Communities In addition to the hard facts and inclusivity through the socio-economic contribution, soft factors such as the ability of migrant businesses to integrate diasporic members and ethnic groups into the local and entrepreneurial ecosystem are almost forgotten. Migrant businesses are often the pivotal point for ethnic community members and are important associates of the diaspora (Elo, 2016). Even though more and more of these companies are starting up in the knowledge-intensive sectors (see the well-known example of BionTech; Schäfer, 2021), most are still in the more traditional sectors, such as trade. The analyses of the data also show this. A breakdown of start-ups by sector shows that most of all start-ups are in the service sector. This also applies to migrant start-ups. On average in 2013/2014, around 21% of new businesses in the trade sector were founded by migrants. In the same period, the share of all start-ups in trade was only 17% (Metzger, 2016). This trend is continuing. The IAB/ZEW Start-up Panel (2016) evaluations in cohorts 2009 to 2015 show that trade, with a share of around 24%, continues to be one of the most important economic sectors in which migrants start-up businesses. This is followed by other consumer-related services and the construction sector, each with shares of 11.8% and 10% respectively (see chart 4 in the appendix). This is not surprising, as it was in these three sectors that migrant entrepreneurs were most frequently employed (IAB/ZEW Start-up Panel 2016). Leicht et al. (2017) conclude similarly, identifying higher shares of migrant self-employed in construction, trade, and hospitality, as well as in non-knowledge-intensive services.

These figures provide evidence that many of the migrant businesses are still operating in the local ecosystem today and play a major role in local regions and neighbourhoods. Interviews have shown that migrant entrepreneurs are often sought out by ethnic and co-ethnic populations to help with problem-solving. On the other hand, they stand as role models for socio-economic development by integrating into society and establishing entrepreneurship. The entrepreneur status makes them interesting for both worlds – ethnic and nonethnic societies. They portray a positive narrative of migration, which plays an important role in the respective countries of arrival, particularly in those countries with strong opposition to migration.

Especially in areas of urban poverty and deprived neighbourhoods, where many migrant enclaves must live and work alongside each other, these businesses can offer opportunities and means to lift socio-spatial inequality.

Examples from the Interviews

A Turkish respondent who runs seven installation businesses in the Ruhr area told us that he gets visits from young people in the neighbourhood and at the local football club he belongs to, who ask him for immunity when they represent to him that they do not want to participate in local drug sales and want to get out. And whether he can give them the names of people who can help them.

Some of the interviewed migrant entrepreneurs pointed out that they provide pro bono advice to other migrant entrepreneurs, as part of their diaspora who want to start a business in the same neighbourhood. They advise them on business models, customers, German start-up policies, and suppliers.

Examples from the Interviews
An entrepreneur who runs a second-generation Greek restaurant reported that he showed his Italian friend, also second-generation, how to open a restaurant and, in addition, how to revitalise an empty bar in the same district. *'I advised him to do something new as well. To be brave. What can happen if you fail? Then you just start over. I told him to go to Rome and check out the latest trends in gastronomy. Implement it here. I help where I can'.*

Next to pursuing opportunities in their country of residence, migrant entrepreneurs actively seize business opportunities across borders, which is called *transnational migrant entrepreneurship* (Drori et al., 2009). With multiple connections to businesses and people abroad, migrant entrepreneurs create unique product offerings and supply chains, thereby enriching local and foreign economies. Some first-generation migrants have created shops and marketplaces in their country of residency whilst sourcing handcrafted, artisanal products like jewellery, bags, and other goods from their country of origin to sustain and strengthen local, indigenous communities.

Examples from the Interviews
An entrepreneur who runs a B2B online marketplace sourcing handmade products from African artisans explains the starting point of this venturing journey highlighting the problematic situation with his residence permit. *'I was born and grow up in Morocco, studied math there, moved to France to study computer science and then moved to Germany to work for SAP, where I also worked for the office of the CTO. I quit my job back in 2019 to start my first start-up inspired by many successful start-up stories that I have witnessed. 3 months after quitting my job I received a letter from the foreign office that I have to leave Germany asap and that my stay is not legal anymore'.*

10.4 Discussion

This chapter provides an overview of migrant businesses in Germany. The quantitative and qualitative examination of the topic revealed that migrant businesses are first and foremost a multi-layered economic phenomenon. In line with our research question, *'Are migrant businesses inclusive and if so, in what way?'*, this chapter presented a multidimensional data analysis to give some answers. In so doing, data was studied for migrant entrepreneurs venturing activities pertaining to (1) local labour markets, (2) regional development, (3) social mobility, (4) diasporic and ethnic communities. We assume that migrant entrepreneurs make up for the lack of inclusiveness in EE by actively executing inclusivity and intersectionality in their venturing efforts.

Based on our results, we summarise that migrant entrepreneurs are an instrument of integration on several levels in local EEs. Migrant self-employed people not only create more jobs and training opportunities for youngsters but also offer more apprenticeships compared to native German businesses, considering their share in the German economy. Their contribution to innovation through the frequent introduction of market innovations and the transnational exchange of knowledge also has great potential for economic regional development in Germany.

Migrant entrepreneurs make an important contribution to local supply and EEs. Urban and neighbourhood development benefits from migrants as local entrepreneurs, especially in small and medium-sized towns, where they contribute to the maintenance of the general infrastructure due to high migration rates, especially in places where 'corner shops' of German origin are increasingly closing for various reasons. At the same time, migrant entrepreneurs have the potential to change the cityscape of metropolises and large cities when migrant businesses 'cluster' (see Duisburg Marxloh, the Dong Xuan Center in Berlin Lichtenberg or the Japanese quarter in Düsseldorf, e.g., along Immermannstraße, also called Little Tokyo on the Rhine).

It is not only individuals who complete the integration process by setting up their own businesses and attaining the status of successful migrants in their country of origin or working as employees for a migrant company that benefits from migrant entrepreneurship. Entire ethnic communities also benefit from migrant entrepreneurship on the ground. Migrant businesses partly take on diaspora structures and are the pivotal point for many questions of orientation in the new homeland. They also function as a kind of information point or door opener about integration and serve as representatives of the respective ethnic group in the majority society.

In line with the above, we can summarize that migrant entrepreneurs are inclusive in EEs through:

1. Their share of the German economy increased by 33% between 2005 and 2016, the founders are younger and less risk-averse.
2. Creation of new jobs and measured by their share of the economy, offer more apprenticeships than German companies on average.
3. Increased introduction of innovations in the market and their role as knowledge brokers, making a significant contribution to the diversity of the regional knowledge base and economic development in Germany.
4. They contribute to the maintenance of general infrastructures in small and medium-sized towns that are characterized by strong outward migration. In metropolitan areas and urban surroundings, on the other hand, they shape the local

economy and can become customer and visitor magnets by building clusters of migrant-led businesses.
5. The self-employment of individuals often leads to a change of status from 'refugee' or 'migrant' to 'entrepreneur', which points out the socio-economic integration and development in the society of arrival.
6. They leverage diasporic structures on the ground and become spokespeople for guidance and development of their community and peers, act as door openers for migrants regarding integration into the majority society and take on representational functions for immigrants.

The aforementioned specifics highlight the inclusive nature of migrant entrepreneurs through taking on the responsibility of fostering diversity, equity, and inclusion in EEs while themselves depend on the social and economic success of their venturing efforts. This status is best described by calling it an *inclusivity tax for migrant entrepreneurs* in which they take on multiple roles and responsibilities such as enabling socio-economic growth for peers from marginalized and underrepresented communities and creating transnational business opportunities whilst trying to maintain and grow their own business facing legal, political, social, and economic challenges in their country of residence.

10.5 Conclusion

As with all research, our study comes with limitations. We make no claim to the representativeness of the study and acknowledge a small sample size and the super-diversity of migrant entrepreneurs in terms of nationality, legal status, and business structure. This is explained by the difficulty in attracting respondents for the said study. The aim of this chapter was to propose a different perspective on migrant entrepreneurship in the discourse of inclusive entrepreneurship. The authors argue that existing entrepreneurship training programs are indebted to co-design and co-deliver to enlarge the participation of entrepreneurs of underrepresented communities. However, efforts should entail changing the narrative on migrant entrepreneurs due to their special role in cultivating an inclusive entrepreneurial ecosystem whilst themselves being subdued to othering by the larger society adding legal and economic repercussions in their country of residence.

Therefore we propose a closer look at measures to minimize the inclusivity tax for migrant entrepreneurs such as providing a safe public space for discussions about the importance and impact of migrant entrepreneurship whilst reframing migrant entrepreneurship in a positive way; drafting entrepreneurial policy mechanism to ensure equitable access to opportunities for social, political, and economic participation; and strengthening migrants integration into society through coordinated action among different actors involved in qualification and training. We suggest delivering sensitization and trainings on intercultural management and diversity, equity and inclusion targeting hub managers, general partners in venture capital and professionals in entrepreneurial ecosystem. It would help to provide highly individualized multilingual training programs for migrant entrepreneurs to enter and scale in the countries of residence market and examine existing policies known to hinder migrant entrepreneurship. In particular we address those around employment rights, self-employment, residence permits, entry visas, and recognition of prior qualifications and experience whilst aiming at developing new initiatives for assisting migrant entrepreneurs. An improved access to finance and market opportunities for migrant entrepreneurs with public policy makers, SMEs, and migrant entrepreneurship support organizations is needed.

Whilst acknowledging the super-diverse potential of migrant entrepreneurship, it also represents a challenge for the entrepreneurial ecosystem and facilitators within. Willingness to participate in inclusive entrepreneurship programs depends on the entrepreneur's character, irrespective of their migration background. Especially the second generation of migrant entrepreneurs seems to be well-informed and has their own network of allies and resources. The qualitative interviews presented in this chapter have shown that second-generation migrants are more inclined to use private advisory structures rather than programs facilitated by the public sector and government. A distinct number of entrepreneurs emphasize the advantages of peer-to-peer exchanges with established entrepreneurs, irrespective of nationality and heritage, whilst describing advice received from other sources as theoretical, institutional, and distant from the reality on the ground.

Nevertheless, migrant entrepreneurship remains a driver of innovation and the requirements of migrant entrepreneurs need to be addressed by policymakers, facilitators of the entrepreneurial ecosystem, larger corporations, and SMEs to foster economic growth, diversity, equity, and inclusion in the respective country of residence. The generation of a positive narrative on migrant entrepreneurship in the public sphere, redesign of legal and economic policies for newcomers, and an individualized training and support system will lead to minimizing the inclusivity tax for migrant entrepreneurs fostering socio-economic growth on a transnational scale.

Finally, an inclusive entrepreneurial ecosystem needs raw models to build around them an environment that is authentic and caregiving. Now, still, migrant entrepreneurs often are excluded from the bigger entrepreneurial ecosystem and lag the sense of belonging. This is the first step to be changed. The attribute *migrant* should be referred to as an asset, because at the end migrant entrepreneurs are businesspeople like all the other entrepreneurs.

References

Aldrich, H. E., & Waldinger, R. (1990). Ethnicity and entrepreneurship. *Annual Review of Sociology, 16*(1), 111–135. https://doi.org/10.1146/annurev.so.16.080190.000551

Aliaga-Isla, R., & Criado, A. (2013). Systematic review of immigrant entrepreneurship literature: Previous findings and ways forward. *Entrepreneurship and Regional Development., 25*, 819–844. https://doi.org/10.1080/08985626.2013.845694

Ancona, A., Cinelli, M., Ferraro, G., et al. (2023). Network-based principles of entrepreneurial ecosystems: A case study of a start-up network. *Small Bus Econ.* https://doi.org/10.1007/s11187-023-00738-6

Asheim, B., & Gertler, M. S. (2005). The Geography of Innovation – Regional Innovation Systems. In J. Fagerberg, D. C. Mowery, & R. R. Nelson (Eds.), *The Oxford handbook of innovation* (pp. 291–317). Oxford University Press.

Boshuizen, J. (2009). *Join the club! Knowledge spillovers and the influence of social networks on firm performance*. University of Twente/CSTM.

Cassarino, J.-P. (2004). Theorising return migration: The conceptual approach to return migrants revisited. *International Journal on Multicultural Societies IJMS, 6*(2), 253–279.

David, A. (2015). *Scientia Est Potentia: Human capital and the role of networks; Migration, inclusion and new qualification for a sustainable regional economy*. [dissertation]. University of Twente.

David, A. (2017). *Migrantisches Unternehmertum. Eine Chance der Arbeitsmarktintegration für geflüchtete Menschen? [Migrant entrepreneurship. An opportunity for labour market integration for refugees?] Forschung Aktuell, 02/2017*. Institut Arbeit und Technik.

David, A., & Coenen, F. (2017). Immigrant entrepreneurship – A chance for labor market integration of refugees? In A. David & I. Hamburg (Eds.), *Entrepreneurship and entrepreneurial skills in europe: Examples to improve potential entrepreneurial spirit* (pp. 77–101). Verlag Barbara Budrich.

David, A., & Coenen, F. (2019). Knowledge in motion: Highly-skilled migration and the role of regional networks. *Advances in Social Sciences Research Journal, 6*(4), 274–293.

David, A., & Terstriep, J. (2018). Innovation of informal ethnic entrepreneurship: A result of the opening of the EU's borders? In V. Ratten & P. Jones (Eds.), *Transformational entrepreneurship*. Routledge.

David, A., & Terstriep, J. (2023). *Transformational hubs for recognised refugees – Policy recommendations by the enter to transform project* (Vol. 6). Institute for Work and Technology. https://doi.org/10.53190/inno/202301

David, A., Barwińska-Małajowicz, A., & Coenen, F. (2012). From brain drain to brain exchange: How to use better highly skilled workers: A conceptual approach. *Unia Europejska.pl, 216*(5), 25–35.

David, A., Giustolisi, A. & Terstriep, J. (2019a). *Migrantische Ökonomie(n) [Migrant Entrepreneurship] (Expertise des Instituts Arbeit und Technik (IAT) der Westfälischen Hochschule Gelsenkirchen Bocholt Recklinghausen im Auftrag der Fachkommission zu den Rahmenbedingungen der Integrationsfähigkeit der Bundesregierung)*. Gelsenkirchen.

David, A., Evans, M., Hamburg, I. & Terstriep, J. (Hrsg.) (2019b). *Migration und Arbeit: Herausforderungen, Problemlagen und Gestaltungsinstrumente. [Migration and Employment: challenges, problems and instruments of governance]*. Verlag Barbara Budrich.

David, A., Terstriep, J., Stoewe, K., Ruthemeier, A., Elo, M., & Schmidt, A. G. (2022). *Migrantisches Unternehmer:innentum in Deutschland. Vorschlag einer Differenzierung. [Migrant Entrepreneurship. Proposal for a Differentiation]. Diskussionspapier der Bertelsmann Stiftung*. Bertelsmann Stiftung. https://doi.org/10.11586/2022002

Desai, S., Naud, W., & Stel, N. (2021). Refugee entrepreneurship: Context and directions for future research. *Small Business Economics, 56*, 933–945. https://doi.org/10.1007/s11187-019-00310-1

Drori, I., Honig, B., & Wright, M. (2009). Transnational entrepreneurship: An emergent field of study. *Entrepreneurship Theory and Practice, 33*, 1001–1022. https://doi.org/10.1111/j.1540-6520.2009.00332.x

Edin, P.-A., Fredriksson, P., & Åslund, O. (2003). Ethnic enclaves and the economic success of immigrants: Evidence from a natural experiment. *The Quarterly Journal of Economics, 118*(1), 329–357. http://www.jstor.org/stable/25053906

Elo, M. (2016). Typology of diaspora entrepreneurship: Case studies in Uzbekistan. *Journal of International Entrepreneurship, 14*, 121–155. https://doi.org/10.1007/s10843-016-0177-9

Erlach, Ch. & Mueller, M. (2020). *Narrative Organisationen. Wie die Arbeit mit Geschichten Unternehmen zukunftsfähig macht*. Springer Gabler.

Gërxhani, K., & Kosyakova, Y. (2022). The effect of co-ethnic social capital on immigrants' labor market integration: A natural experiment. Comparative. *Migration Studies, 10*(15). https://doi.org/10.1186/s40878-022-00289-x

Growe, A. (2009). Knowledge-holders and networking in metropolitan regions. Spatial requirements of knowledge-holders and the combination of politics. *Raumforschung und Raumordnung, 5*(6), 383–394. https://doi.org/10.1007/BF03185713

Heilbrunn, S., Freiling, J., & Harima, A. (Eds.). (2019). *Refugee entrepreneurship: A case-based topography*. Palgrave Macmillan.

Hello Europe, Ashoka. (2022). *Transforming the field of migration through collaborative framework (October 17, 2022)*. Available at SSRN: https://ssrn.com/abstract=4250438 or https://doi.org/10.2139/ssrn.4250438 (with contribution from David, A. & Terstriep, J.).

Kloosterman, R., van der Leun, J., & Rath, J. (1999). Mixed embeddedness: (In)formal economic activities and immigrant businesses in the Netherlands. *International Journal of Urban and Regional Research, 23*(2), 253–267. https://doi.org/10.1111/1468-2427.00194

Kriegesmann, B., Böttcher, M., Lippmann, T. & Wietzke, M. (2015). Wissenschaftsregion Ruhr [Science Region Ruhr] (Langfassung). In *Wirtschaftliche Bedeutung, Fachkräfteeffekte und Innovationsimpulse der Hochschulen und außeruniversitären Forschungseinrichtungen in der Metropole Ruhe*. Regionalverband Ruhr (RVR).

Krueger, N. (2021). Beyond "Getting Asked to Dance": Inclusive entrepreneurial ecosystems. In T. M. Cooney (Ed.), *The Palgrave Handbook of MinorityEntrepreneurship*. Palgrave Macmillan. https://doi.org/10.1007/978-3-030-66603-3_6

Krüger, D., & David, A. (2020). Entrepreneurial education for persons with disabilities: A social innovation approach for inclusive ecosystems. *Frontiers in Education, 5*, 1–17. https://doi.org/10.3389/feduc.2020.00003

Leicht, R., & Langhauser, M. (2014). Ökonomische Bedeutung und Leitungspotenziale von Migrantenunternehmen in Deutschland. [Economic significance and management potential of migrant enterprises in Germany]. In *WISO Diskurs WISO Diskurs: Expertisen und Dokumentation zur Wirtschafts- und Sozialpolitik*. Friedrich-Ebert-Stiftung.

Leicht, R., Berwing, S., Philipp, R., Block, N., Rüffer, N., & Ahrens, J.-P. und Co-Autor/innen: Förster, N., Sänger, R. & Siebert, J.: (2017). *Gründungspotenziale von Menschen mit ausländischen Wurzeln. Entwicklungen, Erfolgsfaktoren, Hemmnisse*. [Start-up potentials of people with foreign roots. Developments, success factors, obstacles]. Studie des Instituts für Mittelstandsforschung (ifm) der Universität Mannheim und des Instituts für sozialpädagogische Forschung Mainz (ism), im Auftrag des Bundesministeriums für Wirtschaft und Energie (BMWi).

Leifels, A. & Metzger, G. (2019). *Gründungen durch Migranten: größerer Wunsch nach Selbständigkeit*. [Start-ups by migrants: greater desire for self-employment]. Fokus Volkswirtschaft Nr. 240, KfW Research.

Lichtenthaler, U. (2009). Absorptive Capacity, Environmental Turbulence, and the Complementarity of Organizational Learning Processes. *Academy of Management Journal, 52*(4), 822–846.

MacKinnon, D., Kempton, L., O'Brien, P., Ormerod, E., Pike, A., & Tomaney, J. (2022). Reframing urban and regional 'development' for 'left behind' places. *Cambridge Journal of Regions, Economy and Society, 15*(1), 39–56. https://doi.org/10.1093/cjres/rsab034

Malecki, E. J. (2018). Entrepreneurship and entrepreneurial ecosystems. *Geography Compass, 212*, e 12359. https://doi.org/10.1111/gec3.12359

Metzger, G. (2016). *Migranten überdurchschnittlich gründungsaktiv – Arbeitsmarkt spielt eine große Rolle*. [Migrants more active than average in setting up businesses – labour market plays a major role]. Fokus Volkswirtschaft Nr. 115, KfW Research.

Metzger, G. (2019a). *KfW-Gründungsmonitor 2019*. [KfW Start-up Monitor] Gründungstätigkeit in Deutschland stabilisiert sich: Zwischenfahrt oder Ende der Talfahrt? KfW Research, Frankfurt am Main.

Metzger, G. (2019b). *KfW-Gründungsmonitor 2019. Tabellen und Methodenband.* [KfW Start-up Monitor, Tables and Methods]. KfW Research/Frankfurt am Main.
Mikrozensus. (2016). *Statistisches Bundesamt* (Destatis).
Mikrozensus. (2019). *Statistisches Bundesamt (Destatis), Stand.* 09.10.2019/09:56:18.
OECD. (2022). *International migration outlook 2022.* OECD Publishing. https://doi.org/10.1787/30fe16d2-en
Powell, A., et al. (2021). *Designing inclusive entrepreneurship ecosystems: A three-city landscape scan.* Centre for Entrepreneurship & Innovation.
Pries, L. (2011). Transnationale Migration als Innovationspotenzial [Transnational migration as a potential for innovation]. In K. Engel, J. Großmann, & B. Hombach (Eds.), *Phönix flieg! Das Ruhrgebiet entdeckt sich neu.* Klartext.
Rabadjieva, M., & Butzin, A. (2019). Emergence and diffusion of social innovation through practice fields. *European Planning Studies.* Published online 13 Feb 2019.
Saxenian, A. (2007). *The new argonauts: Regional advantage in a global economy.* Harvard University Press.
Saxenian, A. (2012). The new argonauts, global search and local institution building. In P. Cooke, M. D. Parrilli, & J. L. Curbelo (Eds.), *Innovation, global change and resilience* (pp. 25–42). Edward Edgar Publishing.
Schäfer, S. (2021). *Innovative Gründer:innen mit Migrationserfahrung in Deutschland.* Status quo, Herausforderungen und Handlungsempfehlungen zur Förderung innovativer Gründungen von Personen mit Migrationserfahrung, Bertelsmann Stiftung.
Schmiz, A. (2014). *Transnationalität als Ressource? Netzwerke vietnamisischer Mitgrantinnen und Migranten zwischen Berlin und Vietnam* [Transnationality as a Resource? Networks of Vietnamese fellow migrants between Berlin and Vietnam]. Bielefeld: transcript.
Stam, E. (2015). Entrepreneurial ecosystems and regional policy: A sympathetic critique. *European Planning Studies, 23*(9), 1759–1769. https://doi.org/10.1080/09654313.2015.1061484
Stockhorst J. (2011). *Verfügbarkeit von hoch qualifizierten Arbeitskräften abseits der Ballungsräume, Regionale Restriktionen und Chancen für Hochtechnologieunternehmen der Medizintechnik, Stadt- und Regionalforschung* [Availability of highly qualified labour away from conurbations, Regional restrictions and opportunities for high-tech medical technology companies, Urban and regional research]. LIT Verlag Dr. W. Hopf.
Stoewe, K. (2022). *Entrepreneurship and integration in the global city.* The cases of refugee-origin entrepreneurship in Birmingham and Cologne. (PhD Dissertation).
Terstriep, J., & Lüthje, C. (2018). Innovation, knowledge and relations: On the role of clusters for firms' innovativeness. *European Planning Studies, 26*(11), 2167–2199.
Trippl, M. & Maier, G. (2007). *Knowledge spillover agents and regional development.* Working Paper of DYNREG – Dynamic Regions in a Knowledge-Driven Global Economy Lessons and Policy Implications for the EU, Vienna.
Wilson, K. L., & Portes, A. (1980). Immigrant enclaves: An analysis of the labor market experiences of Cubans in Miamic. *American Journal of Sociology, 86*(2), 295–319. https://doi.org/10.1086/227240
Zhou, M. (2004). Revisiting ethnic entrepreneurship: Convergencies, controversies, and conceptual advancements. *International Migration Review, 38*(3), 1040–1074.

Chapter 11
Show Me the Evidence! – Where Does Entrepreneurship Education Really Shape the Entrepreneurial Mindset?

Kirsten Mikkelsen, Su-Hyun Berg, and Aurelia Engelsberger

11.1 Introduction

Recent entrepreneurship literature expands our understanding of entrepreneurship education (hereafter, EE; Halbfas & Liszt-Rohlf, 2019; Brock & Kim, 2011; Ebbers, 2019). It enhances our understanding on EE and its impact on students; students from business schools are no longer the only entrepreneurs-to-be, every student can be entrepreneurial through experiencing EE programs. Recently, other institutions such as colleges and universities offered diverse entrepreneurship courses, seminars and curricula that exceed the duration of one semester and aim to develop entrepreneurship expertise as well as soft skills and offer practice-related activities (Brock & Kim, 2011). Furthermore, the discussion on EE was enriched by including a didactical perspective on EE concepts. (Halbfas & Liszt-Rohlf, 2019). This trend can be found at German universities – 18% of all students in Germany have visited at least one entrepreneurship course, with an upward tendency, 7.6% of all students try to start their own business during their studies (Bergmann & Golla, 2020). And recent EE curricular courses are action-oriented since "entrepreneurship requires practice. Learning as a method, in our opinion, is often more important than learning specific content" (Neck & Greene, 2011, p. 68). In addition, European Parliament (2006) acknowledged the significance of EE and published key skills that can be

K. Mikkelsen (✉)
Europe-University Flensburg, Flensburg, Germany
e-mail: kirsten.mikkelsen@uni-flensburg.de

S.-H. Berg
University of Southern Denmark, Technology Entrepreneurship and Innovation, Sonderburg, Denmark

A. Engelsberger
OMIND Consulting, Niefern-Öschelbronn, Germany

K. Mikkelsen, A. Wolf (eds.), *Minds, Brains, and Doxa for Inclusive Entrepreneurship*, International Studies in Entrepreneurship 47,
https://doi.org/10.1007/978-3-031-50164-7_11

achieved by EE: such as (1) creativity, initiative and entrepreneurial skills to implement ideas; (2) innovative thinking and risk-taking; (3) ability to organize projects for a social or commercial activity; and (4) awareness of ethical values and promotion of a responsible corporate management.

While extant studies and political efforts on EE highlighted the importance of EE for fostering the entrepreneurial mindset (hereafter, EM) change (Pittaway & Cope, 2007; Naia et al., 2014; Nabi et al., 2017; Fayolle, 2018), but hardly any study provides quantitative data to prove the visible impact of EE on EM at an individual level. The majority of existing quantitative studies mirror the effects of EE on intentions and attitudes in entrepreneurship (Krueger & Carsrud, 1993, Kickul et al., 2008, Chen et al., 1998), which to date have been in the centre of predictability of entrepreneurial behaviour. Subsequently, this chapter seeks to find an answer to the following question:

"How does EE impact the individual's entrepreneurial mindset?"

The study experimentally employs a tool that originally stems from tracking the open innovation mindset (OIM). It is adapted to measure changes of the individual EM. More specifically, this chapter investigates what entrepreneurial mindset changes can be measured.

Section 11.2 presents the theoretical framework, Sect. 11.3 refines our research settings and approach, Sect. 11.4 analyses research data and Sect. 11.5 wraps up with limitations and concluding observations.

11.2 Theoretical Background and Literature Review

Entrepreneurship Education and Effectuation Approach

Entrepreneurship education is "enabling entrepreneurial thinking and acting capabilities to master socio-economic situations in a mature, competent, reflected and responsible manner" (Bijedić, 2019). Entrepreneurship education thus goes far beyond the qualification to start a new business (ibid.). According to this definition, entrepreneurship education is to be understood as a lifelong learning approach (Bijedić, 2019) and can merely be acknowledged as a life skill (Neck et al., 2020).

Most entrepreneurship education in Higher Education Institutions (HEIs) employed an "about" approach; they were traditionally more teacher-centred and did hardly engage students in activities and projects (Pittaway & Edwards, 2012; Stovang & Nielsen, 2015). The authors reason that entrepreneurship education, particularly if it seeks to be inclusive, should engage effectuation (Sarasvathy, 2001). The effectuation approach aims at improving a state of being. The life of the individual and, by extension, the condition of the whole world is to be improved. It is therefore a concept that roots in meaning and purpose and that functions as a kind of human problem solving. It is a process that is both dynamic and iterative. Through initial self-reflection individuals get to discover their own potential and may formulate a series of potential outcomes. The core questions are "Who am I? What do I know?" and "Who do I know?". While the first question involves a reflection on personal values and inner purpose, the second question relates to one's experience and competencies. The final question is a matter of one's social capital such as network, friends and family. Following the iterative dynamic effectuation process the action with and engagement of other people results in potential outcomes, plans are made and may repeatedly be discarded or reshaped (Sarasvathy, 2001). Effectuation explicitly encourages a multi-perspective. The entrepreneurial environment is characterized by numerous uncertainties (Sarasvathy & Dew, 2005). The effectual reasoning follows the logic "To the extent that we can control the future, we do not need to predict it" (Sarasvathy, 2006).

The effectuation approach follows five principles: bird-in-hand principle, affordable-loss principle, lemonade principle, crazy-quilt principle, pilot-in-the-plane principle (Sarasvathy, 2008). The bird-in-hand principle describes the starting point of the effectuation process. According to this principle, decisions are made based on the available means. "The emphasis here is on creating something new with existing means rather than discovering new ways to achieve given goals" (Sarasvathy, 2008). It can be argued that the effectuation approach emphasizes flexibility in regard to potential outcomes, which is an essential aspect to survive in an environment that is characterized by volatility, uncertainty (and hence unpredictability), complexity and ambiguity (VUCA). One current example is the COVID-19 pandemic, which hit unexceptionally everyone from citizen to organization, from student to startup. Secondly, unlike the causation method, where individuals start scratching together the resources they need to reach a pre-given goal, the effectuation approach encourages more individuals to start up with what they have at hand. Thirdly, the effectuation approach encourages creativity which is crucial for a decision making. Whether it is COVID-19 pandemic or war in Europe in the twenty-first century, it is important to learn to deal with uncertainty. The principle of affordable loss, which is applied in effectual reasoning, can help here by rather acting on what a person is willing to lose instead of focusing on what can be achieved if the project succeeds. Hence effectual reasoning can help reduce the cost of failure and in an EE context help to prepare students to act entrepreneurial, by thinking differently, staying more flexible and learning to deal with uncertainty. Being aware of viable loss might help young people to control for their risk. The trial-and-error approach, with many iterations, is a process that is closer to optimizing the product and more responsive to the needs of the target audience. In the same vein with Neck and Greene (2011), we argue that entrepreneurship education in HEIs should focus on how to act, learn and build in an unknown future on the basis of the effectuation approach.

Entrepreneurial Mindset

Drawing from the current state of entrepreneurship literature, a vast pool of definitions of the EM can be identified. This leads back to the fact that even for the concept of entrepreneurship many different definitions exist. In order to provide a suitable definition for the term EM, it is crucial to understand the context of investigation such as the content to be taught in the courses that eventually gets measured. McGrath and MacMillan (2000) firstly defined the entrepreneurial mindset as a way of thinking "that enables adaptable decision making; a mindset that is both self-reflective and self-regulatory, and that allows the individual to think beyond biases embedded in existing sense-making mechanisms to appropriately interpret the cause–effect relationships represented by environmental feedback". McMullen and Kier (2016) stressed that EM is an "ability to identify and exploit opportunities without regard to the resources currently under their control", which means that entrepreneurial activity has risks to some extent. Shepherd et al. (2010) explained EM as an "ability and willingness of individuals to rapidly sense, act, and mobilize in response to a judgement decision under uncertainty about a possible opportunity for gain". Besides the exploration, identification and exploitation of entrepreneurial opportunities there is also the aspect of creating such opportunities according the effectuation approach.

Following the latter, we understand the EM as a set of qualities and competencies that help future entrepreneurs to deal with and within circumstances of an unforeseeable and unsecure future (Neck et al., 2021). More recent works offer typologies for the entrepreneurial mindset (Larsen, 2022) or, as in Chap. 2 of this book, a taxonomy of the entrepreneurial mindset (Krohn et al., 2021), calling out for a more interdisciplinary understanding of mindsets, where parameters of the interconnected concepts of innovation and entrepreneurship are included.

The definition and measurement of EM is important as it is closely linked to what entrepreneurship educators actually teach. As a kind of metacognition, the entrepreneurial mindset can be improved through EE programs and can be considered as a mind habit that requires learning to shape (Schmidt & Ford, 2003). EM closes the gap between teaching and learning, e.g., creative problem-solving, optimism and resilience (Schulte, 2019). A recent study argues for the positive and significant impact of EM on the individual attitude and behaviour, in particular recognizing opportunity and creating new ideas (Kuratko & Morris, 2018, Schulte, 2019). Moreover, the EM is influenced by the context, spanning from the organizational to the spatial, that generates more complexity (Kuratko et al., 2021). EM is closely related to the concept of a growth mindset (Dweck, 2007), where the ability and willingness to learn, also from mistakes and failures, is crucial (Neck et al., 2021).

Against the background of effectuation, EM as an individual's way of thinking or an ability to capture or create entrepreneurial opportunities faced with an uncertain future – plays an important role on how individuals collaborate with others. A recent German Startup Monitor revealed that more than 60% of successful entrepreneurs rather collaborate than compete (German Startup Monitor, 2020). This is a direct link to knowledge sharing as presented in the context of an OIM. Innovation is known for being connected to entrepreneurial activity. To date there is no clarity about the relation between the (open) innovation and the entrepreneurial mindset. Krohn et al. (2021) point out that innovation and entrepreneurship in themselves are two distinct and yet synergetic phenomena (Kahn, 2022). It is yet to be answered what the nature of the relationship between the (open) innovation mindset and the entrepreneurial mindset is. Despite the awareness of this unanswered question this investigation takes an OIM measurement tool as a starting point. According to Engelsberger et al. (2021), the concept of an open innovation mindset (OIM) can be captured by assessing the already above-mentioned elements: openness to experience, positive attitudes towards knowledge sharing and sourcing (KSS), risk and failure tolerance, creativity and integrative complexity. To adapt this already existing measure to this current study and the context of EE and EM, the authors have added three components of an entrepreneurial mindset that represent elements of the effectuation approach to the measurement tool: entrepreneurial uncertainty, entrepreneurial creation and collaboration.

11.3 Research Setting and Methods

Research Setting

The objective in the present chapter is to investigate entrepreneurial mindset changes and assessing the applicability of the measurement method. The following section explains the specific context and settings of the research designs.

For a long time, the German-Danish border region has been perceived as peripheral, with poor infrastructure and far removed from everything else (Lorenz et al., 2018). While the European startup hotspots like Berlin and Copenhagen have attracted growing attention, it took until 2009 for the Northern Federal State of Schleswig-Holstein to start gathering resources on EE in Higher Education to facilitate entrepreneurial activity among students. Since then, various third-party public funding has had an impact on the establishment of an on campus, cross-university entrepreneurship centre, culminating in the current project @ventureDock. @ventureDock is, funded by BMWK,[1] a joint project of the Europe-University of Flensburg and the University of Applied Sciences Flensburg on Entrepreneurship Education. This unique project on inter-university and interdisciplinary entrepreneurship education does not only target the culmination of startup projects, but particularly aims to initiate a mindset change among a wide range of students from diverse disciplines. Especially non-business students are addressed to reach entrepreneurial potential that to date had not been addressed. This is based on the idea of entrepreneurship being a life skill rather than a business skill. A newly developed

[1] Federal Ministry for Economy and Climate protection.

curricular course is called "Entrepreneurial @Venture – Create your Future!". It is an elective course with five ECTS and open to students of all disciplines (currently 20 study programs) to shape their future. Built on the effectuation approach, this seminar provides insights into the "from problem identification to solution pitch" process enriched with diverse design thinking methods. The seminar aims to promote the entrepreneurial mindset, ultimately enable innovation, growth and mindshift of participants, particularly those coming from non-business disciplines. These learning and development goals are not only useful for starting a new venture, but also make a significant contribution to identifying problems in general and being able to solve them in creative and innovative manner. Eventually it is about enabling students to deal with VUCA (Volatility, Uncertainty, Complexity und Ambiguity) in their everyday life. In the long run it is supposed to enhance young people's employability by equipping them with skills they and potential employers need to ensure a company's innovative competitiveness.

The course additionally contains a peer-mentoring aspect through a student cooperation with University of Southern Denmark, living up to the project slogan "collaboration instead of competition".

For the curricular group projects, the lecturer assigns interdisciplinary groups in advance. Students work in those inter disciplinary groups throughout the seminar sessions and have the chance to arrange flexible consultation appointments with the lecturers regarding the group projects. The content and type of group project is open, it is recommended though, to develop concepts that are rooted in the students' resources.

The seminar begins with an introduction of basic concepts on entrepreneurship and entrepreneurial behaviour. Then the groups identify problems or anomalies in their everyday life and examine them from diverse perspectives in the second session. Based on the knowledge gained, (innovative) ideas will be generated supported by creative and design thinking methods in the third session. These ideas are converted into prototypes in the fourth session. Empathy map and persona help students to sharpen their value proposition. In the fifth session, students learn the basics of storytelling and pitching, which will take a place in the final session. All groups present their projects in the final joint session in front of juries. Juries consist of researchers, practitioners, local politicians and investors. Throughout the whole process students are invited to continuously reflect on the sessions and instructed to keep learning logbooks.

Data Acquisition and Measurement Tool

The following section presents a novel tool for tracking students mindset development and the change of each EM element in particular throughout a semester.

The data collected in this study stem from the OMindset evaluation monthly report and online survey data which was conducted from the first and the last session of the curricular course.

OI mindset (Engelsberger et al., 2021, 2022) is made up of the following 6 dimensions: *openness, creativity, positive attitude towards KSS, risk and failure tolerance, and integrative complexity*. Openness consists of ten items. A sample item for openness is "I see myself as someone who is original, comes up with new ideas" (John & Srivastava, 1999). Creativity consists of 13 items. A sample item for creativity is "I suggest new ways to achieve goals or objectives" (Zhou & George, 2001). Positive attitudes towards KSS based on the NIH syndrome[2] consists of nine items. A sample item is "I like to work with nonrelated or less related subject area" (Bergmann & Golla, 2020). Positive attitudes towards KSS based on the NSH syndrome[3] consists of four items. A sample item is "I have negative attitudes to having other partners receiving and using my knowledge and technology" (Burcharth et al., 2014). Risk tolerance consists of eight items. A sample item is "I enjoy taking risks in most aspects of my life" (Zhang et al., 2019). Failure tolerance consists of four items. A sample item is "I understand when you try something new, you sometimes fail (reverse scored)" (Danneels, 2008). Finally, for integrative complexity, respondents were asked to list arguments supporting the use for knowledge exchange across organizations ("pro") (Carroll & Bright, 2010; Czaja et al., 2016). They were also asked to list arguments against supporting the use for knowledge exchange across organizations ("con").

These components of the OI mindset were then extended by three dimensions: *entrepreneurial uncertainty, entrepreneurial creation and collaboration* based on Sarasvathy's effectuation approach (Sarasvathy, 2001) to capture the EM. Entrepreneurial uncertainty actually relates to how students deal with uncertainty. One of two sample items covering entrepreneurial uncertainty is "I am not intimidated by uncertainty". Entrepreneurial creation consists of two items as well, what "I feel capable to develop solutions to problems" is one example for this. "I am able to involve and convince people of my ideas" is one of two sample items for collaboration. All items for these three dimensions were formulated based on and according the four principles of effectuation and the along critical steps of the iterative dynamic effectuation process (Sarasvathy, 2001). Here collaboration and entrepreneurial creation are related to dealing with uncertainty.

The EM can be captured using the OMindset evaluation tool developed by OMIND platform GmbH that measures the mindset development over time as well as tracks the students' knowledge exchange in real time. Hence, this tool supports us tracking the changes of specific EM elements (KSS) during the EE programs on the individual level.

Particularly the study analyses how a joint interdisciplinary EE program by two universities shapes the individual EM before, during and after the program.

The evaluation questionnaire consists of 30 items altogether.

---

[2] In the face of open innovation, employees may exhibit a tendency to reject new ideas from outsiders, the so-called "Not-Invented-Here" (NIH) syndrome (Antons et al., 2017; Katz & Allen, 1982).

[3] In the face of open innovation, employees may have negative attitudes towards the sharing of internally developed knowledge, the so-called "Not-Sold-Here" (NSH) syndrome (Burcharth et al., 2014).

In total, 95 students participated in the OMindset evaluation throughout the semester and completed two online surveys before and after four interdisciplinary curricular entrepreneurship courses[4] at two German universities – Europe-University Flensburg and Flensburg University of Applied Sciences – offered in two languages (GER and ENG) from September 2021 to February 2022.

The interactive digital course in the fall semester 2021/2022 consisted of six online tutoring sessions, self-study, coaching and mentoring support and hands-on assignments. The tasks were organized as group works, some individual reflection tasks were incorporated. Students were guided through an entrepreneurial journey, from entrepreneurial theory to design thinking methods, prototyping, concept creation and a final pitch. The total workload was 92 h including 24 h of online tutoring sessions, 24 h of self-study and 24 h of group assignments, plus 10 preparation hours of pitch presentation and an individual portfolio.

Spring semester 2022 was made up of the same curriculum but took place in presence on campus.

This research approach and data set is a pioneer attempt in the field of EE research and allows us to visualize the impact of EE on the individual mindset change. All participating students in the EE program received an OMindset evaluation access link after the first and the last seminar of the course. Students were invited to evaluate their entrepreneurial mindset before and after going through the entrepreneurial journey. In addition to the two assessments, students received a link to the knowledge sourcing and sharing (KSS) tracker. As Engelsberger et al. identified KSS to be decisive in executing (open) innovative behaviour measuring KSS is a key aspect also related to entrepreneurial mindset and behaviour. Sending out a KSS tracker link directly after class is meant to keep the evaluation as much as a real-time measurement as possible.

Data Analysis and Results

The data analysis collected via the OMindset evaluation tool supports that interdisciplinary entrepreneurship programs have a direct effect on individual mindset changes in terms of openness to experience, positive attitudes towards knowledge sharing and sourcing, risk and failure tolerance, creativity, integrative complexity, dealing with uncertainty, creation and collaboration (Engelsberger et al., 2021). Figure 11.1 displays the changes of nine EM components measured after the first and the last sessions of interdisciplinary entrepreneurship program in winter semester 2021/2022 with an aggregate number of students of 95. Respondent ratio was initially low and decreasing over the semester (from seminar 1 to 6), which lead to the low number of totals.

[4] Two interdisciplinary Bachelor courses and two Master's courses with identical course contents and time schedule.

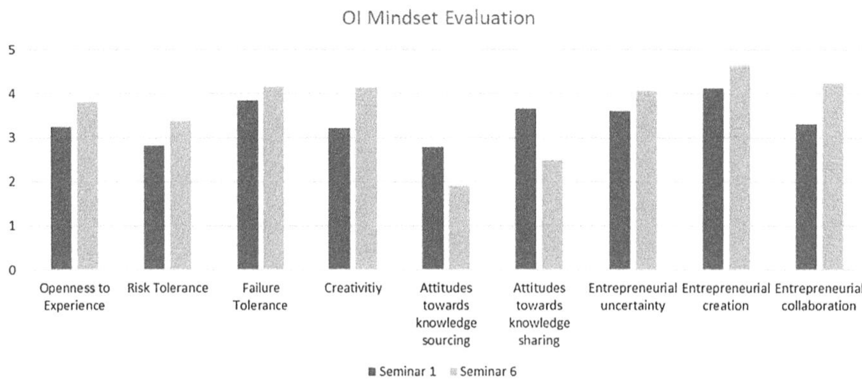

Fig. 11.1 OMindset evaluation result from winter semester 2021/2022. (Source: OMIND Consulting *seminar 1 ($n = 31$) seminar 6 ($n = 6$))

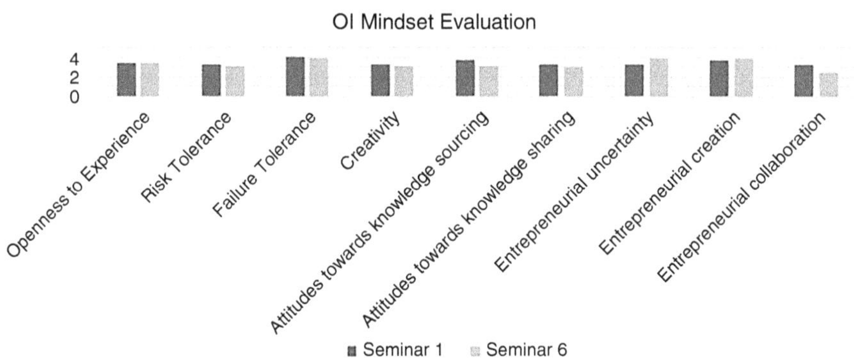

Fig. 11.2 OMindset evaluation result from summer semester 2022. (Source: OMIND Consulting seminar 1 ($n = 6$), seminar 6 ($n = 11$))

However, it could be observed that openness to experience, risk tolerance, failure tolerance, creativity, entrepreneurial creation and entrepreneurial collaboration changed positively once participants completed the first and the last session EE program.

Figure 11.1 shows the OMIND data from the summer semester 2022. Entrepreneurial uncertainty and entrepreneurial creation of participants changed as they attended the EE program throughout the semester. A common EM component which changed in both winter and summer semester is entrepreneurial creation.

Since the EE program during the winter semester completely took place online due to the pandemic circumstances from September 2021 to February 2022 and in presence in summer semester from March to July 2022, it does not allow us to compare two data sources directly. However, both EE programs, either online or presence format, had a positive effect on individual's entrepreneurial creation (Fig. 11.2).

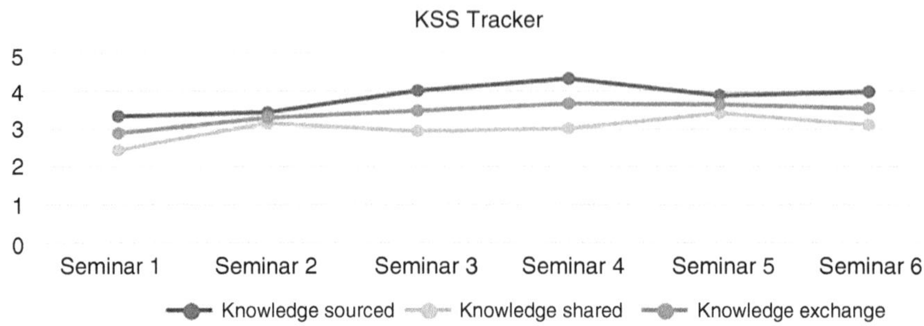

Fig. 11.3 KSS tracking winter semester 2021/2022. (Source: OMIND Consulting; (n = 16))

With openness to experience, the student's readiness to try new things and apply different approaches is captured. This is closely related to the student's tolerance to take a risk while trying something new without knowing whether it will succeed or not. The failure tolerance is more related to the student's ability to forgive himself/herself a mistake when done. Integrative complexity shows the student's ability to view different perspectives of one problem commonly known as "seeing both sides of a coin". This is important in relation to changing perspectives and being able to empathize with others. The positive attitudes towards knowledge sharing – the readiness to share one's own knowledge – seem to be decreased over time. A possible explanation can be that the students felt they were in a competitive situation.

The KSS tracker, which measures attitudes towards knowledge sharing, sourcing and exchange of participants, also demonstrates the changes of individual's attitudes. As participants go through our EE program, their overall attitudes towards knowledge sharing, sourcing and exchange increased during the winter semester (Fig. 11.3). The number of students using the KSS tracker was more stable than with the EM self-assessment tool.

In the following semester, the overall attitudes towards knowledge sharing also increased, as participants attended the six sessions of the interdisciplinary EE program during the semester (Fig. 11.4).[5] The attitudes towards knowledge sharing of all EE program participants – both in winter semester 2021/2022 and summer semester 2022 – increased during the EE program.

11.4 Limitations and Concluding Observations

We are aware of two main limitations of our study. First, the participation rate of each survey was different. Students received an invitation email with a hyperlink to OMIND evaluation and the KSS tracker once they completed the EE seminar. The

[5] Since OMIND Consulting renewed its measuring tool after the winter semester, only two tendencies (attitudes towards knowledge sharing and sourcing) were tracked in the second semester.

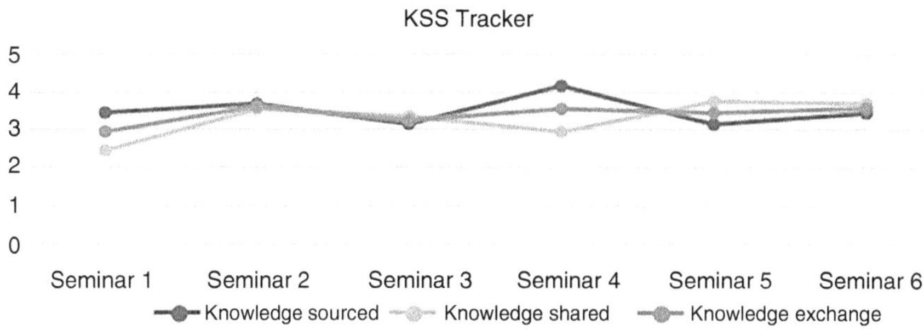

Fig. 11.4 KSS tracking summer semester 2022. (Source: OMIND Consulting; (n = 50))

invitation was valid 14 days. Once the authors and three further EE program instructors received the OMIND evaluation results of the winter semester 2021/2022, they decided to let students perform OMIND evaluation and KSS tracker during the class, not after the class, to increase a participation rate of OMIND evaluation and KSS tracker. Therefore, students received an invitation email with a link to OMIND evaluation and the KSS tracker as the EE seminar started, so they could complete the survey during the seminar. Second, each participant is required to insert a personal code before starting to answer OMIND evaluation questions. A personal code is necessary to collect and compare individuals' responses before and after the EE program. However, 75% of student from the winter semester 2021/2022 misunderstood how to create an individual code by themselves, albeit a detailed instruction and an example of creating a personal code were clearly given. The authors noted that and made it easier to create a personal code by combining two alphabet letters and two numbers. Third, real-time measurement for the winter semester 2021/2022 was restricted as participants received the hyperlink for the KSS tracker after the seminar. OMIND extended the accesses time up to 24 h after the seminar and the time point at when the participant inserted data was not recorded. The extension of access time to KSS tracker much improved for the summer semester (Fig. 11.4) by sending the hyperlink for the KSS tracker 30 min prior to the ending of the seminar. It allowed the participants to complete data transfer much shorter than in the winter semester 2021/2022, thus enhanced the accuracy of the real-time mindset measurement.

In sum, we provided the first quantitative data on the impact of EE on individual mindset change by using OMIND evaluation tool and KSS tracker. An important implication for policy makers and EE practitioners is that EE can have direct effect on individual mindset changes and the discrepancy through EE program can be designed by means of the university. Additionally, given the direct impact of EE on EM it is valid to argue that EE fosters opportunities for new venture creation on campuses, mind-set change, critical thinking and problem solving indeed. The results given based on an interdisciplinary course also underline the importance and opportunity EE has in relation to address students that are widely not seen as being typically entrepreneurial. With the program it is possible to include students from different disciplines and with diverse backgrounds and levels of experience. The EM assessment also helps smaller universities with less tech-oriented studies argue for alternative KPI in terms of goals of EE. It empowers more inclusive approaches to EE. This is of special interest if long term and multiplier effects that influence a (remote) region's competitiveness more indirectly are considered.

References

Antons, D., Declerck, M., Diener, K., Koch, I., & Piller, F. T. (2017). Assessing the not-invented-here syndrome: Development and validation of implicit and explicit measurements. *Journal of Organizational Behavior, 38*(8), 1227–1245.

Bergmann, H., & Golla, S. (2020). Unternehmertum an Hochschulen in Deutschland – Ergebnisse des Global University Entrepreneurial Spirit Students' Survey (GUESS) 2018/2019.

Brock, D. D., & Kim, M. (2011). Social entrepreneurship education resource handbook. *SSRN Electronic Journal, 115*(2), 715. https://doi.org/10.2139/ssrn.1872088

Bijedić, T. (2019). Begriffliche und disziplinäre Genese der Entrepreneurship Education (English title: Conceptual and disciplinary genesis of entrepreneurship education). In *Entrepreneurship education* (pp. 21–40). Springer Gabler. (in German).

Carroll, J., & Bright, A. (2010). Integrative complexity of public beliefs toward wildfire management: Development of a scale. *Journal of Applied Social Psychology, 40*(2), 344–359.

Chen, Chao C./Greene, Patricia G./Crick, Ann (1998), Does entrepreneurial self-efficacy distinguish entrepreneurs from managers?, Journal of Business Venturing, 13, 295–316.

Czaja, M. R., Bright, A. D., & Cottrell, S. P. (2016). Integrative complexity, beliefs, and attitudes: Application to prescribed fire. *Forest Policy and Economics, 62*, 54–61.

de Araújo Burcharth, A. L., Knudsen, M. P., & Søndergaard, H. A. (2014). Neither invented nor shared here: The impact and management of attitudes for the adoption of open innovation practices. *Technovation, 34*(3), 149–161.

Danneels, E. (2008). Organizational antecedents of second-order competences. *Strategic Management Journal, 29*(5), 519–543.

Dweck, C., (2007). Mindset The New Psychology of Success, Ballantine/Penguin Random House, Updated Edition.

Ebbers, I. (2019). Entrepreneurship Education als Möglichkeits- und Ermöglichungsraum – eine erste theoretische Annäherung aus fachdidaktischer Perspektive. In T. Bijedić, I. Ebbers, & B. Halbfas (Eds.), *Entrepreneurship education: Begriff – Theorie – Verständnis* (pp. 43–61). Wiesbaden.

Engelsberger, A., Cavanagh, J., Bartram, T., & Halvorsen, B. (2021). *Multicultural skills in open innovation: Relational leadership enabling knowledge sourcing and sharing*. Personnel Review.

Engelsberger, A., Halvorsen, B., Cavanagh, J., & Bartram, T. (2022). Human resources management and open innovation: The role of open innovation mindset. *Asia Pacific Journal of Human Resources, 60*(1), 194–215.

European Parliament and the Commission of the European Union. (2006). *Empfehlung des europäischen Parlaments und des Rates (in German).*

Fayolle, A. (Ed.). (2018). *A research agenda for entrepreneurship education*. Edward Elgar Publishing.

German Startup Monitor. (2020). *Deutscher startup monitor 2018*. Startups eV, B. D., & Deutschland, P.

Halbfas, B., & Liszt-Rohlf, V. (2019). Entwicklungslinien und Perspektiven der Entrepreneurship Education – eine Analyse von Definitionen. In T. Bijedić, I. Ebbers, & B. Halbfas (Eds.), *Entrepreneurship education: Begriff – Theorie – Verständnis* (pp. 3–20). Wiesbaden.

John, O. P., & Srivastava, S. (1999). *The Big-Five trait taxonomy: History, measurement, and theoretical perspectives.*
Kahn, K. B. (2022). Innovation is not entrepreneurship, nor vice versa. *Journal of Product Innovation Management, 39*(4), 467–473.
Katz, R., & TJ Allen (1982). Investigating the Not Invented Here (NIH) syndrome: a look at the performance, tenure, and communication patterns of 50 R&D Project Groups. *R&D Management 12*(1), 7–20.
Kickul, J., Wilson, F., Marlino, D., & Barbosa, S. D. (2008). Are misalignments of perceptions and self-efficacy causing gender gaps in entrepreneurial intentions among our nation's teens? *Journal of Small Business and Enterprise Development, 15*(2), 321–335.
Krohn, M., Hattenbergb, D. Y., Kruegerc, N. F., & Herstatta, C. (2021). A taxonomy of mindset – Unlocking the synergies of innovation and entrepreneurship through mindset-based perspectives. In *Innovation and product management conference.*
Krueger Jr., Norris F./Carsrud, Alan L. (1993). Entrepreneurial Intentions: Applying the theory of planned behaviour, *Entrepreneurship & Regional Development: An International Journal, 5*:4, S. 315–330.
Kuratko, D. F., & Morris, M. H. (2018). Corporate entrepreneurship: A critical challenge for educators and researchers. *Entrepreneurship Education and Pedagogy, 1*(1), 42–60.
Kuratko, D. F., Fisher, G., & Audretsch, D. B. (2021). Unraveling the entrepreneurial mindset. *Small Business Economics, 57*(4), 1681–1691.
Larsen, I. B. (2022). Fostering an entrepreneurial mindset: A typology for aligning instructional strategies with three dominant entrepreneurial mindset conceptualizations. *Industry and Higher Education, 36*(3), 236–251.
Lorenz, C., Egerer, J., & Gerbaulet, C. (2018). Cross-border cooperation in the European context: Evidence from regional cooperation initiatives. In *Energiewende "Made in Germany"* (pp. 319–344). Springer.
McGrath, R., & MacMillan, I. (2000). *The entrepreneurial mindset.* Harvard Business School Press.
McMullen, J. S., & Kier, A. S. (2016). Trapped by the entrepreneurial mindset: Opportunity seeking and escalation of commitment in the Mount Everest disaster. *Journal of Business Venturing, 31*(6), 663–686.
Nabi, G., Liñán, F., Fayolle, A., Krueger, N., & Walmsley, A. (2017). The impact of entrepreneurship education in higher education: A systematic review and research agenda. *Academy of Management Learning & Education, 16*(2), 277–299.
Naia, A., Baptista, R., Januário, C., & Trigo, V. (2014). A systematization of the literature on entrepreneurship education: Challenges and emerging solutions in the entrepreneurial classroom. *Industry and Higher Education, 28*, 79–96.
Neck, H. M., & Greene, P. G. (2011). Entrepreneurship education: Known worlds and new frontiers. *Journal of Small Business Management, 49*(1), 55–70.
Neck, H. M., Brush, C. G., & Greene, P. G. (2021). Introduction to teaching entrepreneurship. In *Teaching entrepreneurship* (Vol. 2). Edward Elgar Publishing.
Neck, H. M., Neck, C. P., & Murray, E. L. (2020). *Entrepreneurship: The practice and mindset* (2nd ed.). Sage Publications.
Pittaway, L., & Edwards, C. (2012). Assessment: Examining practice in entrepreneurship education. *Education + Training, 54*(8/9), 778–800.
Pittaway, L., & Cope, J. (2007). Entrepreneurship education: A systematic review of the evidence. *International small business journal, 25*(5), 479–510.
Sarasvathy, Saras D. (2001), Causation and Effectuation: Toward a TheoreticalShift from Economic Inevitability to Entrepreneurial Contingency, *Academyof Management Review*, Vol. 26, Nr. 3, S. 243–263.
Sarasvathy, S. D., & Dew, N. (2005). New market creation through transformation. *Journal of Evolutionary Economics, 15*(5), 533–565.
Sarasvathy, S. D. (2006). What makes entrepreneurs entrepreneurial? *SSRN Electronic Journal.*

Sarasvathy, Saras D. (2008). What Makes Entrepreneurs Entrepreneurial?. Darden Case No. UVA-ENT-0065, Available at SSRN: https://ssrn.com/abstract=909038 or http://dx.doi.org/10.2139/ssrn.909038.

Schmidt, A. M., & Ford, J. K. (2003). Learning within a learner control training environment: The interactive effects of goal orientation and metacognitive instruction on learning outcomes. *Personnel Psychology, 56*(2), 405–429.

Schulte, B. (2019). *Unternehmensnachfolgen und Entrepreneurship Education*. Springer Fachmedien Wiesbaden. (in German).

Shepherd, D. A., Patzelt, H., & Haynie, J. M. (2010). Entrepreneurial spirals: Deviationamplifying loops of an entrepreneurial mindset and organizational culture. *Entrepreneurship: Theory and Practice, 34*(1), 59–82.

Stovang, P., & Nielsen, S. L. (2015). DesUni: University entrepreneurship education through design thinking. *Education +Training, 57*(8/9), 977–991.

Zhang, D. C., Highhouse, S., & Nye, C. D. (2019). Development and validation of the general risk propensity scale (GRiPS). *Journal of Behavioral Decision Making, 32*(2), 152–167.

Zhou, J., & George, J. M. (2001). When job dissatisfaction leads to creativity: Encouraging the expression of voice. *Academy of Management journal, 44*(4), 682–696.

Chapter 12
On the Opportunities of the Effectuation Approach and Design Thinking in Heterogeneity-Driven Teaching and Learning Contexts

Florian Frenz

12.1 Introduction

Since the ratification of the UN Convention on the Rights of Persons with Disabilities in 2006, inclusion has been considered a societal task (Wiepcke, 2019, 194). Although there had been previous discussions on inclusion and dealing with heterogeneity (Ackermann, 2015, 34), the UN Convention on the Rights of Persons with Disabilities provides additional legitimacy to the ongoing discourse and particularly formulates the right of persons with disabilities to inclusive education (Dumont, 2019, 250). As a result, special needs schools are increasingly being abolished and inclusive schools are being established, leading to a paradigm shift in educational pedagogy and educational practice. This promotes viewing differences among learners not as problems but as ordinary realities and even as resources for learning (ibid.). However, this idealistic notion poses various challenges for instructional practice.

Budde (2017, 14 f.) argues that schools were traditionally seen as homogenizing institutions and now must engage with learner heterogeneity. This results in the need for instruction to be tailored to the individual needs of learners (Becker & Keller, 2022, 406) rather than following a curriculum that aims to provide the same education to all learners, regardless of their starting points, in order to achieve high levels of homogeneity in performance. These efforts to homogenize are evident in Germany through the establishment of different types of schools aimed at creating homogeneous performance groups (Dumont, 2019, 250). Hence, educational policy, school system, and instructional developments require teachers to conceptually, didactically, and interactively deal with heterogeneity in their professional daily

F. Frenz (✉)
Europe-University Flensburg, Flensburg, Germany
e-mail: florian.frenz@uni-flensburg.de

K. Mikkelsen, A. Wolf (eds.), *Minds, Brains, and Doxa for Inclusive Entrepreneurship*, International Studies in Entrepreneurship 47,
https://doi.org/10.1007/978-3-031-50164-7_12

lives (Bohl, 2017, 257). Consequently, various interdisciplinary strategies and response approaches for dealing with heterogeneity in the school and educational context have emerged and will be further explored in this chapter.

Entrepreneurship education is equally confronted with the developments mentioned above regarding a productive handling of heterogeneity, which fosters entrepreneurial activity. It not only gains increasing relevance in discussions on economic policy and regional development but also within general education (Bijedić, 2019, 22). Entrepreneurship education, which generally aims to foster creativity and innovation in all contexts of everyday life (Ebbers, 2014, 171), must inevitably grapple with its opportunities and challenges in teaching and learning contexts shaped by heterogeneity, given its increasing practical relevance in schools. This chapter aims to provide a foundation for further discussions and debates on heterogeneity-sensitive entrepreneurship education and addresses the following question:

How can entrepreneurship education thrive in heterogeneity-driven teaching and learning contexts?

To explore this question, the following chapter will examine perspectives on heterogeneity in the educational context, with a particular focus on the various forms of response that teachers can employ to address heterogeneity. Furthermore, a positioning within the constructivist learning theory will be established, emphasizing individual-oriented rather than collective-oriented instructional orientation. The subsequent third subsection will delve into perspectives on entrepreneurship education, particularly in the context of school education. It will first trace the development of the concept of entrepreneurship education, followed by an exploration of the effectuation approach by Saras D. Sarasvathy (2001) as a cognitive orientation and design thinking as a methodological-conceptual framework. The discussions from subsections two and three will be integrated in the subsequent fourth subsection to demonstrate possibilities for conceptualizing entrepreneurship education using the effectuation approach and design thinking in heterogeneity-driven teaching and learning contexts. In the concluding fifth subsection, the findings regarding the initial question will be summarized, leading to an outlook on challenges and resulting research opportunities.

12.2 Perspectives on Heterogeneity in the Educational Context

First and foremost, it should be noted that, in an international context, the term “heterogeneity” is often replaced by the term “diversity” (Hummrich, 2017, 159). Within the scope of this article, the term “heterogeneity” is used to refer to any form of diversity and difference. As previously mentioned, the ratification of the UN Convention on the Rights of Persons with Disabilities has led to an increasing political legitimization of inclusive education for individuals with disabilities (Dumont, 2019, 250). Special schools are being phased out, and mainstream schools are being oriented towards inclusion. This development involves a shift in perspective that focuses on the differences among learners not as a problem but as a normal aspect and even as a resource for learning (ibid.). The goal is not to adapt individuals with disabilities to existing societal conditions, but rather to modify societal conditions to accept heterogeneity (Ackermann, 2015, 33). However, Ackermann (2015, 34) also points out that the ratification of the UN Convention on the Rights of Persons with Disabilities has led, in some instances, to a simplification of the discourse on heterogeneity. There are two coexisting debates: one focuses on the inclusion of individuals with disabilities, thereby setting up a continuum between disabled and non-disabled in the recognition of heterogeneity. The other debate, which predates the UN Convention on the Rights of Persons with Disabilities, is conducted from a social science perspective and focuses less on the concept of inclusion and more on the concept of exclusion, considering social divisions of all kinds (ibid.). According to this debate, the concept of heterogeneity includes disability but does not end there. According to Budde (2017, 14), concepts of heterogeneity are based on super-individual differences. Typically, socio-cultural difference categories such as gender, ethnicity, social background, and disability are meant, which play a significant role in individuals' socialization. At the same time, within the context of education, heterogeneity also refers to ability-related differences among learners, which are primarily understood as individual abilities (ibid.). It is essential to recognize that teachers encounter a multitude of learners in their classrooms, each with different learning prerequisites and needs. This inevitably raises the question of how to address this heterogeneity in everyday classroom practice (Fellmann, 2016, 87).

In this regard, it should be noted that the discourse (in education) as a whole has shifted from homogenization efforts towards a focus on heterogeneity (Budde, 2017, 13). It appears that the discourse has at least recognized the need to orient instruction towards individual learners, acknowledging that learners differ in various characteristics and that these characteristics influence teaching and learning processes. Against this backdrop, general education systems are confronted with the challenge of meeting the needs of learners in accordance with the existing heterogeneity in order to enable optimal development for all learners (Dumont, 2019, 250). Initially, four forms of response to heterogeneity in instructional practice can be identified. The most common form, especially in the German school system, is the passive response of ignoring learning and performance differences. This passive form of response should not necessarily be attributed to ill will but rather to a lack of time and the capacity to fully grasp heterogeneity in classrooms, resulting in a failure to address existing heterogeneity (Wischer, 2009, 1). The second, more substitutive form of response is to adapt learners to the requirements of instruction. Two approaches can be distinguished in this regard. On the one hand, it is possible to reduce different learning prerequisites in advance by forming homogeneous learning groups. On the other hand, there is the option of using special programs to enable weaker learners to meet instructional requirements (ibid.). These first two forms of response to heterogeneity can be related to the homogenization tendencies described by Budde (2017, 13). The third form of response describes an active approach to dealing with heterogeneity. In this case, instruction is adapted to the relevant differences among learners by providing differentiated learning opportunities (Wischer, 2009, 1). The fourth form of response involves designing instruction to specifically support individual learners through adaptive teaching methods in quiet and exercise phases, as well as promoting differentiated learning objectives (ibid.).

While passive and substitutive forms of response to heterogeneity were predominant in the German school system, criticism of such approaches to dealing with heterogeneity in instruction has grown, particularly in the 2000s and 2010s. This criticism proves to be multifactorial (ibid., 1 f.). In particular, the differences between strong and weak learners are highly dependent on social background (ibid.). Additionally, there has been an increased public perception, among both the general population and teachers, that heterogeneity in society is on the rise (ibid.). Plausible reasons for this include globalization movements and societal processes of individualization (ibid.). From an educational perspective, continuing reform pedagogical tendencies can be observed, which emphasize viewing learners as individuals who have a claim to be recognized and supported in their individuality (ibid.).

Against the backdrop of these insights, a shift towards a constructivist learning theory focused on the individual learner and the corresponding didactics can be observed (Fellmann, 2016, 87). Heterogeneity should be seen not as a burden but as an opportunity to be utilized (ibid.). This requires a change in perspective from the teacher to the learner (ibid., 89). From the teacher's perspective, this involves individualization and differentiation, which presuppose attributions by the teacher. From the learner's perspective, it assumes that teaching and learning processes are co-constructed and co-directed by the learners themselves, incorporating social and cooperative learning (ibid.). An orientation towards the learner personalizes learning, making it a personal matter (ibid.). However, such a reorientation comes with various challenges and does not mean that teachers are relieved of their responsibilities as educators in the classroom. Both the learners, in terms of their learning experiences, and the teachers, in terms of their instructional practices, are challenged (ibid., 89 f.). Teachers must have a basic trust in learners' learning processes while also developing good tasks that encourage thinking, interpretation, and reflection (ibid.). Learners, in turn, need to build confidence in their own abilities and acquire learning competencies to organize their individual learning as independently as possible (ibid.).

In conclusion, it can be stated, in line with Wischer (2009, 7), that individualization and differentiation are not equally suitable for all learners. Therefore, open-ended instruction and direct instruction should not be pitted against each other (ibid.). Empirical evidence suggests that a combination of differentiating approaches and direct instruction without further differentiation is promising (ibid.). In any case, the following questions, as proposed by Wischer (2009, 7), need to be addressed when providing teaching and learning opportunities in heterogeneous contexts:

1. Do all learners possess the necessary competencies to make use of an open-ended approach?
2. What additional structuring learning aids are necessary?
3. In what way can these aids be provided?

12.3 Perspectives on Entrepreneurship Education

Entrepreneurship is an ongoing relevant topic in economic policy discussions, regional development, research, as well as education and upbringing (Bijedić, 2019, 22). In line with the aforementioned relevance, the present chapter aims to provide approaches for a discussion on heterogeneity-sensitive entrepreneurship education. Particularly, considering the increasing significance of entrepreneurship education in general schooling (Wiepcke, 2019, 194), the discourse on this subject inevitably needs to address the field of heterogeneity and inclusion, also, even if not only, in the light of a self-strengthening male dominance in entrepreneurship (Hägg et al., 2022, 4). To this end, this chapter will first examine the developmental lines of entrepreneurship education that have ultimately led to the current subject-oriented understanding of the concept. Subsequently, an exploration of whether entrepreneurship competencies can be learned will be conducted, with reference to Saras D. Sarasvathy's effectuation approach. The chapter concludes with a general overview of design thinking as a prominent means to methodically and conceptually implement entrepreneurship education.

First and foremost, it should be noted that there is no definitive definition for entrepreneurship education, much like for entrepreneurship itself. On the contrary, the combination of the already controversial term "entrepreneurship" with the equally unresolved term "education" seems to further complicate the definition (Halbfas & Liszt-Rohlf, 2019, 4). For this reason, Brigitte Halbfas and Verena Liszt-Rohlf (2019, 8 f.) have traced the definitional development of entrepreneurship education over the past 30 years and identified four phases. Especially the positioning of contemporary definitions on a continuum between using entrepreneurship education to foster venture creation on one side and using entrepreneurship education to foster problem-solving-oriented, innovative, and creative entrepreneurial thinking and action represents a relevant perspective.

The first phase, from 1987 to 1999, particularly in the German-speaking region, showed a very limited conceptual exploration of entrepreneurship education, with the primary understanding focusing on qualification for starting a venture (ibid.). The second phase of definitional development can be identified from the turn of the millennium until 2003, during which an increase in definitional discussions can be observed (ibid.). In this period, a shift towards the individual occurred, and the existing definitions specifically dealt with a subject-oriented qualification for entrepreneurship rather than an object-oriented qualification focusing on venture-creation of the entrepreneurial subject, signifying a transition from an object-oriented to a subject-oriented approach (ibid.). The third phase, from 2004 to 2007, can be pinpointed (ibid.). During this period, the definitional contributions to entrepreneurship education became more diverse (ibid.). This is particularly evident in the fact that, in addition to considering the object and subject of entrepreneurship, the societal impacts of ventures were also addressed (ibid.). Following a relatively quiet phase, the fourth phase began in 2012 and extended until 2017 according to Halbfas and Liszt-Rohlf's work (ibid.). In this phase, the diversity of German-language definitions reached its peak, and didactic approaches gained increasing influence (ibid.). It can be concluded that, in addition to the shift from an object-oriented to a subject-oriented approach, there has also been a definitional opening of the concept of entrepreneurship education. While the first two phases particularly focused on education for starting a venture, the understanding transformed into fostering entrepreneurial personality (Bijedić, 2013, 38) and enabling the application of entrepreneurial thinking and action competence (Ebbers, 2019, 46).

This chapter aligns with a conceptual understanding of entrepreneurship education as a subject-oriented development of problem-solving, creative, and innovative entrepreneurial thinking and action that can be applied in all aspects of life and professional situations enabling learners to actively contribute to societal developments and creatively address shortcomings (Ebbers, 2014, 171). Thus, entrepreneurship education is not necessarily associated with starting, succeeding, or taking over a business, nor is it strictly linked to independent or dependent employment. Rather, it revolves around fostering future-oriented competencies and entrepreneurial thinking and action in a broad sense.

A popular approach that has early attempted to scientifically illuminate entrepreneurial thinking and action is the effectuation approach by Saras D. Sarasvathy. Sarasvathy's work, which emerged around the turn of the millennium, aimed to explore whether it is possible to teach and learn to be an entrepreneur (Sarasvathy, 2001, 2). In the course of this inquiry, Sarasvathy confronted 30 successful founders from various industries, with different-sized companies, with a 17-page problem-setting and documented the process of problem-solving through verbal narration by the participants (ibid.). The analysis of the transcribed speech data revealed a series of sometimes surprising but teachable principles (ibid.). The underlying rationality of these principles is referred to by Sarasvathy as "effectual reasoning," which represents a reversal of the conventional causal decision logic in management (ibid.). Causal decision processes begin with a predefined goal and are focused on finding the fastest, cheapest, and most efficient way to achieve that goal (ibid.). In contrast, effectual reasoning does not start with a specific goal but rather with a given set of means from which goals can continuously emerge (ibid.). These means are divided into three categories:

1. Who I am – Traits, Tastes, and Abilities.
2. What I know – Education, Training, Expertise, and Experience.
3. Whom I know – Social and Professional Networks.

Based on these means, entrepreneurs conceive possible scenarios that can be achieved with them (ibid., 3). They usually start very small with the means closest to them and directly translate them into actions (ibid.).Effectual reasoning is based on several principles, each of which represents a corresponding reversal within the causal decision logic (ibid.). While causal reasoning focuses on expected return, effectual reasoning emphasizes affordable loss (Affordable Loss Principle) (ibid.). While causal reasoning relies on competitive analysis, effectual reasoning relies on strategic partnerships (Strategic Partnerships Principle) (ibid.). While causal reasoning utilizes existing knowledge and predictions of the future, effectual reasoning emphasizes the use of contingencies as a resource (Leveraging Contingencies Principle) (ibid.). Effectual reasoning always follows the logic that the future does not need to be predicted when it can be designed (ibid.).

Designing is a core element of Design Thinking. Design Thinking has emerged as a prominent approach to methodically and conceptually implement Entrepreneurship Education. Firstly, it is assumed that everyone is a designer, as they shape their lives on various levels every day (Clark, 2021, V). Design Thinking has evolved into a recognized approach in academia and business, benefiting institutions, and companies worldwide by providing a new way of problem-solving and innovation (Krohn & Meinel, 2022, 1). Within a problem-solving process, expert knowledge from different individuals is combined, harnessing the collective innovative power of a team (ibid.). In essence, Design Thinking involves multidisciplinary teams generating user-centered problem solutions within a dynamic environment through an iterative process (ibid.). Particularly in startups, Design Thinking is the method that fosters innovation and creativity (Sim-schek & Kaiser, 2019, 17). To achieve this, Design Thinking promotes a mindset and working culture with an open perspective to understand what people truly need in specific situations (Meinel & Thienen, 2016, 310). In most cases, Design Thinking is designed as a process. The number of phases can vary widely. However, all Design Thinking processes share a commonality: at the beginning of the process, there is a phase dedicated to understanding the problem and the target audience, and only once a team has achieved a shared and unified understanding of the problem and target audience, ideas for solutions are generated, which are then built and tested through prototyping. However, the Design Thinking process is never sequential (Gürtler & Meyer, 2019, 31). Rather, Design Thinking thrives on the principles of iteration and continuous reflection, with the omnipresent possibility of revisiting previously taken steps (ibid.).

Design Thinking creates spaces for innovation and is particularly facilitated by a team culture characterized by mutual respect and trust (ibid., 25). It also requires courage to fail and an open feedback culture (ibid.). Consequently, the composition of the team is crucial for Design Thinking. It is important to consider multiperspectivity, multiprofessionalism, and interdisciplinarity (Simschek & Kaiser, 2019, 25). It is not about individuals being brilliant inventors, but rather about team members fertilizing, challenging, and inspiring each other with their different perspectives and experiences (Gürtler & Meyer, 2019, 18). When Design Thinking is successfully applied, participants gain an understanding that the world is malleable and develop creative self-confidence (Meinel & Thienen, 2016, 314).

While the Effectuation approach by Sarasvathy and Design Thinking are not the only approaches underlying Entrepreneurship Education, they are nevertheless popular and particularly fruitful in the educational context. The following chapter will highlight practical implications of these approaches, as well as a described subject-oriented Entrepreneurship Education, for an inclusive entrepreneurship education.

12.4 Practical Implications for Inclusive Entrepreneurship Education

This chapter attempts to present practical implications for inclusive entrepreneurship education by synthesizing the understanding provided, as well as the different approaches and responses to heterogeneity in teaching and learning contexts, with the current understanding of subject-oriented entrepreneurship education, incorporating the Effectuation approach by Sarasvathy and Design Thinking as a popular methodological and conceptual framework for entrepreneurship education. These implications are presented as theses, each of which will be further elaborated upon. Although these theses may appear biased, they must be critically examined and discussed. It is explicitly not the intention of this chapter to promote entrepreneurship education as a panacea for all educational and practical challenges, but rather to highlight potentials that have so far remained largely unexplored.

T1: Inclusive entrepreneurship education empowers to initiate change in order to enable better inclusion.

Inclusive entrepreneurship education, particularly through its explicit positioning regarding the utilization of heterogeneity as a resource, can empower learners to initiate the change that enables better inclusion. Within the framework of inclusive entrepreneurship education in school-based teaching and learning settings, students learn to develop problem-oriented and user-centered solutions. One key focus within inclusive entrepreneurship education can be the promotion of better inclusion. Therefore, students are encouraged to identify barriers to improved inclusion, understand those affected by these barriers, engage in dialogue with them, and ultimately develop solutions in collaboration with them. Although this typically occurs within a limited scope, such as the students' school-related realities, the transfer of acquired skills empowers learners to tackle similar challenges innovatively and creatively in the future. Essential conditions for success include a high sensitivity to various dimensions of heterogeneity among both the teachers and the students, a supportive environment, and a direct connection to real-life experiences.

T2: Inclusive entrepreneurship education can foster the entrepreneurial self-confidence of marginalized groups.

When Design Thinking is successfully applied, participants gain an understanding that the world is malleable and develop a creative self-confidence (Meinel & Thienen, 2016, p. 314). Particularly through experiences of success and encouragement from the environment and the teacher, marginalized groups, in the context of inclusive entrepreneurship education, can develop a new sense of entrepreneurial self-confidence. A key aspect of this is enabling experiences of self-efficacy and emancipation through empowerment. When individuals from marginalized groups, regardless of whether they are disabled individuals, migrants, women, or other groups, feel that their actions can have an impact, this can lead to further actions that ideally reinforce their self-efficacy expectations in the long term. Marginalized populations, in particular, often feel powerless in advocating for their positions in society. Inclusive entrepreneurship education has the potential to liberate individuals from marginalized populations from this sense of powerlessness, empower them to act and foster emancipation. An essential condition for success is an empowering environment that allows ideas to be implemented quickly and at an early stage. Additionally, it requires a teacher who demonstrates a culture of learning from mistakes and enables learners to learn from their failures.

T3: Inclusive entrepreneurship education enables individuals to recognize their individual means and potential beyond the confines of the educational setting.

Especially for learners whose individual abilities and skills lie outside the traditional academic curriculum, it can be challenging to recognize their own worth and realize their potential for (high) performance. Inclusive entrepreneurship education, incorporating the Effectuation approach by Sarasvathy, allows learners to identify problems and develop their own ideas for solving them. Learners need to be sensitized that when considering their personal means, they should think beyond the boundaries of academic subjects. Marginalized populations, in particular, possess means, especially perspectives, that non-marginalized populations do not have access to. For example, they can bring firsthand perspectives on the impact of non-inclusive structures and enrich the problem-solving process within the framework of Design Thinking with their unique insights. In addition to that, learners may, in alignment with the Effectuation approach, learn to cooperate with people with different opinions and perspectives rather than compete in order to, e.g., win an argument. To achieve this, it requires a teacher who explicitly emphasizes that what is learned and taught in school is not the only relevant aspect of everyday life, and that individual experiences, perspectives, abilities, and skills are equally valuable, if not more so, than excelling in specific academic subjects such as mathematics.

T4: Heterogeneity in teaching and learning settings utilizes uncertainty as a resource.

In line with the Effectuation approach by Sarasvathy, according to Effectual Reasoning, uncertainty is considered a resource (Leveraging Contingencies Principle). Heterogeneity in teaching and learning settings can create such uncertainty since heterogeneity is not at all set in stone and continuously promotes new situations, challenges, and chances to cope with, enabling learners to learn how to deal with and leverage uncertainty as a resource. For the teacher, instructing a heterogeneous group brings daily encounters with unforeseeable events since heterogeneity is not limited to rigid dimensions alone; learning groups can vary greatly in terms of performance and motivation from one day to another. As a result, teachers must be able to respond to new situations regularly, regardless of their lesson plans. Rather than ignoring or attempting to homogenize the learning group, it is beneficial to acknowledge and, ideally, utilize the existing heterogeneity. This requires great flexibility and resilience on the part of the teacher. By demonstrating a productive approach to uncertainty, students can observe and incorporate this mindset into their work within the context of inclusive entrepreneurship education.

T5: Heterogeneous teaching and learning settings require entrepreneurial teachers.

In the previous theses, this has already been implied. For a productive, appreciative, and respectful approach to heterogeneity, a teacher needs to be flexible, creative, innovative, and resilient, capable of handling uncertainty. In a teaching and learning setting characterized by heterogeneity, the teacher must work with the available means, if one may refer to the learners as such, every day, even if they have a previously prepared plan. The teacher must be able to deviate from the plan and create a lesson based on the presence of the learners and their individual characteristics, aiming to challenge and support them individually as much as possible. All these skills and abilities that a teacher must possess to succeed in heterogeneously structured teaching and learning settings are also part of entrepreneurial skills.

These theses by no means claim to be exhaustive, but hopefully provide a starting point for further reflection on inclusive entrepreneurship education, especially in teaching and learning settings characterized by heterogeneity.

12.5 Conclusion and Outlook

The aim of this contribution is to answer the question of how entrepreneurship education can thrive in heterogeneity-driven teaching and learning contexts. To achieve this, an overview of perspectives on heterogeneity and inclusion in the education system and educational practice was initially provided. Subsequently, an examination of the conceptual development of entrepreneurship education, along with an overview of the Effectuation approach by Sarasvathy and Design Thinking, was used to contextualize entrepreneurship education in the field. In the fourth synthesis chapter, theses were developed and explained, highlighting the potentials and conditions for inclusive entrepreneurship education. The following theses have emerged from this process:

T1: Inclusive entrepreneurship education empowers to initiate change in order to enable better inclusion.
T2: Inclusive entrepreneurship education can foster the creative self-confidence of marginalized groups.
T3: Inclusive entrepreneurship education enables individuals to recognize their individual means and potential beyond the confines of the educational setting.
T4: Heterogeneity in teaching and learning settings generates uncertainty as a resource.
T5: Heterogeneous teaching and learning settings require entrepreneurial teachers.

Based on these theses, it is now necessary to engage in further considerations and translate them into conceptual and empirical work. It should not be overlooked that a contribution like the present one can hardly capture the entire complexity of the education system and educational practice. Therefore, the theses developed here should be critically examined in response to the initial question, and their validity in practice should be tested.

By presenting the five described theses, this article highlights potential benefits and corresponding success factors, thus opening up new avenues for research in the field of inclusive entrepreneurship education, particularly in heterogeneity-driven teaching and learning settings. It is hoped that these insights will find fertile ground, as there can be mutual benefits between heterogeneity-driven teaching and learning settings and entrepreneurial thinking and actions. In conclusion, the following sentence encapsulates the essence of this contribution: Uncertainty and multiprofessionalism are to be seen as a chance in an entrepreneurial context, just as heterogeneity is in the educational context.

References

Ackermann, K.-E. (2015). Politische Bildung im inklusiven Bildungssystem – grundsätzliche Fragen. In C. Dönges, W. Hilpert, & B. Zurstrassen (Eds.), *Didaktik der inklusiven politischen Bildung* (pp. 30–44). Bundeszentrale für Politische Bildung.

Becker, E. S., & Keller, M. M. (2022). "Ich fand die Unterrichtsstunde interessant – du etwa nicht?". Heterogenität im situationalen Interesse und Zusammenhänge mit Klassen- und Unterrichtsmerkmalen. *Zeitschrift für Erziehungswissenschaft, 25*, 405–425.

Bijedić, T. (2019). Begriffliche und disziplinäre Genese der Entrepreneurship Education. In T. Bijedić, I. Ebbers, & B. Halbfas (Eds.), *Entrepreneurship education* (Begriff – Theorie – Verständnis) (pp. 21–40). Springer.

Bijedić, T. (2013). Entwicklung unternehmerischer Persönlichkeit im Rahmen einer Entrepreneurship Education. In *Didaktische Lehr-Lern-Konzeption und empirische Analyse für die Sekundarstufe II*. Rainer Hampp.

Bohl, T. (2017). Umgang mit Heterogenität im Unterricht: Forschungsbefunde und didaktische Implikationen. In T. Bohl, J. Budde & M. Rieger-Ladich (eds.), *Umgang mit Heterogenität in Schule und Unterricht* (Grundlagentheoretische Beiträge, empirische Befunde und didaktische Reflexionen) (pp. 257–273). Verlag Julius Klinkhardt.

Budde, J. (2017). Heterogenität: Entstehung, Begriff, Abgrenzung. In T. Bohl, J. Budde &M. Rieger-Ladich (eds.), *Umgang mit Heterogenität in Schule und Unterricht* (Grundlagentheoretische Beiträge, empirische Befunde und didaktische Reflexionen) (pp. 13–26). Verlag Julius Klinkhardt.

Clark, D. B. (2021). Foreword: Why Design Thinking? In D. Scott & J. Lock (eds.), *Teacher as designer* (Design thinking for educational change) (pp. V–VIII). Springer.

Dumont, H. (2019). Neuer Schlauch für alten Wein? Eine konzeptuelle Betrachtung von individueller Förderung im Unterricht. *Zeitschrift für Erziehungswissenschaft, 22*, 249–277.

Ebbers, I. (2019). Entrepreneurship Education als Möglichkeits- und Ermöglichungsraum – eine erste theoretische Annäherung aus fachdidaktischer Perspektive. In T. Bijedić, I. Ebbers & B. Halbfas (eds.), *Entrepreneurship Education* (Begriff – Theorie – Verständnis) (pp. 43–61). Springer.

Ebbers, I. (2014). Gezeiten der Ökonomischen Bildung. In C. Müller, H.-J. Schlösser & A. Liening (eds.), *Bildung zu Sozialen Marktwirtschaft* (Schriften zu Ordnungsfragen der Wirtschaft) (p. 171). Lucius & Lucius.

Fellmann, A. (2016). Wie kann Heterogenität im Schulalltag gelebt werden? Arbeiten im gemeinsamen Unterricht und in Lernwerkstätten al seine mögliche Lernkultur. *Pädagogische Hochschule Vorarlberg. F6E Edition, 23*, 87–95.

Gürtler, J., & Meyer, J. (2019). *Design thinking. 30 Minuten*. GABAL.

Halbfas, B. & Liszt-Rohlf, V. (2019). Entwicklungslinien und Perspektiven der Entrepreneurship Education – eine Analyse von Definitionen. In T. Bijedić, I. Ebbers & B. Halbfas (eds.), *Entrepreneurship education* (Begriff – Theorie – Verständnis) (pp. 3–20). Springer.

Hägg, G., Politis, D. & Alsos, G. A. (2022). Does gender balance in entrepreneurship education make a difference to prospective start-up behaviour? *Education + Training*, Vol. ahead-of-print No. ahead-of-print. https://doi.org/10.1108/ET-06-2021-0204

Hummrich, M. (2017). Umgang mit Heterogenität in international vergleichender Perspektive. In T. Bohl, J. Budde & M. Rieger-Ladich (eds.), *Umgang mit Heterogenität in Schule und Unterricht. Grundlagentheoretische Beiträge, empirische Befunde und didaktische Reflexionen* (pp. 159–174). Verlag Julius Klinkhardt.

Krohn, T. & Meinel, C. (2022). Introduction: Design Thinking in the Field of Education. In C. Meinel & T. Krohn (eds.), *Design thinking in education* (Innovation Can Be Learned) (pp. 1–6). Springer.

Meinel, C., & von Thienen, J. (2016). Design thinking. *Informatik Spektrum, 39*(4), 310–314.

Sarasvathy, S. D. (2001). *What makes entrepreneurs entrepreneurial?* https://22657557.fs1.hubspotusercontent-na1.net/hubfs/22657557/Public%20Documents%20For%20Site/what-makes-entrepreneurs-entrepreneurial-sarasvathy.pdf

Simschek, R., & Kaiser, F. (2019). *Design Thinking. Innovationen effektiv managen*. UVK Verlag.

Wiepcke, C. (2019). Social Entrepreneurship Education zur Förderung von Inklusion. In T. Bijedić, I. Ebbers & B. Halbfas (eds.), *Entrepreneurship Education* (Begriff – Theorie – Verständnis) (pp. 193–212). Springer.

Wischer, B. (2009). *Umgang mit Heterogenität im Unterricht – Das Handlungsfeld und seine Herausforderung: TIPP (Teachers in Practice and Process)*. Heterogenität ruft nach Dialog. https://www.lernende-schulen.at/pluginfile.php/278/mod_resource/content/3/Fachartikel_Beate_Wischer.pdf?forcedownload=1

Chapter 13
The Role of the University in the Creation of Personal Entrepreneurial Competencies

Sandra Misiak-Kwit and Jinyue Yang

13.1 Introduction

In recent years, entrepreneurship has caught great attention from a variety of stakeholders due to its significant impact on economic development. Yet, there are still a number of questions that researches are seeking an answer to: What is the essence of entrepreneurship? What characterizes the entrepreneurship? What competencies are necessary for being an entrepreneurial person? Where do these competencies originate? Despite the volumes of information and resources from existing literature, the authors of this chapter undertook an investigation of the role of university, especially the quality of teaching (QoT), in the creation of personal entrepreneurial competences (PECs) in order to address the aforementioned questions.

The demand for professional learning of PECs is a direct outcome of the importance of entrepreneurship in society, which is reflected at the individual level by desire of increasing financial income, sense of independence, success, and self-actualization; at the societal level by decreasing unemployment rates, safety of the community, and economic growth (Tekin & Asar, 2021). In addition, the competencies set for global leadership to ensure improved efficiency and effectiveness of management was also fundamentally altered by the changes brought about by globalization at the end of the twentieth century, including the demand for high levels of PECs (Muzam, 2022).

S. Misiak-Kwit (✉)
University of Szczecin, Szczecin, Poland
e-mail: sandra.misiak-kwit@usz.edu.pl

J. Yang (✉)
The Doctoral School, University of Szczecin, Szczecin, Poland
e-mail: jinyue.yang@phd.usz.edu.pl

K. Mikkelsen, A. Wolf (eds.), *Minds, Brains, and Doxa for Inclusive Entrepreneurship*, International Studies in Entrepreneurship 47,
https://doi.org/10.1007/978-3-031-50164-7_13

Furthermore, a number of studies have also indicated that young people, especially university students and graduates are one of the most powerful forces of entrepreneurship in many countries. China and Poland have both seen fast economic development in the past few decades. Both countries have undergone economic reforms that foster entrepreneurship. As a result, in the EU, according to the open data on Eurostat (2022), the development of entrepreneurial skills and the education programs of youth for cultivation of PECs have been supported by a number of EU grants and non-profit organizations since these are seen as crucial components of creating a global society and developing sustainable economy. Similar to the EU, according to the National Burial of Statistics of China (2021), China also made steps to help young people and university students to obtain PECs in the past years. For example, it opened creative programs at institutions of higher learning and provided financial aid and top-notch educational training to young people who desire to pursue PECs. The two countries have a certain level of similarities, but at the same time, also a lot of differences. One of the most crucial ones is the fact that the university education models are different. Polish university model was developed on the basis of German research university model, and influenced by the cooperate university model and the Bologna process (Kolanowska et al., 2018). Although it is inspired by Chinese tradition and culture as well as other western models, the Chinese university model was created by combining the German research university model and the Chinese university model with Chinese characteristics (Yuaz, 2018). The teaching philosophies in two nations are also different due to the disparities in cultures and educational systems. It is essential to pinpoint those critical success elements for the entrepreneurship developing of the aforementioned nations. Since university students and graduates have a crucial contribution in developing entrepreneurship, as a result, the significance of finding out whether there is a relation between satisfaction with the quality of teaching at universities and satisfaction with the creation of PECs tends to be critical and constitutes the main objective of this chapter.

The authors used structured questionnaires to collect the primary data from the respondents. This research is aimed at university students and university graduates in China and Poland in order to fulfill the aim of this chapter. A set of questions related to the aim of the research were sent out to 216 individuals including 112 Chinese and 104 Poles. The participants were selected randomly among university students and graduates in China and Poland. The choice of this group was dictated by the fact that they practically experienced the teaching process at the university and are able to assess the role of university in the creation of their PECs. It is also worth noting that the respondents have not participated in any program related with entrepreneurship education. The authors, for the purpose of the study, assumed that indicated competences can be often taught during many different courses, i.e., related with stress management, negotiations, marketing, and many others. The findings of this chapter could be useful to a variety of higher education stakeholders both inside and outside of the countries that were the subject of the research, such as students who want to develop their entrepreneurial skills. Another group of beneficiaries are people who want to pursue education or training at universities in order to achieve similar objectives. This might be possible thanks to an acquired knowledge and a better understanding of the role of universities in creating PECs. Further, among groups that can benefit from this research results are family members of the students, university policy makers and educators, (since they may develop instructional programs in relevant disciplines based on the satisfaction of education receivers), government policy makers (since governments in the studied nations are primarily responsible for funding public universities, they may make financing decisions referring to the findings), and the private investors of educational programs of universities. Finally, the general public is also affected significantly by economic development in terms of entrepreneurship, educational support by the states, the employment opportunities, and so on. Therefore, the possibility to discover similarities and differences of view regarding acquisition of PECs and their importance in analyzed countries constitute an additional value of this chapter. Due to the Covid-19 outbreak and geographic distance, data was obtained through internet platforms. The online platforms for collecting data throughout the research were Google questionnaire and the WeChat[1] e-questionnaire program. The Pearson correlation coefficient, the Shapiro-Wilk test, and Kruskal-Wallis H test were used as statistical tools for the primary analysis.

The structure of this chapter encompasses four sections. The first section delves into the literature review on the definitions of entrepreneurship, entrepreneur, entrepreneurial person, entrepreneurial competencies, as well as PECs. The research methodology, respondents' characteristics, and the statistical model that was used to analyze the research data are all introduced in the second section. The third section gives an insight on the role of university in the creation of PECs in China and Poland. Finally, the chapter ends with an overview and conclusions of the research.

13.2 Literature Review and the Concept and Significance of PECs

Numerous researchers and economists have highlighted the importance of entrepreneurship and the recognition of the entrepreneurs' role in the economy across the world. Over a long period of time, entrepreneurship has been identified as one of the key factors for economic growth of a country (Smith, 2010). There are a lot of definitions of entrepreneurship in the existing literature, yet, there is not a unified definition of it. According to Patharkar and Kishnami (2021), entrepreneurship is the capacity and willingness to establish and operate one's own business, which is essentially a new company that offers creative products or services. "Deploying a broader interpretation of innovation is one example of entrepreneurship that incorporates not just economic objectives, but also political and social goals that benefit

[1] Wechat is a Chinese multi-functional instant messaging, social media, and mobile payment app developed by Tencent.

the larger community," Missias and Brugar (2018) argued in their work. According to Gartner (1989), entrepreneurship is "the act of founding a new company where none existed before." Furthermore, Lumpkin and Dess (1996) argued that "the essential act of entrepreneurship is new entity." Entrepreneurship is described by the National Council for the Social Studies (NCSS) (2013) as a characteristic of persons who take on the risk of integrating industrial resources to produce goods and services for profit. Furthermore, according to Stevenson and Jarillo (1990), "entrepreneurship is the process by which individuals or groups pursue opportunities without regarding to resources they currently control."

Along with the development of entrepreneurship, the definition of an entrepreneur has been revised over time and by a lot of researchers. The term "entrepreneur" was originally derived from the French verb "entreprendre," meaning "to undertake." Since the eighteenth century, "entrepreneur" has been used in English to refer to many sorts of business owners (Hébert & Link, 1988). Table 13.1 presents some of the most prevalent definitions of entrepreneur based on various studies.

As shown in Table 13.2, authors characterized entrepreneur differently based on their findings and ways of thinking. However, the above-mentioned definitions share certain commonalities. For example, the three most commonly mentioned characteristics of entrepreneurs include "risk taking," "new business," and "creative thinking talents."

Relating to the aim of this chapter, the highest significance would be placed on definitions that underline the importance of entrepreneurial characteristic of an individual. Vries and Kets (1977) described an entrepreneurial person as one who fulfills a number of functions which can be summarized as innovative abilities, management-coordinating skills, and the risk taking functions. According to Katana (2016), there are certain characteristics of an entrepreneurial person that include creativity, risk-taking, decision and problem-solving skills, discipline, willingness and ability of learning, flexibility of thinking and acting, communication skills, and so on. Currently, the skills related to the usage of mobile technologies also gain on significance (Wiścicka-Fernando, 2021). The authors classified the characteristics of an entrepreneurial person into three primary areas, including inner traits, social skills, and managerial competencies, which are presented in Table 13.2.

Table 13.2 lists 27 main characteristics that a successful entrepreneurial person should possess. They are crucial to those who want to pursue entrepreneurship and be successful. Hence, personality can be analyzed as the internal determinant of entrepreneurship. In the literature, several dozen different features can be found that may be ordered into the diamond of internal determinants of entrepreneurial attitude (Misiak-Kwit, 2020) (Fig. 13.1).

Five contemporary areas in the diamond create a profile of an entrepreneurial person. Each area consists of set of features and competences that predispose to be an entrepreneurial individual. The five areas in the diamond have strong connections with PECs of an individual. Each area contains different entrepreneurial competencies. To integrate with the environment and shape its element, an individual should possess such PECs as willingness to take risk, recognition of needs, intuition, etc. To build long-term relationships such PECs as leadership, ability to gain

Table 13.1 The definitions of entrepreneur – by school

Author	Definition	School
Hawley (1907)	Risk taking is the fundamental characteristic of an entrepreneur	Risk theory
Hornaday and Bunker (1970)	"The successful entrepreneur was defined as a man or woman who started a business where there was none before"	
Howell (1972)	Entrepreneur is the small group of persons who are new firm founders. The term is also used to suggest that the persons "have some significant ownership stake in the business (they are not only employees) and that their intention is for the business to grow and prosper beyond the self-employment stage"	
Hull and Bosley (1980)	A person who manages and runs a business venture while taking on risk in order to make a profit	
Antoncic and Hisrich (2003)	An entrepreneur is a person who has innovative thinking abilities, is a leader, and is willing to take risks	
Thornton (1998)	The entrepreneur is "the bearer of risks inflicted by changes in market demand"	
Evans (1949)	"The person or group of persons who assume the task and responsibility of combining the factors of production into a business organization and keeping this organization in operation... He commands the industrial forces, and upon him rests the responsibility for their success or failure" "Entrepreneurs – Very broadly defined – Are those who organize, manage, and actively control the affairs of the units that combine the factors of production for the supply of goods and services"	Dynamic theory
Kirzner (1997)	An entrepreneur is "a decision-maker whose entire role arises out of his alertness to hitherto unnoticed opportunities"	
Bygrave and Hofer (1991)	"An entrepreneur is someone who perceives an opportunity and creates an organization to pursue it."	Dynamic & Risk Theory
NCSS (2013)	"Individuals who are willing to take risks in order to develop new products and start new businesses. They recognize opportunities, enjoying working for themselves, and accept challenges."	
Brockhaus (1980)	An entrepreneur is defined as a main owner/manager of a business who does not work elsewhere.	Behavior school
Collins (2003)	"An entrepreneur is someone who specializes in taking critical decisions about the coordination of scarce resources."	

Source: Own compilation

trust, EI, and assertiveness are needed. Another area in the diamond, effectiveness and desirability of actions, requires organizational capabilities, time management, aspirations, negotiation skills which can also be determined as PECs. Inner attitude of an individual is fourth area of the diamond and comprises such PESs as passion, independence, self-realization, flexibility, confidence, and many others. Finally, PECs that enable the implementation of changes include creativity, imagination, decisiveness, courage, innovativeness, and the like. Therefore, acquisition of certain competences and entrepreneurial education is gaining on significance.

Table 13.2 Characteristics of an entrepreneurial person based on Vries and Kets (1977) and Katana (2016)

Inner traits	Social skills	Managerial competencies
Willingness and ability to learn new knowledge	Appropriate appearance	Creativity and innovation
Flexible thinking and acting	Communicativeness	Risk taking abilities
Driven for accomplishment	Resourcefulness	Decision-making skills
Consistency in achieving personal goals	Friendliness	Problem-solving skills
Imagination	Listening skills	Developmental vision
Eager for independence	Assertiveness, abilities to set broderies	Consistency in achieving organizational goals
Courage and initiative	Emotional intelligence	Propensity to lead, honesty and responsibility
Self-confidence	Empathy	Resilience of uncertainty
Self-discipline	Sense of humor	Work discipline

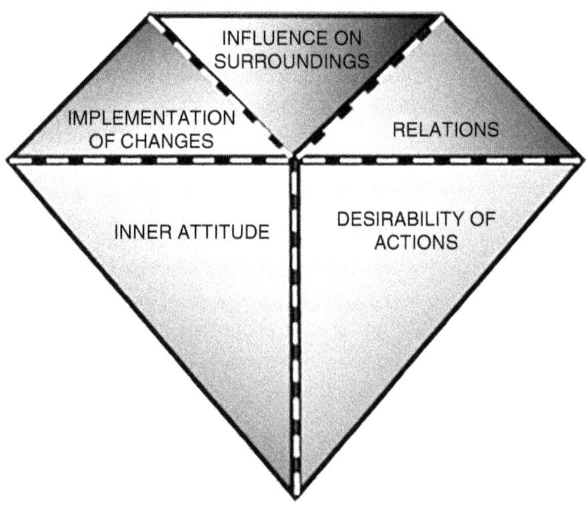

Fig. 13.1 Diamond of internal determinants of entrepreneurial attitude. (Misiak-Kwit, 2020)

According to the Cambridge Dictionary (2022), competency is connected with individuals' job performances in a wide range of areas and refers to fields of work at which a person is competent. Therefore, taking into consideration the broad perspective of entrepreneurship, entrepreneurial competencies literally means the competencies of being an entrepreneurial person and/or an entrepreneur who is starting and running an own enterprise. These competencies include a variety of aspects, such as creativity and innovation, decision-making, problems-solving, communicative skills, as well as other leadership abilities. Moreover, such competencies, relating to human resource development, also make a positive contribution to company's success (Smerek & Vetráková, 2020).

Entrepreneurial competencies (EC) are a collection of actions that help to produce the desired effects and consequences of entrepreneurial intentions, according to Kurtz and Bartram (2002). Referring to the study of Ploum (2019), EC are characterized as the capacity to perform consistently efficiently in a certain professional field, such as job, position, and organizational environment. The concept describes a comprehensive collection of business-related information, skills, mindsets, and competencies. According to Ratković et al. (2022), EC include the ability to turn innovative ideas into projects, keep a business alive, ability to manage a company, initiative, taking responsibility, taking risks, solving problems, planning and managing projects, having leadership skills, being optimism, perseverance, being passionate, resilience, having self-confidence, empathy, and so on.

Similarly, a number of researches defined PECs. According to Mitchelmore and Rowley (2010), PECs involve competencies such as learning, cognitive, innovating, problem-solving, decision-making, coping with uncertainty and risks, sustaining temporal tension, critical thinking, and analytical thinking skills. In general, the PECs are grouped into three categories: conceptual, organizing, and commitment competencies. Conceptual entrepreneurial competencies represent entrepreneurs' innovation and creativity abilities, which can be related to the ability of thinking out of box and the possibilities of coming up with innovative ideas (Mamun et al., 2016). Organizing competencies, on the other hand, are usually connected with the leadership abilities of entrepreneurs, such as taking up responsibilities, coping with unknown challenges and making decisions (Mau & Lau, 2000). In case of commitment competencies, according to McClelland (1973), initiative, dedication, hard-working, commitment, determination, and proactive orientation are some of the basic characteristics of successful entrepreneurs. Furthermore, according to Wickramaratne et al. (2014), PECs not only have a significant indirect influence on the general performance of a firm, but also can affect the entrepreneurial orientation of firm's owner/manager. In a nutshell, PECs are the critical personal abilities of individuals which allow them to be an entrepreneurial person and/or run a business successfully.

On the basis of literature review, there is no big difference between the definitions of EC and PEC, both including a set of competencies that a successful entrepreneurial person should possess. After integration of the competencies, the authors have chosen ten PECs for empirical research, such as leadership skills, communicativeness, personal time management, initiative, self-confidence, creativity and innovation, problem solving skills, persistence, information seeking, and risk taking and risk management.

Furthermore, Mesquita et al. (2016) suggested that trainings in academic courses could be utilized to directly learn and enhance such personal entrepreneurial competences. Ratković et al. (2022) also indicated that the recognition and development of PECs in society are influenced by labor market and high-standard educational institutions as well as the professional education of the young people.

It can be clearly stated that entrepreneurial education plays a crucial role in the development of individual careers, companies, regions, countries, and global economy. Moreover, the type history and reputation of chosen university gain on significance (Smerek & Kováčiková, 2019). The educational system's goals are indicated by the labor market according to the competency-based approach (Prokopenko et al., 2020), but also the ability to influence this market (where the students are the changemakers) should be taken into consideration. Such impact is also possible through job creation and self-employment (Wasliczuk et al., 2021).

13.3 Research Methodology

The main objective of this chapter was to verify whether there is a relation between satisfaction of university students and graduates with the quality of teaching (QoT) and their satisfaction with creation of PECs at universities in China and Poland. One of the reasons to compare both countries is the emphasis on the quality and development of higher education. Secondly, despite differences in population, Human Development Index in China and Poland is quite close. More information regarding comparison of those two countries is presented in Table 13.3.

The comparison relates also to the data presenting the area of education, like Literacy Rate and the average IQ score considered as a smartness of a country. Although, the Literacy Rate is higher in Poland, China acquired higher IQ score.

In order to fulfill the objective of the chapter and discover similarities and differences, the authors conducted the survey in analyzed countries. The questionnaire used in this study was translated into Chinese and Polish, taking into account that not everyone was able to fill in the questionnaire in English. The data was collected through Google questionnaire for participants from Poland and the WeChat e-questionnaire program for participants from China. In order to have comparable findings, the same amount of respondents were invited to participate in the survey in analyzed countries. However, there is a slight difference between the respond rates in two countries. There were 112 and 104 completed questionnaires from Chinese and Polish respondents, respectively, representing 99.1% and 94.6% respond rates. The data collecting procedure took around 2 months (began from 27th, December, 2021 to 15th, February, 2022). The questionnaire follows the Polish and Chinese civil law and ethical standards. Furthermore, it is on the basis of voluntariness, anonymity, and confidentiality.

Table 13.3 Comparison of the basic data from the area of education

Description	China	Poland
Literacy rate (2015)	96.36%	99.79%
Smartest countries (2023) – IQ	104.1	96.35
GDP per capita (in $)	17,192 (rank 77)	34,103 (rank 41)
Unemployment rate by World Bank	5.2% (2019)	3.2% (2020)
Human Development Index (2021)	0.768	0.876
Annual growth of HDI (1990–2021)	0.95	0.65
Gender inequality index value (2021)	0.192	0.109

Source: Word Population Review (2023) and Human Development Reports (2023)

There were four demographic and three field questions in the questionnaire concerning described issue. Following the demographic questions such as country, age, gender, education level, and type of Higher Education Institution (HEI) (public or private), the respondents were then asked to rank their satisfaction with the QoT and with the level of creation of PECs at their universities at the first field question. They were asked to rate their satisfaction from 1 to 5, where 1 is very dissatisfied, 2 is dissatisfied, 3 is neither satisfied nor dissatisfied, 4 is satisfied, and 5 is very satisfied. The second field question allows respondents to assess the importance of the 10 most relevant and critical PECs in the scale from 1 to 5, where 1 is not important and 5 is very important. The ten chosen PECs include Leadership skills, Communicative skills, Personal time management, Initiative, Self-confidence, Creativity and innovation, Problem solving skills, Persistence, Information seeking, and Risk taking and risk management. Finally, the third question requires respondents to rank the possibility of acquiring the ten aforementioned PECs in the scale from 1 to 5, where 1 is not possible and 5 – strong possibility of acquisition. For the data analysis, Microsoft Excel and SPSS were utilized.

Furthermore, the Pearson correlation coefficient was applied to find out the relationship between the independent and dependent variables of the study. The Pearson correlation coefficient is often utilized in science to determine the relation between rank variables (Daniel 1990). In this research, the independent variable is quality of teaching (QoT), while the dependent variable is the creation of PECs. The measurement unit is the satisfaction of students with the QoT and the creation of PEC at their universities. In order to fulfill the main objective of the chapter, the authors created a conceptual framework I (Fig. 13.2).

The conceptual framework I shows the hypothetical relationship between the satisfaction with QoT and satisfaction with creation of PECs. Accordingly, the formulated hypotheses are:

H_0: There is no relationship between satisfaction with QoT and satisfaction with creation of PECs;

H_a: There is a relationship between satisfaction with QoT and satisfaction with creation of PECs.

The Shapiro-Wilk test (1965) was run to explore the normality of the distributions. A part of the quantitative approach for the analysis conducted in order to fulfill the aim of the paper is also Kruskal-Wallis H test. The Kruskal-Wallis H test was conducted to determine whether there is a difference in the satisfaction with QoT

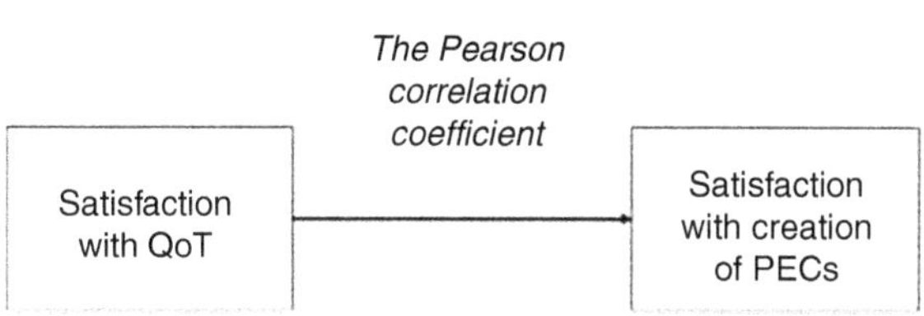

Fig. 13.2 Conceptual framework of study I. (Source: Own elaboration)

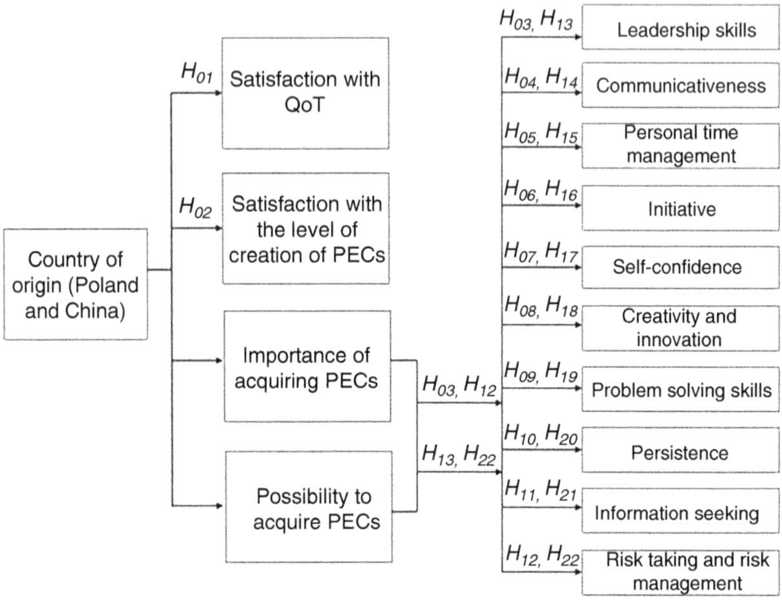

Fig. 13.3 Conceptual framework of study II. (Source: Own elaboration)

and satisfaction with the level of creation of PEC based on the respondents' country of origin. Moreover, Kruskal-Wallis H test (Theodorsson-Norheim, 1986) was calculated also for importance and possibility of acquisition of chosen PECs. The null hypothesis states that both group means are equal, whereas the alternative hypothesis that not all group means are equal (at least one of the means is different from the others). The conceptual framework II is presented in Fig. 13.3.

Considering social and demographic characteristic of the sample, the basic information is presented in Table 13.4. It illustrates that proportions of responses are comparable in China and Poland. Furthermore, the statistics indicate that in the analyzed countries, there was a minor variation in the number of male and female respondents, leading the authors to infer that the study is based on gender balanced participation. The data also shows that the majority of the respondents in both countries hold a bachelor's degree (74.3% and 52.9% in China and Poland, respectively). When it comes to the number of respondents with a post-graduate degree, Polish outnumbered Chinese respondents. It is worth mentioning that the number of university students who participated in Poland was slightly higher than in China, but the percentage of respondents with a bachelor's degree was lower in Poland, while the percentage of respondents with a high school diploma was higher. Due to that fact it is significant to implement advanced teaching methods that support entrepreneurial education and give free space for self-development. Moreover, most respondents were studying or graduated from public universities, so assessment concerns essentially quality of teaching of public education.

Table 13.4 The characteristics of respondents from China and Poland

	China		Poland	
Country of region	No.	%	No.	%
Total number of respondents	112	100	104	100
Gender				
Male	53	47	50	48
Female	54	48	51	49
Prefer not to say	5	5	3	3
Age				
18–21	13	12	12	12
22–25	19	17	54	52
26–29	48	43	20	19
30–35	29	26	12	12
36–40	1	1	4	4
More than 40	2	2	2	2
Level of education				
High school diploma	4	4	21	20
Bachelor's degree and specialized degree	86	77	55	53
Master's degree	21	19	24	23
Doctoral degree	1	1	4	4
Higher education institutions (HEI)				
Public HEI	107	96	87	84
Private HEI	0	0	9	9
Public HEI abroad	0	0	3	3
Private HEI abroad	2	2	2	2
Other	3	3	3	3

Source: Own research data

The Role of University in the Creation of PECs

During the study, respondents were asked to rank their satisfaction with the quality of teaching and the level of creation of personal entrepreneurial competencies at their university. Therefore, the authors are able to indicate subjective perception of analyzed aspects. The average rank assigned to the satisfaction with the QoT equals 3.01 in China and 3.14 in Poland. Satisfaction with the level of creation of personal entrepreneurial competencies received average rank amounting 3.01 in China and 2.94 in Poland. The data clearly indicate that the respondents are neither satisfied nor dissatisfied with quality of teaching and the level of creation of PECs. The average rank for both variables is the same in China, whereas polish respondents are more satisfied with the quality of teaching then with the level of creation of personal entrepreneurial competencies.

To deepen the analysis, it is worth to analyze specific data concerning satisfaction with QoT and creation of PEC (Table 13.5).

Table 13.5 illustrates the satisfaction rate of Chinese and Polish university students with the QoT and with the level of creation of PECs based on their own experiences and views. The QoT and the creation of PECs at Chinese and Polish universities were ranked on a scale of 1 to 5, where 1 is very dissatisfied, 2 is

Table 13.5 The satisfaction with quality of teaching and with the level of creation of personal entrepreneurial competencies by respondents from China and Poland – in %

Quality of teaching at the university				
1	**2**	**3**	**4**	**5**
China				
10%	12%	47%	29%	2%
Poland				
4%	18%	45%	25%	8%
Creation of personal entrepreneurial competencies at the university				
1	**2**	**3**	**4**	**5**
China				
6%	16%	49%	27%	2%
Poland				
13%	21%	33%	27%	7%

dissatisfied, 3 is neither satisfied nor dissatisfied, 4 is satisfied, and 5 is very satisfied. The data in the table clearly show that the majority of the respondents in both countries were neither satisfied nor dissatisfied with the QoT at their universities, with the satisfaction rates in China and Poland of 47% and 45%, respectively, which confirms the data presented in Table 13.5. Furthermore, more Chinese respondents than Polish respondents expressed strong dissatisfaction with the QoT at their universities (10% vs. 4%). In addition, there was a higher rate of respondents who were very satisfied with the QoT at their universities in Poland than in China (8% vs. 2%). When it comes to the satisfaction with the level of creation of PECs at universities, nearly half of the Chinese respondents were neither satisfied nor dissatisfied, while 33% of Polish respondents felt the same. However, the number of respondents who felt negative about the creation of PECs is lager in Poland than in China. In the contrary, more respondents from Poland than from China expressed higher satisfaction with the creation of PECs at their universities (7% vs. 2%).

As a next step, the authors intended to gain knowledge on importance of acquisition of chosen PEC in the eyes of respondents (Fig. 13.4).

Figure 13.4 shows the differences and similarities of the average rank assigned to the importance of acquisition of chosen PECs by Chinese and Polish respondents. The importance of the acquisition for each chosen PEC was then evaluated and listed in sequences separately. As shown in Fig. 13.4, the acquisition of "creativity and invention," "problem solving skills," and "communicativeness" were regarded as the three most crucial PECs from the perspective of Polish respondents, while "self-confidence," "problem solving skills," as well as "creativity and innovation" were considered as the three most important PECs from the viewpoint of Chinese respondents. However, "self-confidence" was ranked as the seventh place in the eyes of Polish respondents in comparison with Chinese respondents. Moreover, respondents from both countries considered "initiative" and "leadership skills" as the least important PECs. In addition, the average rating values for each PEC are relatively different. Despite of the "leadership skills," Chinese respondents ranked the importance of acquisition of each PEC higher than Polish respondents (average value of 2.51 from Chinese respondents vs. 3.74 from Polish respondents).

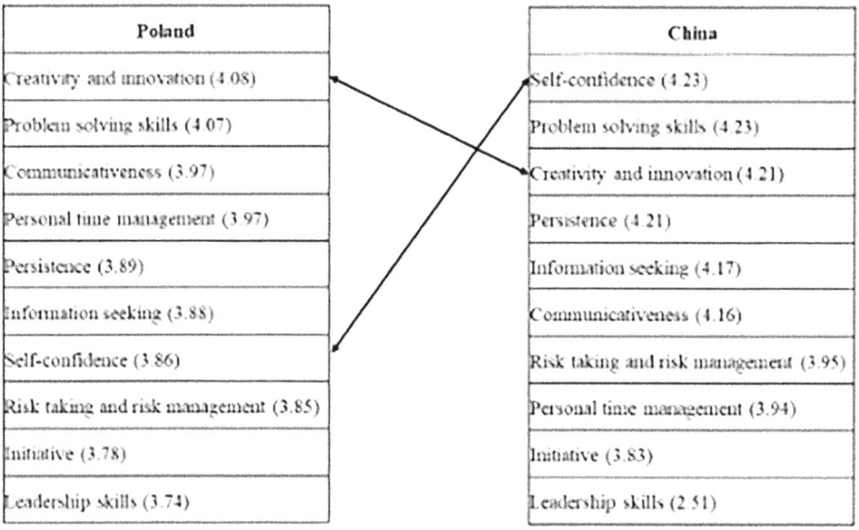

Fig. 13.4 The average rank assigned to the importance of acquisition of chosen personal entrepreneurial competencies by respondents from China and Poland

Next, the detailed results were compared; Table 13.6 presents the percentage variations between the respondents' perspectives from China and Poland about the importance of acquiring the chosen PECs.

The importance of the acquisition of each PEC was rated on a scale of 1–5, where 1 is not important and 5 is very important. As shown in Table 13.6, 64% of Chinese respondents rated "self-confidence," while 39% of Polish respondents chose "creativity and innovation" as the most important PEC to acquire. On the other hand, 26% Chinese respondents considered "leadership skills" as the least important PEC to acquire, while it is hard to tell which PEC was the least important to acquire from the perspective of the Polish respondents based on the percentages. That is why it was significant to compute the average ranking scores in order to differentiate the relative importance of each PEC.

Figure 13.5 illustrates the average rank assigned to the possibility of the acquisition of chosen PECs by respondents from China and Poland. The possibilities of the acquisition for each chosen PEC was then evaluated and listed in sequences.

Taking into consideration the data presented in Table 13.7, it is clear that "personal time management," "communicativeness," and "problem solving skills" were rated as the PECs with highest possibility to acquire from the Polish university education, while "communicativeness," "problem solving skills," and "information seeking" were considered as the PECs with highest possibility of acquiring from Chinese university education. Compared to Polish respondents, Chinese respondents thought that "personal time management" is less possible to acquire during university studies. The three PECs with the least probability of acquisition, in the opinion of Polish respondents, were "risk taking and risk management," "leadership skills," and "initiative," while for Chinese respondents – "leadership skills," "persistence," and "risk taking and risk management."

Table 13.6 The importance of acquisition of chosen personal entrepreneurial competencies by respondents from China and Poland – in %

	1	2	3	4	5
China					
Leadership skills	26%	26%	19%	29%	0%
Communicativeness	8%	3%	10%	23%	56%
Personal time management	9%	3%	8%	46%	35%
Initiative	8%	3%	17%	43%	29%
Self-confidence	8%	4%	10%	14%	64%
Creativity and innovation	8%	2%	12%	18%	61%
Problem solving skills	9%	3%	6%	21%	62%
Persistence	8%	3%	11%	17%	62%
Information seeking	8%	2%	13%	20%	58%
Risk taking and risk management	8%	2%	15%	37%	38%
Poland					
Leadership skills	0%	5%	39%	33%	23%
Communicativeness	1%	4%	24%	39%	32%
Personal time management	1%	4%	24%	39%	32%
Initiative	0%	9%	29%	39%	23%
Self-confidence	1%	6%	27%	38%	28%
Creativity and innovation	1%	3%	22%	35%	39%
Problem solving skills	0%	1%	29%	32%	38%
Persistence	1%	5%	27%	38%	29%
Information seeking	0%	11%	22%	36%	32%
Risk taking and risk management	0%	7%	31%	33%	30%

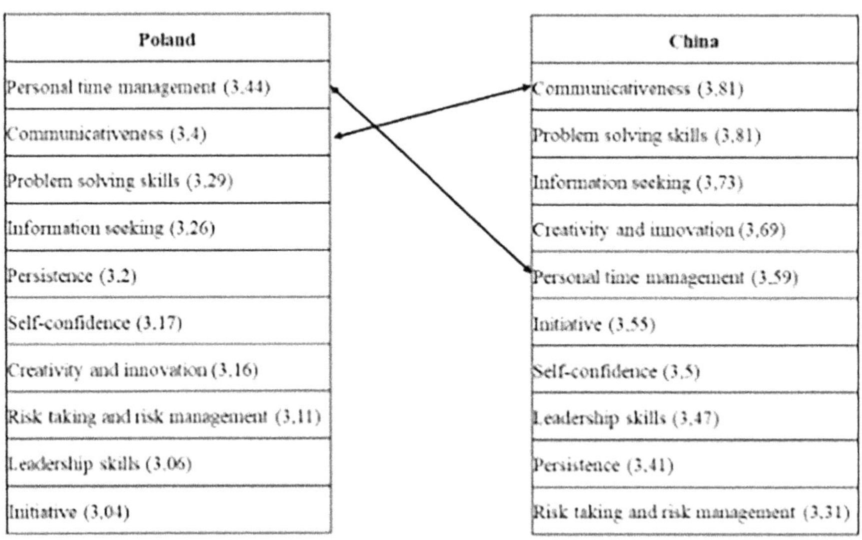

Fig. 13.5 The average rank assigned to the possibility of acquiring chosen personal entrepreneurial competencies by respondents from China and Poland

Table 13.7 The possibility of acquiring chosen personal entrepreneurial competencies by respondents from China and Poland – in %

	1	2	3	4	5
China					
Leadership skills	11%	6%	26%	39%	18%
Communicativeness	9%	4%	21%	31%	36%
Personal time management	8%	6%	22%	45%	19%
Initiative	7%	6%	38%	22%	27%
Self-confidence	11%	5%	15%	29%	40%
Creativity and innovation	13%	2%	29%	18%	39%
Problem solving skills	11%	5%	15%	29%	40%
Persistence	13%	4%	37%	24%	23%
Information seeking	11%	4%	19%	33%	33%
Risk taking and risk management	13%	3%	44%	20%	21%
Poland					
Leadership skills	8%	22%	35%	27%	9%
Communicativeness	7%	8%	38%	35%	13%
Personal time management	6%	13%	30%	36%	16%
Initiative	9%	19%	38%	28%	7%
Self-confidence	8%	16%	38%	26%	12%
Creativity and innovation	8%	18%	35%	29%	11%
Problem solving skills	6%	14%	39%	28%	13%
Persistence	13%	13%	28%	30%	15%
Information seeking	5%	16%	37%	32%	11%
Risk taking and risk management	14%	12%	32%	33%	10%

Table 13.7 displays more detailed data concerning the probabilities of obtaining the selected PECs from the perspectives of the Chinese and Polish respondents. On a scale of 1–5, the possibilities of acquiring each PEC from the universities' education in the eyes of respondents from the analyzed countries were computed.

As shown in Table 13.7, "self-confidence" and "problem solving skills" were equally considered by respondents from China as the PECs with the highest possibility (40%) to acquire during university studies. "Personal time management" was rated by the Polish respondents as the PEC that has the highest possibility (16%) to obtain during university studies. However, the acquisition of "risk taking and risk management" was rated by Polish respondents as having the least opportunity (14%) of being acquired, while "creativity and innovation," "persistence," as well as "risk taking and risk management" were viewed by Chinese respondents as the PECs with the least possibility (13%) to obtain during university studies.

Comparing the importance and possibility of acquisition of PEC, it should be stressed that according to Polish respondents "problem solving skills" and "communicativeness" are both most important and most obtainable. Such statement, according to respondents from China, is true regarding "problem solving skills."

Furthermore, to examine an association between satisfaction with QoT and satisfaction with creation of PECs, the Pearson correlation coefficient was applied.

Multiple R and R Square is 0.48 and 0.23 for China and 0.59 and 0.35 for Poland, respectively. First of all, the authors can state that there is a relationship based on the data set. In both analyzed countries, there is a moderate positive relationship between satisfaction with QoT and satisfaction with creation of PECs. However, satisfaction with QoT has rather weak effect on satisfaction with creation of PEC. In Poland 35% and in China 23% of the variability observed in the satisfaction with creation of PECs is explained by the regression model.

Further, the normality test was run. The null hypothesis assumes that the data come from normal distribution, whereas the alternative hypothesis assumes that the data do not come from the normal distribution. According to the test results, Shapiro-Wilk test Sig. = 0.00; thus, it can be concluded that data do not come from the normal distribution. Meaning, H_0: Sample data coming from the normal distribution was rejected. Due to that fact, a non-parametric method – Kruskal-Wallis H test – was selected for further investigation. A Kruskal-Wallis H test was conducted to determine whether there is a difference in:

- Satisfaction with the quality of teaching (H_{01}, H_{a1}).
- Satisfaction with the level of creation of personal entrepreneurial competencies (H_{02}, Ha_2).
- The importance of acquiring chosen competencies.
- Leadership skills (H_{03}, Ha_3).
- Communicativeness (H_{04}, Ha_4).
- Personal time management (H_{05}, Ha_5).
- Initiative (H_{06}, Ha_6).
- Self-confidence (H_{07}, Ha_7).
- Creativity and innovation (H_{08}, Ha_8).
- Problem solving skills (H_{09}, Ha_9).
- Persistence (H_{010}, Ha_{10}).
- Information seeking (H_{011}, Ha_{11}).
- Risk taking and risk management (H_{012}, Ha_{12}).
- The possibility of acquiring chosen competencies.
- Leadership skills (H_{013}, Ha_{13}).
- Communicativeness (H_{014}, Ha_{14}).
- Personal time management (H_{015}, Ha_{15}).
- Initiative (H_{016}, Ha_{16}).
- Self-confidence (H_{017}, Ha_{17}).
- Creativity and innovation (H_{018}, Ha_{18}).
- Problem solving skills (H_{019}, Ha_{19}).
- Persistence (H_{020}, Ha_{20}).
- Information seeking (H_{021}, Ha_{21}).
- Risk taking and risk management (H_{022}, Ha_{22}).

based on the respondents' country of origin, where one variable was denoted as variable from Poland and second variable as variable from China. The summary of the testing hypotheses is presented in Tables 13.8, 13.9, and 13.10.

Table 13.8 The summary of the testing hypotheses – part I, satisfaction; Poland ($n = 104$), China ($n = 112$)

Country	Mean rank	χ^2	*df*	Sig.	α
Satisfaction with QoT					
Poland	110.64	0.269	1	0.604	0.01
China	106.51				
Satisfaction with the level of creation of PECs					
Poland	106.53	0.220	1	0.639	0.01
China	110.33				

Table 13.9 The summary of the testing hypotheses – part II, the importance of acquiring PECs; Poland ($n = 104$), China ($n = 112$)

Country	Mean rank	χ^2	*df*	Sig.	α
The importance of acquiring PECs					
Leadership skills					
Poland	138.66	49.763	1	**0.000**	0.01
China	80.49				
Communicativeness					
Poland	96.99	7.887	1	**0.005**	0.01
China	119.28				
Personal time management					
Poland	105.27	0.606	1	0.436	0.01
China	111.50				
Initiative					
Poland	103.33	1.524	1	0.217	0.01
China	113.3				
Self-confidence					
Poland	91.66	16.659	1	**0.000**	0.01
China	124.14				
Creativity and innovation					
Poland	99.22	5.205	1	0.023	0.01
China	117.12				
Problem solving skills					
Poland	97.17	7.760	1	**0.005**	0.01
China	119.02				
Persistence					
Poland	93.13	13.826	1	**0.000**	0.01
China	122.77				
Information seeking					
Poland	9.742	9.742	1	**0.002**	0.01
China	120.50				
Risk taking and risk management					
Poland	102.00	2.391	1	0.122	0.01
China	114.53				

Table 13.10 The summary of the testing hypotheses – part III, the possibility to acquire PECs while studying; Poland ($n = 104$), China ($n = 112$)

Country	Mean rank	χ^2	*df*	Sig.	α
The possibility to acquire PECs					
Leadership skills					
Poland	95.56	9.106	1	**0.003**	0.01
China	120.42				
Communicativeness					
Poland	94.57	10.774	1	**0.001**	0.01
China	121.43				
Personal time management					
Poland	102.89	1.775	1	0.183	0.01
China	113.71				
Initiative					
Poland	94.47	10.942	1	**0.001**	0.01
China	121.53				
Self-confidence					
Poland	97.92	6.227	1	0.013	0.01
China	118.32				
Creativity and innovation					
Poland	93.11	12.974	1	**0.000**	0.01
China	122.79				
Problem solving skills					
Poland	90.87	17.037	1	**0.000**	0.01
China	124.88				
Persistence					
Poland	103.17	1.556	1	0.212	0.01
China	113.45				
Information seeking					
Poland	93.02	13.180	1	**0.000**	0.01
China	122.87				
Risk taking and risk management					
Poland	104.13	1.062	1	0.303	0.01
China	112.55				

A Kruskal-Wallis H test showed that there was no statistically significant difference between the satisfaction with the QoT and satisfaction with the level of creation of PECs across two groups of respondents based on their country of origin.

A Kruskal-Wallis H test showed that there was statistically significant difference between the importance of acquiring six PECs across two groups of respondents based on their country of origin – information seeking, problem solving skills, self-confidence, leadership skills, communicativeness, and persistence. A Kruskal-Wallis H test showed that there was no statistically significant difference between the importance of acquiring the other four PECs across two groups of respondents based on their country of origin.

A Kruskal-Wallis H test showed that there was statistically significant difference between the possibility to acquire six PECs across two groups of respondents based on their country of origin – information seeking, problem solving skills, initiative, creativity and innovation, communicativeness, and leadership skills. A Kruskal-Wallis H test showed that there was no statistically significant difference between the possibility to acquire the other four PECs across two groups of respondents based on their country of origin.

13.4 Conclusions

The main objective of this chapter was to verify whether there is a relation between satisfaction of university students and graduates with the QoT and their satisfaction with creation of PECs at universities in China and Poland. In order to fulfill the aim of this chapter, the authors conducted a literature review on the concept of entrepreneurship, entrepreneur, EC, and PEC. Furthermore, a quantitative research on the satisfaction with the acquisition of PECs and with the possibility of acquiring PECs from universities, as well as their importance in analyzed countries was conducted.

Based on the literature review, there are no big differences between EC and PEC, the definition of PEC is based on the characteristics of an entrepreneurial person, which including a set of competencies that a successful entrepreneurial person should possess, such as leadership skills, communicativeness, personal time management, initiative, self-confidence, creativity and innovation, problem solving skills, persistence, information seeking, and risk taking and risk management. Furthermore, a large number of researchers also suggested that PECs can be obtained throughout educational training, particularly in HEIs.

After analyzing and evaluating the research data, the authors found that the majority of respondents in both countries were neither satisfied nor dissatisfied with the QoT at their universities. Apparently, more Chinese respondents than Polish respondents (10% vs. 4%) also expressed strong dissatisfaction with the QoT at their universities, while more Polish respondents than Chinese respondents (8% vs. 2%) were very satisfied with the QoT at their universities. Furthermore, regarding the satisfaction with the level of creation of PECs at universities in analyzed countries, the research findings (shown in Table 13.5) clearly indicate that the respondents are neither satisfied nor dissatisfied. When it comes to the importance of acquisition of chosen PECs, "problem solving skills" as well as "creativity and innovation" were considered as very important PECs by respondents from both analyzed countries, while "initiative" and "leadership skills" were rated as the least important PECs by respondents from both countries. However, Polish respondents believed "communicativeness" to be more crucial than "self-confidence," which Chinese respondents valued it as one of the most significant PEC. The results also show that there are some disparities in respondents' perceptions of the possibilities of obtaining the chosen PECs while studying at universities in analyzed countries. "Communicativeness" and "personal time management" were considered as the

PECs with highest possibilities of acquisition from higher education, while "risk taking and risk management" as well as "initiative" were viewed as the PECs with lowest possibilities of acquisition during university studies, from Chinese and Polish respondents' perspective, respectively.

In conclusion, based on the research findings, the authors conclude that there is a moderate positive relationship between the satisfaction of university students and graduates with the QoT and their satisfaction with creation of PECs at universities in analyzed countries. Moreover, according to the research data, the average rank assigned to the satisfaction with QoT correlates with the averaged rank of possibilities of the acquisition of PECs. In other words, the probability of acquiring PECs increases with higher university QoT satisfaction. A Kruskal-Wallis H test showed that there was statistically significant difference between the importance of acquiring six PECs across two groups of respondents based on their country of origin – information seeking, problem solving skills, self-confidence, leadership skills, communicativeness, and persistence. A Kruskal-Wallis H test also showed that there was statistically significant difference between the possibility to acquire six PECs across two groups of respondents based on their country of origin – information seeking, problem solving skills, initiative, creativity and innovation, communicativeness, and leadership skills. Thus, it can be stated that respondents from Poland and China have statistically significant different points of view regarding both importance and possibility of acquisition of four personal entrepreneurial competencies – information seeking, problem solving skills, leadership skills, and communicativeness.

Finally, it is also worth to mention limitations of the study. Due to the small sample size, the research conclusions cannot be generalized. The research process in both countries was also hindered by epidemiological situation. Notwithstanding the limitations, the differences between Polish and Chinese respondents are highlighted and can be a solid basis for further studies on larger samples.

References

Antoncic, B., & Hisrich, R. D. (2003). Clarifying the intrapreneurship concept. *Journal of Small Business & Enterprise Development, 9*(2), 7–24.

Brockhaus, R. (1980). Risk taking propensity of entrepreneurs. *Academy of Management Review, 23*(1), 509–520.

Bygrave, W., & Hofer, C. (1991). Theorizing about entrepreneurship. *Entrepreneurship Theory and Practice, 2*(16), 13–22.

Cambridge Dictionary. (2022). *The definition of competency*. Retrieved April 07, 2022, from https://dictionary.cambridge.org/dictionary/english/competency

Collins, C., Locke, E., & Shane, S. (2003). Entrepreneurial motivation. *Human Resource Management Review, 2*(13), 257–280.

Daniel, W. W. (1990). Spearman rank correlation coefficient. In *Applied nonparametric statistics* (2nd ed.). PWS-Kent.

Eurostat. (2022). *Young people in Europe – A statistical summary – 2022 edition*. Retrieved January 03, 2023, from https://ec.europa.eu/eurostat/en/web/products-catalogues/-/ks-06-22-076

Evans, J. G. (1949). The entrepreneur and economic theory: A historical and analytical approach. *The American Economic Review, 1*(39), 336–348.
Gartner, W. B. (1989). Who is an entrepreneur? Is the wrong question. *Entrepreneurship Theory and Practice, 13*(4), 48–60.
Hawley, F. (1907). *Enterprise and the productive process*. Putnam.
Hébert, R. F., & Link, A. N. (1988). *The entrepreneur: Mainstream views & radical critiques*. Praeger.
Hornaday, J., & Bunker, C. (1970). The nature of the entrepreneur. *Personal Psychology, 1*(23), 47.
Howell, R. (1972). Comparative profiles: Entrepreneurs versus the hired executive: San Francisco peninsula semiconductor industry. In A. Cooper & J. Komives (Eds.), *Technical entrepreneurship: A symposium* (pp. 66–67). Center for Venture Management.
Hull, D., & Bosley, J. (1980). Reviewing the heffalump: Identifying potential entrepreneurs by personality characteristics. *Small Business Management, 1*(18).
Human Development Reports. (2023). Retrieved May 12, 2023, from https://hdr.undp.org/data-center/thematic-composite-indices/gender-inequality-index#/indicies/GII
Katana, C. (2016). Entrepreneurship in students' awareness – Knowledge, attitudes, commitment. *Scientific papers of the Silesian University of Technology. Organization and Management Series,* 98, 39–45.
Kirzner, I. (1997). Entrepreneurial discovery and the competitive market process: An Austrian approach. *Economic Literature, 1*(25).
Kolanowska, E., Górowska-Fells, M., & Płatos, B. (2018). *The system of education in Poland.* Foundation for the Development of the Education System.
Kurtz, R., & Bartram, D. (2002). Competency and individual performance: Modelling the world of work. *Organizational Effectiveness, 10*(1), 227–235.
Lumpkin, G., & Dess, G. (1996). Clarifying the entrepreneurial orientation construct and linking it to performance. *Academy of Management Review, 21*(1), 135.
Mamun, A. A., Muniady, R. A., Permarupa, P. Y., Zainol, N. R. B., Nawi, N. B. C., & Malarvizhi, C. A. (2016). Social capital and entrepreneurial competencies: A study among women microentrepreneurs in Malaysia. *The Journal of Developing Areas, 50*(5), 383.
Man, T., & Lau, T. (2000). Entrepreneurial competencies of SME owner/managers in the Hong Kong service sector: A qualitative analysis. *Journal of Enterprising Culture, 8*(3), 235.
McClelland, D. (1973). Testing for competence rather than for intelligence. *American Psychologist, 28*(1), 1.
Mesquita, C., Lopes, R. P., & Bredis, K. (2016). Entrepreneurship in higher education as a horizontal competence. In M. Peris-Ortiz, J. Gómez, F. Vélez-Torres, & C. Rueda-Armengot (Eds.), *Education tools for entrepreneurship. Innovation, technology, and knowledge management* (pp. 223–241). Springer.
Misiak-Kwit, S. (2020). *Determinants and consequences of entrepreneurship in Poland. Theoretical approach*. University of Szczecin.
Missias, M. T., & Brugar, K. (2018). Entrepreneurship. *Counterpoints, 527*(26).
Mitchelmore, S., & Rowley, J. (2010). Entrepreneurial competencies: A literature review and development agenda. *International Journal of Entrepreneurial Behavior and Research, 16*(2), 92.
Muzam, J. (2022). The challenges of modern economy on the competencies of knowledge workers. *Journal of the Knowledge Economy, 14*, 1635. https://doi.org/10.1007/s13132-022-00979-y
National Burial of Statistics. (2021). *Catalog of statistical survey items of government departments in 2020*. Retrieved January 03, 2023, from: http://www.stats.gov.cn/xxgk/zftjdcxmsp/bmtjdcxm/202201/t20220124_1826972.html
National Council for the Social Studies (NCSS). (2013). *The college, career, and civic life (C3) framework for social studies state standards*. Silver Spring.
Patharkar, N., & Kishnani, N. (2021). *Entrepreneurship*. The Bhopal School of Social Sciences.
Ploum, L. (2019). Competencies for sustainable entrepreneurship. In W. L. Filho, A. Azul, L. Brandli, P. Özuyar, & T. Wall (Eds.), *Decent work and economic growth. Encyclopedia of the UN sustainable development goals* (pp. 82–92). Springer.

Prokopenko, O., Osadchenko, I., Braslavska, O., Malyshevska, I., Pichkur, M., & Tyshchenko, V. (2020). Competence approach in future specialist skills development. *International Journal of Management, 11*(4), 645–656.

Ratković, T., Šlogar, H., & Šokčević, S. (2022). Entrepreneurial competencies of university students. *Economics and Sociology, 15*(4), 129–135.

Shapiro, S. S., & Wilk, M. B. (1965). An analysis of variance test for normality (complete samples). *Biometrika, 52*(3–4), 591–611. https://doi.org/10.1093/biomet/52.3-4.591

Smerek, L., & Kováčiková, V. (2019). University as a factor in the employee selection process in Slovak enterprises, conference paper. In *Conference: 33rd IBIMA conference: Education excellence and innovation management through vision 2020* (pp. 271–278).

Smerek, L., & Vetráková, M. (2020). Difference in human resources development in various types of companies. *Polish Journal of Management Studies, 21*(2), 398–411. https://doi.org/10.17512/pjms.2020.21.2.28

Smith, D. (2010). The role of entrepreneurship in economic growth. *Undergraduate Economic Review, 6*(1).

Stevenson, H., & Jarillo, J. (1990). A paradigm of entrepreneurship: Entrepreneurial management. *Strategic Management Journal, 1*(11).

Tekin, B., & Asar, M. (2021). Role of entrepreneurship self-efficacy and risk-taking tendencies in the relationship between financial literacy and entrepreneurial intention. *Social Entrepreneurship Review, 1*, 7–33. https://doi.org/10.15678/SER.2021.1.01

Theodorsson-Norheim, E. (1986). Kruskal-Wallis test: BASIC computer program to perform nonparametric one-way analysis of variance and multiple comparisons on ranks of several independent samples. *Computer Methods and Programs in Biomedicine, 23*(1), 57–62. https://doi.org/10.1016/0169-2607(86)90081-7

Thornton, M. A. (1998). Richard Cantillon and the origin of economic theory. *Journal des Économistes et des Études Humaines, 8*, 61–74.

Vries, D., & Kets, M. F. R. (1977). The entrepreneurial personality: A person at the crossroads. *Journal of Management Studies (Wiley-Blackwell), 14*(1), 35–37.

Wasliczuk, J., Chukhray, N., Karyy, O., & Halkiv, L. (2021). Entrepreneurial competencies and intentions among students of technical universities. *Problems and Perspectives in Management, 19*(3), 10–21. https://doi.org/10.21511/ppm.19(3).2021.02

Wickramaratne, A., Kiminami, A., & Yagi, H. (2014). Entrepreneurial competencies and entrepreneurial orientation of tea manufacturing firms in Sri Lanka. *Asian Social Science, 10*(18).

Wiściska-Fernando, M. (2021). The use of mobile technologies in online shopping during the Covid-19 pandemic - an empirical study. *Procedia Computer Science, 192*(1), 3413–3422. https://doi.org/10.1016/j.procs.2021.09.114

Word Population Review. (2023). Retrieved January 07, 2023, from https://worldpopulationreview.com/countries.

Yuaz, Z. (2018). Dual priority agenda: China's model for modernizing education. *ECNU Review of Education, 1*(1), 5–33. https://doi.org/10.30926/ecnuroe2018010102

Chapter 14
Become an Entrepreneur? No, That Is Not My Way. Intersectionality and Sensitizing Students for Entrepreneurship

Julia Große, Verena Liszt-Rohlf, and Alexandra Baldwin

14.1 Introduction

Policymakers assume that universities have a particular relevance to economic activities like starting new businesses and the support required to do this. Based on this assumed relevance of universities, different cultures and different forms of support geared towards promoting entrepreneurial thinking and entrepreneurship have emerged at universities (Altmeier, 2019; Halbfas, 2006; Ferreira et al., 2018). In the context of these efforts, entrepreneurship education has emerged as a young research discipline; its subject focus lies on the qualification of (nascent) entrepreneurs. In the context of this subject orientation, Metzger emphasizes that entrepreneurs are the main drivers in this field and their intentions for starting a business deserve particular attention. Metzger thematically emphasizes entrepreneurs' founding intention, which is subject to various factors and, in a broader sense, has an impact on the founding activity within a country (Metzger, 2015). Throughout this paper, founding intention is defined as "the subjectively perceived probability of becoming professionally self-employed within a certain period of time after a cut-off date" (Walter, 2008: 8).

If we look at the general implementation of founding support at universities in Germany, it appears that numerous support programs target students who are already interested in founding or who have a concrete intention to start a business; yet, there is only marginal evidence of entrepreneurship education targeting students who

J. Große
University of Kassel, Kassel, Germany

V. Liszt-Rohlf (✉) · A. Baldwin
Department of Business Studies, University of Applied Sciences Burgenland, Eisenstadt, Austria
e-mail: verena.liszt-rohlf@fh-burgenland.at

K. Mikkelsen, A. Wolf (eds.), *Minds, Brains, and Doxa for Inclusive Entrepreneurship*, International Studies in Entrepreneurship 47,
https://doi.org/10.1007/978-3-031-50164-7_14

have no intention of becoming entrepreneurs and who could be sensitized to the topic of entrepreneurship. It is therefore assumed that universities hardly meet the requirement to consider "all" students (Högsdal et al., 2020; Gründungsradar, 2020; Walter, 2008).

Furthermore, it seems evident that due to globalization and other social development processes, the student population at universities is becoming increasingly diverse. According to the theory of planned behavior, this constitutes a corpus of different background factors of social inequality that influence the development of students' founding intentions and would therefore have to be taken into account when promoting entrepreneurship at universities (Jungbauer-Gans & Gottburgsen, 2021; Geldof, 2016; Ajzen & Fishbein, 2005).

However, it has not yet been scientifically clarified which social background factors influence the founding intentions of students. When looking at the diverse backgrounds from which students stem, it appears safe to assume a degree of social inequality among the student body. Studies from the field of family entrepreneurship show that most founders come from families in which at least one other person has founded a company or has an entrepreneurial role model in their immediate environment (Allen, 2021). Other categories of social inequality, such as gender, are also indirectly assumed to influence the intention to start a business. However, the consideration of individual categories of social inequality in research on diverse students, such as gender, class, or ethnicity, is controversial in the context of sociological research. Recent theories from feminist research indicate that there are interactions between categories of inequality (intersections), which generate inequality within social structures (as in this case of founding new businesses), and that the social position of students on the labor market and thus their capacity to start their own business can reinforce hidden discrimination. These interactions and relations between social inequality categories cannot simply be merged in their effect, as is often the case in quantitative studies, but have to be looked at separately (Winker & Degele, 2010). In the context of researching founding intentions, however, these interactions are hardly taken into account.

Accordingly, in the context of this research, universities would have to include the social (unequal) starting points when supporting students in terms of founding. In this context, it is questionable to what extent the intersectional inequality of students influences the development of a student's own intention to start a business. In order to be able to deal with these questions, we used the multi-level approach of an intersectionality analysis by Winker and Degele (2010) and carried out narrative interviews in the context of qualitative empirical research. Based on the state of the method, the following subordinate questions could be derived:

- To what extent can identity constructions of economics students at the University of Kassel be differentiated in terms of their intention to found a company at the end of their Bachelor's degree?
- What symbolic representations go hand in hand with rejecting to start one's own company?
- Do social structures of domination prevent the emergence of entrepreneurship intentions among students?

Answering the research questions is expected to advance current theory on entrepreneurship intentions. First, the theory of planned behavior or founding intention research could be developed further. The background factors that have received little attention so far can be better specified when applying the method. Secondly, with the new application of intersectionality analysis in entrepreneurship education, the method could advance entrepreneurship education and the field could experience a methodological enrichment.

14.2 Entrepreneurship Education and Founding Support

The current discussion of the subject of starting a business first raised political interest through Birch. He described how small and medium-sized enterprises create a large proportion of new jobs and referred to them as "gazelles". Some authors have since claimed that interest in entrepreneurship, especially as a discipline, began with these remarks (Hindle, 2007; Aronson, 2004). However, the transfer and location of entrepreneurship education in universities has entailed controversy since then. Hindle (2007) discusses what reasons may speak against entrepreneurship education in universities, especially in Business Schools. In this regard, he cites McMullan (1987), among others, who argues that entrepreneurship requires primarily experiential teaching-learning methods and environments that are fundamentally at odds with typical university (economics) teaching-learning methods (Hindle, 2007; McMullan & Long, 1987). Economics teaching-learning methods in this context are often referred to as "managerialism" oriented. Here, management theory is seen as the basis for entrepreneurship education. This is grounded in the belief that the environment is predictable and known, justifying a linear planning approach (Johannisson, 2018).

Other authors also point out limitations in this regard. For example, Johannisson (2018) writes from a process philosophy perspective that entrepreneurship is a phenomenon that represents a more profound human activity than simply introducing a radical innovation to a market. Rather, in relation to entrepreneurship, he writes of a way of life that recognizes change as a natural state (entrepreneurship as a processual phenomenon) (Johannisson, 2018). Entrepreneurship is thus a processual phenomenon that requires not only cognitive but also affective and conative skills. He also subsumes situated insights that students need to attain. Accordingly, these should promote the entrepreneurial spirit of students. (Johannisson, 2018).

The critical view that universities are places that support founding and entrepreneurship that the above-mentioned authors expressed only shows a small section of the scientific dissent on this topic. Especially, as the traditional goal of universities – the dissemination of knowledge to the global community, and the collaboration between universities and industries – has changed. Universities have become inherently more internally entrepreneurial and support proactive solutions to societal problems. As a result, there is an increased exchange with other institutions, which means that the perception of universities within society is transforming (Ferreira et al., 2018). Yet, in this paper, the critique of typical praxeological entrepreneurship support is taken up in an attempt to address the central question: "To what extent is the intention to start a business influenced by intersectional inequality?"

At the beginning of the development of entrepreneurship education, higher education institutions had no coordinated educational programs of their own and no role models in theory or practice to fall back on. The result of this unsystematic development process of entrepreneurship education was a confusing, multi-layered, difficult-to-access collection of fragments and approaches of the most diverse character, which emerged in the specific requirement contexts of the individual universities (Halbfas, 2006). To date, this development process has not yet been completed and various forms of entrepreneurship education have evolved at universities: "There is still much work required for universities to be seen as entrepreneurial." (Ferreira et al., 2018: 12). Whereby entrepreneurship education must also always be considered in the overall context of an entrepreneurial ecosystem at universities and no generalized silver bullet can be identified in this regard (Ferreira et al., 2018).

In summary, many different educational programs and strategies have emerged in the context of entrepreneurship education, which are difficult to compare. Thus, academic articles on this topic often deal with "best practice" concepts (see, for example, excerpts from Chapter IV, The Role and Impact of Entrepreneurship Education – Fayolle et al., 2019).

The responsibility for start-up awareness at universities is centrally assigned to the various events in teaching, as teaching events here are considered the core for competence transfer. According to the Gründungsradar, approximately 7489 teaching events featured a start-up in Germany in 2019. These included 3602 curricular events with an average of 4.4 ECTS credits and 3874 extracurricular events. In most cases, extracurricular events are offered by central institutions or the university administration. Overall, the higher education institutions in Germany were able to reach around 200,000 participants with start-up-relevant content in 2019. In this regard, 168 out of 183 higher education institutions state that they cover at least five of the following topics: Introduction to entrepreneurship, entrepreneurship mindset, start-up-relevant business knowledge, business plan, idea development and design sprints, prototyping, legal and tax aspects, start-up financing, intrapreneurship and soft skills (Gründungsradar, 2020), whereby the content presented here not only raises awareness but also qualifies students to start a business, as is recorded in the funnel model under the segment "teaching" (ibid.). It should also be critically noted to what extent students who are fundamentally reluctant to start their own business are inclined to participate in extracurricular events on the topic of start-ups. Bijedic also points out that in the university context only "those who want to start a business" are supported. "Entrepreneurship support in the tertiary sector is mainly focused on preparing those willing to start a business, mostly in terms of expertise, infrastructure and resources." (Bijedic, 2019).

Entrepreneurial Intentions

Research on the topic of founding intentions or entrepreneurial intentions first gained special attention about 30 years ago with the work of Shapero (1982, 1984). Subsequent work by Bird (1988) and Gartner (1985) produced contributions that turned to both cognitive intention approaches and a process view. In this regard, social psychological approaches such as Bandura's work on self-efficacy (1982) or the "Theory of Planned Behavior" by Ajzen (1991) achieved particular attention in research. To date, many diverse publications have appeared in the research context of founding intentions, which according to Fayolle (2013) can be systematized as follows (Fayolle & Liñàn, 2014; Liñàn & Fayolle, 2015).

Core Model – Methodological Issues and Theoretical Deepening

1. The role of personal level variables in the emergence of entrepreneurial intentions.
2. The relationship between entrepreneurial education and the entrepreneurial intention of its participants.
3. The role of context and institutions in the development of entrepreneurial intention.
4. Entrepreneurial process and the link between intention and behavior.

Within this framework, many of the empirical studies are based on quantitative research practices. Regarding qualitative and quantitative studies, two research directions can be identified in summary: Studies dealing with personal (motives for founding, characteristics of founding individuals) and organizational (differences between departments at universities) determinants (Walter, 2008).

Personal determinants like motives for founding lead to human behavior, including business creation, and the behavior itself is difficult to explain in all its complexity. On a psychological level, it can be approached from different angles. Social and personality psychologists explain person-related determinants in all their complexity with the consideration of fully functioning individuals processing available and existing information in the context of biological and environmental factors. Ajzen (1991) developed a comprehensive and empirically well-supported model for this purpose (Ajzen, 1991; Ajzen, 2012). This theory of planned behavior draws on the preceding theory of reasoned action (1988). Ajzen considers intention (motivating factor) to be a central momentum for individuals' behavior. Basically, the stronger the intention of an individual to perform a certain behavior, the more likely the actual implementation. In addition, actual implementation of a behavior also depends on non-motivational factors. Ajzen refers to these as the availability of necessary resources for a behavior, such as time, money, and skills. According to Ajzen, if individuals have these resources and are motivated to perform a behavior, this behavior will occur with a high degree of certainty. Moreover, a high degree of perceived control over one's own behavior can overcome obstacles and lead to direct implementation of the behavior (Ajzen, 1991, 2020).

Various background factors significantly influence these processes. According to Ajzen, background factors do not have a direct effect on the development of an intention and are rather to be understood as an indirect influence and affect the various types of conviction as upstream determinants. Examples include personal characteristics such as age, gender, income, education, race, ethnicity, culture, knowledge, and information. General attitudes, human capital, or personality traits such as self-efficacy are also subsumed under these factors. Due to the large number of background factors, Ajzen and Fishbein (2005) suggest a well-founded selection of suitable ones (cf. Lange, 2012; Ajzen & Fishbein, 2005).

The background factors raised here tend to be neglected in most studies about founding intentions, when discussed in the context of entrepreneurship education and the theory of planned behavior. However, the fundamental influence of personal characteristics such as gender, age, ethnicity, etc. points to an influence of social inequality of individuals when it comes to the intention to establish a company. In the educational context of higher education, migration and mobility (globalization), for example, present new challenges and feature increasingly diverse student populations. Studying and teaching face differentiated demands in this regard. The organizational objective of higher education institutions is measured here along the achievement of international academic excellence to the social guarantee of equality and equal opportunities (Jungbauer-Gans & Gottburgsen, 2021; Geldof, 2016). The increasing diversity of students at universities described here and the influence of social inequality (described as background factors) on the intention to start a business raise the fundamental question of which founding-relevant background factors (indirectly) influence the intention of students to start a business.

Influencing Sociological Determinants on Students' Intention to Start a Business

In the context of entrepreneurship education at universities, approaches prevail that emphasize the effect of role models. Studies that predominantly focus on entrepreneurial behavior have shown that entrepreneurs often have a reference person, such as their mother or father, who were entrepreneurs themselves. In this regard, entrepreneurial individuals likewise reported having experienced necessary values, norms, and skills early on that are important for an entrepreneurial future (Dyer & Handler, 1994). Possible explanations for this are also offered by research findings about family entrepreneurship. According to this research tradition, the answer to the question of how families sustain their own business over generations is "socialization." Socialization is a process by which members of a social group, such as the family in this case, absorb and internalize the values, ideals, behaviors, procedures, and expectation of the social groups (Allen, 2021; Berger & Luckmann, 1966; Dyer, 2021). Socialization is to be distinguished from the concept of education, as it happens willfully, consciously, and intentionally. Part of socialization are expectations and norms regarding manners, tone of voice, and the meaning of gestures, e.g., the first place of socialization is usually the family. The research field of family entrepreneurship assumes that entrepreneurship at the individual level appears to be a particular way of thinking and acting that arises, among other things, from family socialization (Allen, 2021; Sarasvathy, 2008).

At this point, research on role models becomes relevant. Role models who motivate students can be described as "individuals who (i) influence role aspirants' achievements, motivation, and goals by acting as behavioral models, (ii) are representations of the possible, and (iii) act as inspirations" (Morgenroth et al., 2015). The dominant function of role models could be learning by example, which means that role models (iv) "give advice and hands-on support" (Bosma et al., 2012a, b, p. 413).

Role models usually have a personal relationship with the person who looks up to them. It is advantageous if the role models are perceived as successful by the students and have similarities to the students (in terms of gender, race) (Dasgupta, 2011; Ahn et al., 2020). It is even assumed that not only similarities but even relationships can be decisive with regard to the effect of role models. There are different views on this in science, which on the one hand confirm this effect on entrepreneurial intention or whether it is a matter of influences from the wider family environment (such as grandparents) (Laspita et al., 2012; Pablo-Lerchundi et al., 2015). If role models are observed away from personal relationships, as this is the case for students and entrepreneurs, they may still be affected. Here, it depends on the respective role model and his or her experiences. If the experiences are negative (many hours of work), this can have a deterrent effect. However, this effect can be reduced through personal interaction (Fellnhofer & Mueller, 2018; van Auken et al., 2006; Austin & Nauta, 2016) or discussing positive experiences (like demonstrating a feasible and desirable career option) (Karimi et al., 2014). For women in particular, personal interaction and relationships have a particularly strong effect on entrepreneurial intention (BarNir et al., 2011). Regarding the target group focused in this paper, it is worth mentioning that students prefer role models who also embrace desires and aspirations in their presentations (Radu & Loué, 2008). Additionally, it has become clear in one study that students with little self-esteem should learn from success (not failure) stories from role models (Chen et al., 2016). Taking this idea further, there is evidence that promotion-focused students who favor pursuing desirable outcomes are more likely to benefit from positive experiences of role models. Students who are more prevention-focused are more likely to benefit from experiences of role models who present avoidance strategies for undesirable outcomes (Lockwood et al., 2002).

Other sociological contextual models are hardly covered except for research on the existence of networks and personal forms of capital, but influences of the latter on the intention to start a business as a whole are feasible (Bosma et al., 2012a, b). Sporadically different categories of inequality like class and gender are anticipated in these studies, whereas a capture of social inequality in an intersecting changing context also in the sense of the insights of the "Doing Difference" approach of Fenstermaker and West (2002) is not found in the literature (Fenstermaker & West, 2002). According to this popular approach by Fenstermaker and West (2002), gender, for example, emerges in relation to class and ethnicity in a simultaneous process (Winker & Degele, 2010; Fenstermaker & West, 2002). Work that captures aspects of social inequality tend to be studies that address family contextual conditions and role models (Winker & Degele, 2010; Fenstermaker & West, 2002; Bosma et al., 2012a, b). Yet, articles from the UK context of entrepreneurship education point to a need for intersectional inequality analyses. Martinez and Agwunobi (2018), among others, write that the need to take up the social context of entrepreneurship is undeniable and that it is necessary to refrain from a one-dimensional superficial consideration of individual categories of inequality (Martinez & Agwunobi, 2018). In general, there are different concepts of diversity in science, which have different effects on the study thereof. In the following, different concepts are discussed in more detail.

14.3 Diversity and Intersectional Inequality of Students

Diversity Understanding and Perspectives

Diversity is regarded worldwide as an undisputed concept for describing human differences and as a normative guiding concept for dealing with them (diversity management). Social protests in the U.S. human rights movement in the late 1950s are described as the beginning of the discussion on the topic of "diversity." These can be understood as triggers for scholarly engagement with the topic (Vedder, 2009). Terms such as diversity, heterogeneity, and diversification are usually used synonymously in the research context in order to be able to proceed flexibly through conceptual contingency (Leontiy & Schulz, 2020; Bührmann, 2020; Hofmann, 2012). Fundamentally, a distinction is made between biological and social diversity. Both terms are based on different scientific disciplines. Biological diversity originates from the natural sciences and focuses on "hierarchies of similarities and dissimilarities between different species and sub-species…" (Bührmann, 2020: 36). In this regard, according to Bührmann (2020), extensive taxonomies in the form of trees have often emerged in the past, with the human species represented as the crown. Within these taxonomies, subcategories of the human species are often represented, to which the emergence of race theories can be attributed (Bührmann, 2020; Torrens & Barahona, 2012). In the context of social diversity, various understandings of diversity have emerged from the social science field. American diversity research practice often considers dimensions such as race, gender, ethnicity (nationality), age, physical condition such as age, religion, and role within an organization (Krell & Sieben, 2011; Bührmann, 2020). Bührmann (2020) also identifies three different concepts of diversity.

The *positivist understanding of diversity*, which is indicative of the field of diversity management in human resources, assumes diversity as a given, assuming a strict normalization of diversity and your dimensions of diversity. In this respect, the dimensions of diversity are partly seen as unchangeable, but also changeable. Within the positivist understanding of diversity, members of marginalized (mostly exotic) groups are centrally focused on. Differences between these various groups are dramatized and persons subscribe to them. Classifying individuals into one of these different groups entails that certain characteristics are inferred. The *critical understanding of diversity*, in contrast to the positivist understanding, does not take diversity for granted. Adherents of this current assume that diversity and its relevant dimensions are only produced in the "doing" within socio-cultural contexts (socially constructed). There is no question of a functional increase through diversity, as would be the case in the positivist sense, but rather existing power and domination relations are considered. Furthermore, the assignment of different characteristics to individuals belonging to a certain social group is strictly rejected and an intersectional, anti-discriminatory perspective is demanded. The goal is often to reduce "social inequality" in a social context (Bührmann, 2020). The *reflexive understanding of diversity* first constructed by Bührmann (2020) built on elaborations by Butler (1992), Foucault (1977), and Fenstermaker and West (2002), among others. The phenomena regarding different understandings of diversity are recognized as true in that they are operative. "Moreover, it is assumed that there is no dimension of diversity, for whatever reason, that is considered particularly relevant to explore. Rather, what is considered particularly relevant and why is of interest." (Bührmann, 2020: 49). The focus is not only on the oppressed and exoticized groups, but also on privileged groups and individuals, highlighting and analyzing (intersectional) differences and commonalities. However, the objective is also to be understood as anti-discriminatory, under which, however, the researcher's perspectives and standpoints (of the researcher) must also be explicated (Bührmann, 2020). Here, Bührmann raises three aspects to be reflected upon. These include the situatedness of the researcher in the research field, the implications of the methodological research design used, and the explicit and implicit epistemological presuppositions of the research practice (Bührmann, 2020).

These different understandings of diversity presented here offer three approaches to examining the phenomenon of influencing background factors in the context of students' intentions to start a business. However, the comparative presentation should not obscure the fact that each one of the understandings presented can be taken and have merit in the context of a different discourse. In this paper, the reflexive understanding of diversity is prioritized, as it is considered beneficial to find out which relevant dimensions of diversity, in the context (of equal founding support at universities) of students' founding intentions are at work and why (Bührmann, 2020). Consequently, the anticipation of particularly relevant differences is therefore rejected.

The (Historical) Development of the Intersectional Multi-level Approach

Historically, intersectionality grew out of feminism. Intersectionality is based on the teachings of the American "Combahee River Collective" of Black Feminism from 1977–1982, where the manifesto "All the women are white, all the blacks are men, but some of us are brave" linked for the first time the themes of the black civil rights movement to women's studies. This title highlights the problematic tendency to view "race" and "gender" in inequality analyses as mutually exclusive "categories of experience and analysis" (Crenshaw, 2010). The discourse on "triple oppression theory" that began in this regard then looked at the differences of women within the women's movement. In the process, a multiple oppression thesis emerged in inequality studies, but it was emotionally charged, causing the oppression of black women to fall out of focus (Lutz, 2001). The diversity debate that followed subsequently gained prominence. Central to this are the debates on "multiculturalism" (identity issues) and "minority or ethnic studies" (negotiation processes in the public sector). (Knapp, 2005).

In sociological research practice, various approaches to the analysis of intersectionality have become established (McCall, 2005). The intercategorical approach is favored by McCall because it fundamentally questions the existence of social inequality and interrogates relationships of different categories of inequality. The consideration of several categories within inequality research belongs to the "common sense" today. Race, class, and gender are the most commonly used categories since these categories alone are difficult to implement in an empirical analysis (Winker & Degele, 2010). The authors understand intersectionality as "… a system of interactions between inequality-creating social structures (i.e., of power relations), symbolic representations and identity constructions that are context-specific, topic-oriented and inextricably linked to social praxis." (Winker & Degele, 2011: 54).

This understanding of intersectionality anticipates the most diverse categories of difference and their social construction processes theoretically and methodologically on different levels. The relevance of different categories of inequality depends on the object of investigation and on the level of investigation. Levels of investigation in this respect are:

- Social structures incl. Institutions (macro level).
- Interactively produced processes of identity formation (micro level).
- Cultural symbols (representation level) (Winker and Degele, 2010).

At the macro level, categories are deductively established: class, gender, race, and body. These characteristics are crucial for the distribution of resources and the social position of members of society from their position in the labor market and their responsibility for the reproduction of the labor force. To this end, the four structural categories describe processes and relations within the logic of capitalist accumulation. In this context, relations of domination are racism, classism, bodyism, and sexism (Winker and Degele 2010). The interconnectedness of categories is described at the micro level by the Doing Difference approach. Gender emerges in conjunction with ethnicity and class. Symbolic representations at the representational level support the relations of domination described above and are equally visible through them. Norms, values, and stereotypes are elaborated on this level (Winker & Degele, 2010).

14.4 Research

Intersectional Multi-level Analysis as a Research Method

The present study uses the multi-level approach of an intersectionality analysis by Winker and Degele (2010), which follows eight steps. These eight steps of analysis build on the data basis derived from six qualitative narrative interviews and the analysis based on open coding (inductive) as set forth in the framework of grounded theory (Winker & Degele, 2010).

Step 1: The first step is to identify categories of difference regarding the interviewees (students). The authors justify this (in simplified terms) by stating that: "we know who we are when we know from whom we delineate ourselves. This is true even when the 'Other' is not even referenced; delineation can also be implicit." (Winker & Degele, 2011: 58). Therefore, the students' own identity constructions are analyzed first.

Step 2: Thereupon, based on the results of the preceding interview situations, values and norms that operate within a society can also be identified, made visible, and recorded. "These can be hegemonic representations, but also norms and values that create opposing public sociopolitical movements." (Winker & Degele, 2011: 59).

Step 3: Subsequently, on the basis of the identity constructions on the micro level, references to social structures are established and deductively assigned to the categories of class, gender, ethnicity, and body anticipated in this approach. In this context, social structures refer to structures in which subjects act and which they (re)produce, such as institutions, laws, and organizations.

Step 4: In the fourth step, the most important categories for the interviewee are compiled iteratively. Here, particular attention should be paid to categories that can be found on the micro, meso, and macro levels and that are interwoven and overlapping.

Step 5: From the fifth step on, the analysis refers to all examined cases.

The typing starts with the summary of the analyzed interviews and their subject constructions under the aspect of different strategies to overcome uncertainties. In this process, the subjects under investigation are divided into types based on one or more characteristics (such as able vs. not able, financial security, etc.). "The types generated in this way are more similar in certain characteristics than others, so that their similarity to each other must be explained by a plausible parameter value." Degele and Winker (2011: 60). The types formed here, have on the one hand, the greatest possible internal homogeneity and, on the other hand, a sufficient degree of external heterogeneity in comparison with each other. Here Degele and Winker (2011: 60) follow: "McCall's (2005: 1774) proposal for the preliminary adoption and strategic use of categories." Here, analytical distance and precise descriptions are required. In this regard, it must be emphasized that the dimensions of comparison have yet to be established as a priori. The dimension is social practice. The subject matter has, therefore, not been explicitly separated, for example, from men's to women's. "Only when the types have been established is there an analysis of the extent to which they are gendered, ethnicized, etc." Degele and Winker (2011: 60).

Step 6: In the sixth step, additional data sources on the macro level are to be collected and examined in depth for the analysis. It is particularly important to take up the structural power relations, whereby the "not naming" of categories can also be addressed.

Step 7: In the seventh step, prevailing ideologies are traced on the basis of the symbolic representations in order to clarify which social contexts are significant for the values and norms recorded in step 2. An example of this would be the achievement principle, which can be shared value for all educated groups.

Step 8: Step eight concludes by looking at numerous cross-case interactions, interrelationships, and different dimensions of inequality. At the structural level, we must begin by answering the question which classism, heteronormativity, racism, and bodyism can be identified in the field and to what extent they are interwoven. Subsequently, their impact on the micro level must be examined. The relationship between the macro level and its power relations and their symbolic representations will still be raised. The result here should derive conclusions about the extent to which structures and representations mutually support each other.

Field Access and Sampling

The sampling in this study is developed through "theoretical sampling," a procedure developed from Grounded Theory and is particularly suitable for research questions with an explorative character. Grounded theory methodology attempts to elaborate new theoretical ideas about a subject area within a given framework of rules. The theory is grounded by relating revisable generalization claims to bounded social phenomena (Glaser & Strauss, 1998, S. 53 ff). The use of this theory is justified by the marginal prior knowledge available in the context of the subject matter being researched here. A limitation that can be justified in the context of the theoretical reference points of this paper is the selection of the sample based on students who refuse to start their businesses and have no interest in dealing with the subject area. Through this limitation, possible insights can be generated in the context of the demand for equal start-up support and the sensitization of universities to start-ups. Of course, according to the guiding question of this paper, the counter-groups (such as students who have already founded and students who have the desire to start a business) would also have to be examined here to contrast a difference. However, in the context of the limitations of this paper, this is not possible. Nevertheless, for the following study to yield useful insights for start-up promotion in higher education on the influence of intersectional inequality, the sampling is narrowed as described above (ibid.).

In the context of intersectional inequality, the question of how to account for different positionings in the research field needs to be addressed. This is made possible in this study by the fact that the sample's composition should reflect the possible diversity in the research field. However, this cannot be implemented in its entirety because " ... already here limits become apparent since it is simply impossible to take into account all conceivable intersections of expressions of several difference-categories and life situations." (Ganz & Hausotter, 2020: 74 f.). Nevertheless, an attempt is made to map all possible differences by means of the greatest possible contrast since it is precisely this contrast that is the concrete concern of intersectional research (cf. Ganz & Hausotter, 2020: 75, ibid.).

Case selection is handled very roughly according to the principles of grounded theory and is not made based on specific theoretical presuppositions. Students who reject self-employment and have no interest in exploring the topic area form the basis of the samples. For example, the University of Kassel was selected, and six students from the Department of Economics were interviewed. Students were accessed through a social media platform to network within the university. An advertisement briefly stated the research interest of this study; the placement and wording were carefully selected to avoid priming the research subjects. The possible participants were called as follows:

Who can take part in the study?
Students of the Faculty 07 – Economics at the University of Kassel, who ...

- Are enrolled in the Bachelor's degree program.
- Have not yet dealt with the subject area of "Entrepreneurship" (study or private).
- Cannot imagine ever founding or taking over their own business and/or.
- Cannot imagine being self-employed in general.

Interview Questions

Compliant with the form of a narrative interview, students were asked " ... to tell what is important to them – and not what they think the researcher wants to hear" (Ganz & Hausotter, 2020: 70) at the beginning of the interview. Furthermore, especially with regard to the intersectional research context, it should be pointed out that people who, for example, have been confronted with discriminatory experiences are often not taken seriously regarding these experiences. This should also be addressed in advance, and the interviewees should be approached with confidence (Ganz & Hausotter, 2020).

In terms of content, the narrative impulses are oriented towards both the epistemological interest of this thesis, the sampling developed for it, and the orientation of the intersectional research approach according to Degele and Winker (2017). Thus, the first step to be taken within the intersectional multilevel analysis is to describe the identity constructions of the interviewees. The first question impulse therefore aims at encouraging the students to construct their identity on the basis of their own narrated story and, moreover, to put themselves in relation to "others." The second narrative impulse aims to shed light on the students' attitudes towards starting their own business. Here, only reasons are considered which, in the view of the interviewees, speak against founding their own company and/or make the topic of founding one's own company seem uninteresting in itself.

Analysis

The results recorded in the interview (in the form of speech) were then transcribed, coded, and analyzed in an open process. Coding was done using an interpretive coding technique based on the concept-indicator model. Here, a researcher forms interpretative categories from the data material (Breuer et al., 2019). Based on this elaboration, it is then decided which additional data should be collected. Theory is generally developed through case contrasting and ends when no further case contributions are found in the research process (theoretical saturation) (Ganz & Hausotter, 2020; Glaser & Strauss, 1998, Breuer et al., 2019).

14.5 Results

The aim of this work is to shed light on the influence of social background factors in the context of students' rejection of starting their own business. In the context of increasing diversity at universities and newer research directions regarding inequality research, a method from intersectionality research was chosen for the study. The research motivation in this regard arose from the findings of the various research traditions on inequality research in the context of entrepreneurship education. As described at the beginning, findings such as those from "family entrepreneurship" show that individuals are more inclined to start businesses if they have role models in their family. They already experience the values and norms that are associated with entrepreneurship in childhood (cf. Dyer & Handler, 1994, p. 71 ff.). However, it is not only the social background that is assumed to have an influence; the gender of individuals also seems to have an effect on the development of their intention to start a business. However, the focus of studies that examine a single category of inequality such as "gender" bears the risk of overlooking equally conditioning factors and overlapping influences such as "race," "class," and "body" (ibid.), or even the influence of age and health. In addition, categories of inequality are context-specific and also interwoven (cf. Degele & Winker, 2017, p. 18, Fenstermaker & West, 2002, p. 237). Furthermore, analyzing entrepreneurship education at universities suggests that students who have no intention of starting a business or categorically reject starting their own business remain completely unaffected by the promotion of entrepreneurship at universities. In the context of equal entrepreneurship education, all students are to be included with regard to becoming sensitized to entrepreneurship. The study takes a closer look at students who refuse to start their own business, who do not develop their own intention to start a business and who usually remain under the radar of university entrepreneurship programs. More precisely, these are students who are not interested in the subject area, do not participate in any related events like entrepreneurship education courses, and do not see themselves as entrepreneurs in the future (ibid). The method chosen here was able to provide initial findings about reasons why students reject starting their own businesses on the micro, meso, and macro level.

Identity Level of the Students (Micro Level)

In terms of the identity level of the students, structural references to all four inequality categories (race, class, gender, and body) could be derived in the context of intersectional inequality and the rejection of starting their own business. With regard to the first guiding question, to what extent students of economics at the University of Kassel differ, two distinct groups could be identified in the course of the study. The biggest difference between the two groups was tied to their social class situation. According to Degele and Winker (2017), the type formation is carried out using the stage model of empirically based type or group formation (cf. Degele & Winker, 2017, p. 122). Basically, the central themes of the entire identity construction are worked out in the context of attitudes towards starting one's own business. Central themes are: capable vs. not capable, work-life balance, financial security (e.g., in case of unemployment, illness and old age), fear of investment and loss of capital, good business idea vs. bad business idea, psychological stress, disturbances in the social environment, poor vs. rich, city vs. country, taking responsibility for staff, parents' profession, challenges, external image as a future entrepreneur, and social advancement. It is striking that all students grew up in rural areas or spent part of their childhood there. In addition, all students shy away from the high workload that can go hand in hand with setting up a business. Another important common feature of the cases is educational advancement, with four out of six students describing their educational advancement in detail. Educational advancement can therefore be seen as central to the construction of one's own identity.

Types of Intersectional Inequality

Students who belong to the group "Search for Financial Security" (SfFS) are primarily concerned about their finances. This includes, for example, financial security in case of illness and in old age. Concerns of this kind are demonstrably due to interactions regarding the inequality categories "body" and "class." Further distinctions can be made in the group of SfFS.

It is evident that two of the students in this group are more emotionally charged in their reasons for not starting their own business. Students of this type describe dramatic worst-case scenarios (group: thinking in worst-case scenarios – (TiWS): two person) in their stories and explicitly reject starting their own business. In addition, the expectations of the family seem to play a major role for the students in this group. In this respect, it is also significant that the students in this group have a migration background. In addition, possible psychological stress and the effects of starting a business in the prevailing social environment are a central topic for both.

The group "Lack of Self-efficacy" (LoSe: two person), on the other hand, concentrates on financial security, both in the case of unemployment, illness, and old age. For the students in this group, self-efficacy and the belief in their own abilities play an important role. For example, one of the students has the confidence to start her own small business, whereas another completely shies away from possible challenges and conflicts entailed in such a move.

The group of "Collectivistic Orientation" (CO: two person) differs categorically from the group SfFS through a more collectivist baseline attitude. Money, riches, and success are at the back of the list for these students in terms of career choice, which can be deduced from their class position. Here, the potential workload and assuming responsibilities tied to setting up one's own business stands in opposition to their desire to be together with family and friends (Fig. 14.1).

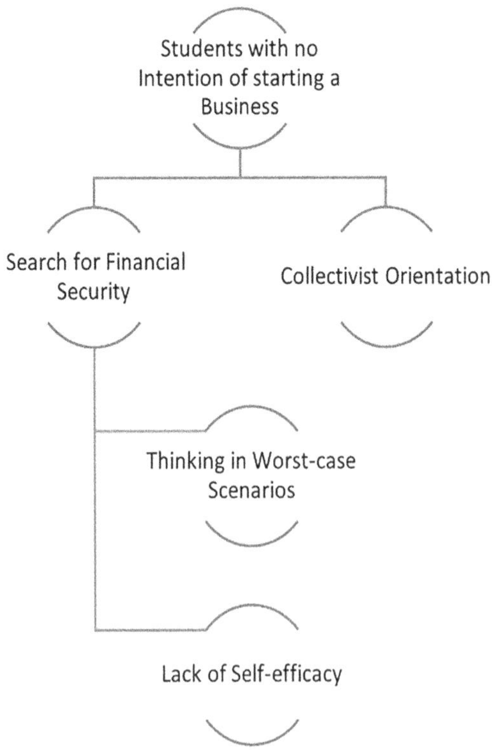

Fig. 14.1 Types of intersectional inequality of students who refuse to start their own business

Symbolic Representations of the Students (Meso Level)

An interesting phenomenon emerges from the groups formed. For example, group CO seems to reject the achievement principle, at least in part, for their own lives. The group CO perceives entrepreneurship as activity that is to be performed alone and constantly, which is out of the question for the students of this group. Status, wealth, and possessions are also not important to them. Group CO wants a life without much pressure to perform. Their choice of occupation tends to be less performance-oriented.

Group SfFS, on the other hand, seems to have accepted the achievement principle and accepted related demands. The students have risen socially through hard work and through achievement. However, in the context of the merit principle and its demand to take responsibility for one's own body, health, and that of others, they shy away from starting their own business. The fear of all students in this group seems to be, among other things, (self-inflicted) relegation because in the context of starting their own business it is uncertain to what extent their performance will pay off. The loss of the social environment is also included in this group.

In the TiWS group, the effect of symbolic representation through immigration is also assumed. The students describe the expectations of society and the family. It seems as if they are subject to a certain compulsion to conform. For one of the students, this leads to an unconditional will to rise, whereas the other student wants to fulfill patriarchal duties on the basis of her gender. This desire to conform results from a desire to adopt values and norms of the affluent West, and at the same time a desire to integrate and fulfill traditional gender roles. The students both want to take responsibility for the family according to the roles they have been assigned.

Societal Structures Including Institutions (Macro Level)

The question of whether social relations of domination prevent students' intentions to start their own businesses can be confirmed for the group of SfFS. The structuring categories and the intersections of "class," "gender," "race," and "body" determine, especially in the group SfFS, the social position of students on the labor market and also affect their attitude towards starting their own business. Here, the students compare starting a business with a permanent job. A permanent position has the advantage that standard contributions for social insurance (pension, health, accident, nursing care, and unemployment insurance) are automatically covered to a certain level. In this context, the structural category "body" is also mixed in. In our society, bodies are to be understood as cultural assets. Only physically healthy people are in demand and health is attributed to individual lifestyle. Health is therefore subject to optimizing, which also manifests itself in the performance principle (class) (cf. Degele & , Winker 2017). In addition, parental benefits and maternity leave benefits are based on income from employment (cf. Bundeszentrale für politische

Bildung – 2009). As a company founder, students would have to take care of their individual insurance coverage. Health and care insurance is obligatory in Germany. Insurance in all social areas, both private and statutory, is offered by various institutions. For example, it is possible to remain insured under the statutory pension scheme despite setting up your own business. There are also many options for additional insurance coverage, such as sick day benefits in the form of continued salary payments in the event of illness (cf. Berlin Chamber of Industry and Commerce – 2022). The state does not provide coverage for entrepreneurs in the context of social insurance in Germany. As can be seen from the individual analysis, the students in the SfFS group come from the petit bourgeoisie and some from the working class. In this context, it must be assumed that they do not have a financial background that could per se protect them when starting their own business. The structures in which students from the sub-group TiWS find themselves entail that they would lack sufficient (financial and social) safeguards if they were to start their own business. In the case of the whole group "SfFS," for example, the parents are particularly careful with their financial resources. In addition, the group "LoSe" is familiar with financial upheaval due to the separation of their parents. This restricted this group's financial situation. In this case, there are further aspects in the context of desired financial security. In general, it must be stated that the group SfFS would have to provide financial and social security for themselves. However, they not only lack the capital, but also the experience, knowledge, and the network to do so. The group "TiWS" emphasizes that they do not know anyone who could be a positive example for them. All of them lack role models from their family or environment. In terms of financial security, the respondents fear that they cannot hedge against unsuccessful business models and lack of profits.

Interactions of the Different Levels in the Overall View

As has been shown in the typology and the following chapters, interactions between class and body are central patterns for group SfFS. Thus, norms of self-responsibility have an effect, both for one's own health and for the preservation of the social position that has been fought for. Setting up a business seems too uncertain per se for the students in group SfFS, as the outcome of founding is not foreseeable. The students cannot guarantee that they can handle the personal responsibility associated with founding. This insecurity is reinforced in the context of experiences and references to poverty – and immigration, as well as by the high expectations of families to meet gender role expectations. On the identity level of the students, the adoption of these values and norms leads to the rejection of starting their own business. At the structural level, students find structures that support them in terms of personal responsibility. Thus, entrepreneurs are obligated to take care of their own social and economic security. Nothing else is propagated to students by the state or other structural stakeholders. Symbolic representations and the structural level therefore reinforce each other in terms of their effect. Particularly complex interactions can be